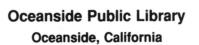

CHARIOTS OF FIRE

CHARIOTS OF FIRE

PHILIP KAPLAN

MBI

For Téa

This edition first published in 2003 by MBI, an imprint of
MBI Publishing Company,
Galtier Plaza, Suite 200, 380 Jackson Street, St. Paul, MN 55101-3885 USA

Page 236 is an extension of this copyright page.

This book was produced by Aurum Press Limited, 25 Bedford Avenue, London WC1B 3AT, Great Britain

ISBN 0-7603-1724-0

1 3 5 6 4 2
2003 2005 2007 2008 2006 2004
Printed and bound in Singapore by Imago

CONTENTS

LANDSHIPS

below: Sumerian chariots and spearmen of the world's first organized army. right: *Mark V Going Into Action*, a painting by W.B.Adeney.

tank (tángk) *n.* 3. An enclosed, heavily armoured combat vehicle that is mounted with cannon and guns and moves on caterpillar treads.

MECHANIZED LAND WARFARE began with the chariot, the predecessor of the armoured car, whose ancestry is much older than that of the tank. Like the tank, the early chariot was operated as a military vehicle by a team or crew consisting of a driver, a bowman (who could also hurl a javelin when necessary), and a shield bearer to afford some protection for the others. Archeologists in Russia have established that Bronze Age warriors in Central Asia used chariots as mobile platforms from which they shot arrows and threw javelins at their adversaries.

A little-known mountain warrior race from the region now called Kurdistan, the Hyksos or "Princes of the Lands", are believed to be the first people to have fought in war chariots. In 1700 BC the Hyksos moved into northern Egypt, establishing a dynasty that would last for 400 years. Their chariot-based mobile striking force was probably the key to their success. They were ultimately overthrown by an even more powerful chariot force of the Egyptian army. The great armies of the Pharoah Thutmose III in 1479 BC, of the Assyrian army in the ninth century BC and of King Solomon in *c.* 972-931 were renowned for the might and capability of their war chariot corps. But it was Cyrus, king of Persia in the sixth century BC, who is credited with developing the chariot into a first-class fighting vehicle. His long-axled, two-man design was extremely strong and more resistant to overturning than any previous chariot. The axles were mounted with protruding scythes, the horses protected by armour. It was light and very fast. There was also a much larger, wagon-like version featuring a tower with a battering ram, and a capacity for twenty men. According to the Greek commander, Xenophon, this forerunner of the tank was thought by Cyrus

to have magnificent battlefield potential.

When Alexander the Great invaded India in 327 BC he soon faced the forces of the rajah Porus and a battle line that incorporated 200 large and powerful elephants. The massive beasts had been made more formidable by the attachment of swords to their trunks and lances to either side of their bodies. Porus's elephants were used as "infantry tanks" to break the enemy lines enabling supporting cavalry to get through to the opposition forces. A howdah, or fighting cage, sat on the back of each beast and probably carried up to four fighting men. The sight of these giant "living tanks" undoubtedly frightened the opposing army and its horses. So impressed was Alexander with the power and presence of the elephants in a military context that he acquired a considerable number of them for his own forces.

Hannibal is the military commander best known for the use of elephants in a principal combat role and he employed them quite effectively until the day of his final battle, in 202 BC, at Zama when his Roman opponent, Scipio, outsmarted him. Hannibal planned to use his eighty elephants in a terrifying charge intended to breach the Roman centre. But as the animals approached the Roman line the air was rent with the blare of many trumpets and horns from the Roman side. The elephants were bewildered, then terrified. They panicked and fled in retreat through Hannibal's own troops. Like Alexander, however, the Romans were intrigued by the possibilities that elephants seemed to offer in a combat situation and they, too, incorporated them into their armies and continued using them for nearly 200 years.

In 53 BC the Roman General Crassus took an army of 40,000 men into Asia Minor to face a numerically inferior force of Parthians at the battle of Carrhae. His army suffered 50 per cent casualties and half of the remaining men were

below: Albert Stern, a driving force behind the development of the first British tank. above right: Little Willie under construction at Foster's Lincoln works in 1915. below right: King George V inspecting Little Willie in 1918.

captured. He had encountered a new and extremely potent kind of fighting force—10,000 mounted archers supported by 1000 camels carrying additional arrows. The Parthians simply surrounded the Romans, closed to a comfortable firing distance and continued shooting until the Romans had ceased to resist.

In 55 BC the troops of Julius Caesar, on reconnaissance missions to what the Romans were then calling Brittannia, were greeted by audacious spear attacks from light chariots. According to Caesar, the British charioteers drove across the battlefields at great speed, hurling javelins at their enemies from a distance, causing confusion and disorganization among the Roman ranks. The British javelin throwers then dismounted and attacked their enemies on foot. The chariot drivers meanwhile continued on and then halted, their horses facing away from the action, ready to carry their comrades off in a swift getaway should that be necessary. Such attacks took a high toll of the Romans, both in casualties and psychologically, and it is believed by some that this demoralizing effect may have led to Caesar's withdrawal from Britain.

The use of chariots in such roles, however, was in decline at that point. Warring societies had long since concluded that armed soldiers on horseback were of greater value. It is likely that the idea of putting a man on a horse, to gain an intelligence advantage in a battlefield situation, is much older even than the military use of the chariot. The horse provided the mounted reconnaissance rider with significant advantages including height for increased observational capability and considerable speed for approach to and escape from enemy forces.

As the development of body armour for knights on the battlefield began, and horses were being bred for a more refined combat role, the chariot lost its military allure. The horse-mounted soldier, or cavalryman, was now an army's means of

breaking the ranks of opposing infantry. But with the development of firearms in the fourteenth century, the role of the horse as the principal means of giving fighting man mobility was destined to end. The poor animal was soon unable to carry his master efficiently, overburdened as they had both become with the increasingly heavier armour necessary for their protection against the shot from guns. In the next century, soldiers began to discard their heavy armour as the concepts of battlefield mobility and agility to evade enemy missiles came into favour. They began to believe in substantial firepower as a means to achieve both battlefield success and survival. But while mounted cavalry remained an essential part of all armies through World War I, most military minds were soon fascinated by the idea of a soundly-made vehicle which could provide ample protection for those manning it, in addition to the capability to effectively engage the enemy.

Among the earliest such vehicles was that of Italian physician, Guido da Vigevano. In 1335 he devised a windmill-powered cart with an exposed wooden gear train; but, being utterly dependent on wind for its power, da Vigevano's cart had no future. A century and a half later, artist-engineer-inventor Leonardo da Vinci proposed the development of an armoured fighting vehicle, drawing sketches for a bowl-shaped four-wheeled contraption with gun positions mounted between the body, which was to be covered with iron plate armour, and a sort of parasol cover. Da Vinci's "armoured car" was to be human-powered, its eight-man crew turning cranks and transferring power to the wheels through a crude gearing system, but there appears to have been little provision for steering. Its low ground clearance would have caused it to bog down easily and the low power-to-weight ratio would certainly have brought quick physical exhaustion to the crew. Of his creation Da Vinci said: I am building secure and covered chariots which are invulnerable, and when they advance with their guns in the midst of the enemy, even the largest enemy masses are bound to retreat; and behind them the infantry can follow in safety and without opposition . . . . These take the place of elephants and one may hold bellows in them to terrify horses or one may put carabiniers in them. This is good to break up the ranks of the enemy.

It was a sort of progress toward the concept and development of the tank, but it would be another 400 years before a real solution would be found.

In the period between 1419 and 1434, one Jan Jiska led a group of Central European religious dissidents in the Hussite Wars, deploying a kind of war wagon, essentially a defensive cart designed to provide mobility as well as armoured protection. These "Wagon Laagers", as they were called, had thick, timbered sides and pillbox-like slits from which guns or crossbows could be fired. Several such vehicles could be connected together and formed into a defensive circle if Jiska's followers found themselves threatened with enemy attack while on open ground. Variations on such war carts were in use into the latter part of the nineteenth century, being employed by the Boers in South Africa.

The "assault car" design of the mathematician John Napier in 1596 provided for a "round chariot of metal". It was to be fully-armoured to protect it against the musket fire of the time. The power source was to be "those within, the same more easie and more spedie than so many armed men would be otherwise". The role of his assault car was described by Napier: "The use thereof in moving serveth to break the array of the enemies battle . . . by continual discharge of harquebussiers through small holes, the enemy being abashed and uncertain as to what defence or pursuit to use against a moving mouth of metal".

In 1838 the engineer John George of Saint Blazey, Cornwall, England, petitioned the House of Commons claiming, together with his son, to be the sole inventors of what he referred to as a "modern steam war chariot". He described the

9

vehicle as being "coke-burning, with sides armoured against muskett and grape shot". It was crewed by three men and was, he said, "capable of cutting a 23-foot opening in an enemy rank." It could "penetrate the densest lines, the firmest cahorts and the most compact squadrons with as much certainty as a cannon ball would pass through a partition of paste board." George and his son proposed bringing a demostration model of their machine to London for the edification of the Commons which, in the event, expressed no interest in the scheme.

While working on an armoured fighting vehicle design in 1854, Englishman James Cowan decided to try enclosing one of James Boydell's traction engines in an iron skin which was open at the top. The machine featured several cannon that protruded through gun ports. It moved on short, reinforced board "feet" that were fitted to the circumference of the road wheels, forerunners of linked caterpillar tracks on which future tanks and other armoured vehicles would roll.

Cowan's steam traction vehicle found little favour among the members of the Select Committee appointed by the then British Prime Minister, Lord Palmerston. In their estimation, Cowan's design failed to properly provide internally for the functions of the boiler, flywheel and breech-loading guns, for other machinery, coal and ammunition storage, and for the driver and gunners. Palmerston thought Cowan's armoured fighting vehicle repellent and publicly described the thing as "barbaric" and "uncivilized". The committee rejected Cowan's design and he promptly attacked their decision in the press, referring to the members as "washed out Old Women and Senile Old Tabbies". The more visionary and creative thinkers of the day, meanwhile, were in agreement that the future of land warfare lay in a vehicle combining terrific firepower, self-propulsion and greatly improved protection. Progress was slowly being made. The unpleasant Cowan affair would

mark the birth of the tank, a killing machine the world would find irresistible.

In the 1880s the invention of relatively small internal combustion engines by the Germans Gottlieb Daimler and Karl Benz led the world away from steam as a power source for the developing armoured fighting vehicle. Internal combustion power would prove to be the only practical choice. The British government meanwhile, through its War Office, maintained a posture of indifference; ignoring or rejecting various armoured fighting vehicle designs. In 1895 it gave the ho-hum to a small, open-topped armoured car with two mounted machine guns, the brainchild of American entrepreneur Edward Pennington. The bathtub-shaped machine featured Pennington's patented pneumatic tyres and a 1/4 inch-thick armour plate skirt around the hull. The skirt ended eighteen inches above the ground and sported a chain mail fringe to protect the tyres. The car was crewed by two gunners and the driver. It excited no one in the government and was not produced.

Pennington's effort was followed by a relatively similar self-propelled fighting vehicle, the Military Scout, designed by British inventor Frederick Simms and powered by a 1.5hp De Dion engine. It was armed with an air-cooled Maxim machinegun and was thought by many to have much promise, a view not shared by the War Office.

Simms persisted in his efforts and developed a small, petrol-engined, armoured rail-car based on Pennington's design. It saw service in the Second Boer War. Following this success he went on to design a larger version for the road. It was built by Vickers and was the first true armoured car. Well armed, with a Vickers-Maxim one-pounder gun at the rear and two Maxim water-cooled machineguns at the front, Simms' "War Car", as it was called, could achieve a maximum speed of 9mph with its Simms-Daimler 16hp engine. The War Car was shown at the 1902 Crystal Palace exhibition to great acclaim by the press and public. The War Office,

however, was once again unimpressed, causing Simms to redirect his interests away from armoured fighting vehicles.

It was the need to be able to move across open countryside while under ample armour protection that caused Richard Hornsby & Sons, who had developed a track system for use on oil-engined tractors, to experiment successfully with a militarized version in 1905, but the War Office declined to support the venture beyond that stage. Still, with the efforts of Daimler and Benz, and the Hornsby experiment, two key components of the tank, a reliable power plant and a track system to replace wheels, had been put in place.

The years before 1914 saw various, strictly limited, developments in the field in France, Italy, Germany and Great Britain, the resulting vehicles being employed in local conflicts with varying degrees of success. The blinkered, reactionary, intransigent war ministries and general staffs of the time stolidly maintained their hostile attitudes, delaying and sabotaging developments wherever possible. Their inability to learn from and properly interpret their own battlefield experience, coupled with their persistent delusions about future tactics and requirements, left them in the dark and generally ill-prepared for the coming Great War.

It should have been abundantly clear to most military commanders at the start of World War I that neither massed ranks of infantry nor charging cavalry could survive in the face of fire from breech-loading, rifled weapons. But most commanders refused to consider any alternative to sending their troops "over the top" to cross a pocked, denuded wasteland through an unspeakable hail of bullets. "War is good business. Invest your sons", wrote a wag of the day.

The first armoured fighting vehicles to see wartime service were armoured cars with mounted machineguns built by the Belgians and by the

above left: Little Willie at the Tank Museum, Bovington, Dorset, England. far left: Lieutenant Colonel Ernest Swinton, whose 1914 idea led to the creation of the tank. left: Major J.F.C. Fuller, who predicted battles between tanks and foresaw tactics for use by the new "mechanical horse," as he referred to it.

Well, boy, you're off to war. / I'd go again myself / If I was fit. Just reach my sword from off that dusty shelf. / Ah, thanks! The thrill it carries! / This battered hilt to hold. / I'm mutilated, boy, but still / I'm far from being old.

Eight months ago I used to dream / Of glory's honoured crown; / Eight months, and in that hasting time / My idols tumbled down. / I dreamt the thrill of battle; / The roaring charge; the check; / I never thought that I'd return / A battered, useless wreck.
—from *The Veteran*
by Sergeant Frank S. Brown

There's a little wet home in the trench, / That the rain storms continually drench, A dead cow close by, with her hooves in the sky, / And she gives off a beautiful stench.

Underneath us, in place of a floor, / Is a mess of cold mud and some straw, / And the Jack Johnsons roar as the speed through the air O'er my little wet home in the trench.
— *Canadian Song*
Anonymous

British Royal Navy, which were tested and put into action in on the Western Front in 1914. But, in the mud, which became a major feature of the battlefields, these wheeled vehicles, while promising, proved wholly unsuitable. Ironically, in 1912 Lancelot de Mole, an ingenious Australian engineer, had produced a design for a practical armoured tank vehicle which was, in fact, superior to that which the British Army would deploy on the Somme in 1916. When de Mole submitted his idea to the War Office, he got nowhere with it. In 1915, while serving with the Australian Imperial Force, he again tried to interest the War Office in his invention and again was rebuffed.

"Caterpillar landships are idiotic and useless. Nobody has asked for them and nobody wants them. Those officers and men are wasting their time and are not pulling their proper weight in the war. If I had my way I would disband the whole lot of them. Anyhow, I am going to do my best to see that it is done and stop all this armoured car and caterpillar landship nonsense!" declared Royal Navy Commodore Cecil F. Lambert, Fourth Sea Lord, in 1915. Lambert disapproved of the Royal Naval Armoured Car Division which had been set up in October 1914 with the enthusiastic support of Winston Churchill, then First Lord of the Admiralty, to develop a new line of purpose-built armoured cars. Following the German defeat in the battle of the Marne, some Royal Navy units were sent from England to protect the air base at Dunkirk. Their remit also included the rescue of pilots who had been shot down in the area and, to that end, the Admiralty Air Department elected to provide some armoured cars. They bought 100 vehicles from Rolls Royce and had some of them shipped directly to France where they were fitted with a box-like arrangement of armour covering the main unit and rear wheels, and other small, raised armoured boxes to cover the front wheels and the driver's head. The rest of the Rolls Royce cars were modified

in England and went into action in the autumn of 1914 where they operated effectively but also showed that their crews were inadequately protected from overhead sniper fire. This vulnerability led to the development of a new version with a top-mounted machinegun turret and overhead armour, the first examples of which arrived in France in December 1914. While a great improvement over their predecessors, these armoured cars entered service at a point in the war when all significant movement on the battlefields had stopped and the two armies were dug in behind wire barriers and fortifications. The armoured cars showed promise, but the wheeled vehicles were not capable of crossing the trenches or the wire.

In February 1915 Churchill formed the Naval Landships Committee to design and construct a new tracked armoured vehicle based on an idea put forward in 1914 by Lieutenant Colonel Ernest Swinton, Royal Engineers. He reasoned that a caterpillar-tracked, armoured vehicle could be designed and built to destroy machinegun positions and barbed wire barriers and, most importantly, to cross the great trenches and other obstacles on the battlefield with relative ease. Initial trials of the "Machinegun Destroyer" as it was known, were disappointing, but Churchill and the Landships Committee determined to press on. Utilizing two Bullock Creeping Grip tractors imported from the United States, they devised a vehicle called the Lincoln No. 1 Machine. The suspension units and track were then redesigned and modified and the resulting new vehicle soon delivered the performance the committee sought. They called it Little Willie.

The British Army was interested in the possibilities of such a vehicle, but required one with roughly twice the capability of Little Willie. They needed a vehicle able to cross a trench eight feet wide and climb a four-and-a-half-foot parapet. Two members of the committee, William Tritton and Lieutenant

W.G. Wilson, met the challenge with a new design that combined aspects of the Lincoln Machine with Little Willie, resulting in an entirely new vehicle whose tracks ran round the perimeter of its rhomboid sides. The overall height was minimized by the use of sponsons on either side of the vehicle, each mounting a naval six-pounder gun, rather than a top-mounted turret There were fixed front and rear turrets, the front turret accommodating the commander and the driver who sat side by side. The rear turret housed a machinegun. There were four Hotchkiss machine guns in all and four doors behind the sponsons as well as a manhole hatch in the top of the hull. To the rear of the hull was a towed two-wheel steering tail. The new machine was known as Big Willie, but more commonly as Mother. It was eight feet in height and 26 feet 5 inches long, not counting the added steering tail. The overall weight was 28 tons and power was provided by a 105 hp Daimler sleeve-valve engine.

The audience for the February 1916 trial of Mother at the Hatfield Park, Hertfordshire estate of the Marquess of Salisbury included Lloyd George, the Minister of Munitions, Field Marshal Lord Kitchener, the Minister of Defence, some other cabinet members and representatives of the Army and the Admiralty. The machine was put through its paces over a specially prepared obstacle course containing a variety of ditches, craters, streams, wire entanglements and wide trenches, acquitting itself quite well in the view of the Landships Committee members. While Kitchener was not enthusiastic about what he saw, the Army representatives were most impressed and an order for 25 machines was awarded to Foster's and one for 75 to the Metropolitan Carriage, Wagon and Finance Company. Fifty of the vehicles were to be built with the same armament as the Mother prototype. Perversely, these would be referred to as 'males', while the balance of the vehicles were to be armed with six machineguns, four of them mounted in

smaller side sponsons. These were the 'females' and their role was to prevent the males from being swamped by enemy infantry. Shortly after the Hatfield Park trial, the King took a ride in the prototype and concluded that a large number of the vehicles would be a considerable asset to the Army.

The strange vehicles taking shape in secrecy in the workshops at Foster's were being called "tank" by workers and executives, an odd way of referring to a new weapons system, destined to completely alter the future of land warfare. It was an attempt to conceal what they were doing; the term Landship being too much of a giveaway and no longer suitable. Swinton had talked with Lieutenant Colonel W. Dalby Jones about the matter and they had considered "container" and "cistern" before finally agreeing on "tank", which seemed, they reasoned, to imply some sort of agricultural machine or product that would be percieved as part of the company's normal output. Broad hints were even put about that, on completion the products were to be shipped to Russia. So, the word *tank* entered into common usage and soon became the generic word for the machine.

The pressure on the manufacturers to get the Mark I tank into production inevitably resulted in a vehicle that was something less than perfect. The makers took this first production tank from drawing board to assembly in only twelve months. Among its many drawbacks was a gravity-fed fuel system that could starve the engine when the vehicle was manoeuvring with its front end in a steep climbing or descending attitude. The fuel tank was located inside the vehicle, greatly increasing the fire risk. A particularly bizarre design characteristic required the teamwork of four men to steer the vehicle, even with the help of the wheeled steering tail. David Fletcher, Librarian of the Tank Museum, Bovington, England, a leading authority on tanks and author of *The British Tanks 1915-19*, describes the steering procedure of the early tanks: "Four of the crew served the guns; a gunner and loader on each side.

There are certain brisk people among us today Whose patriotism makes quite a display. / But on closer inspection I fancy you'll find / The tools that they work with are axes to grind.

Apparently guiltless of personal greed, / They hasten to succour their country in need; / But private returns in their little top shelves / Show it's one for the country and two for themselves.

Unselfish devotion this struggle demands, / All helping each other whole heart and clean hands. / No quarter for humbugs; we want to be quit / Of men who are making, not doing their bit.

Jones challenges Brown, and Brown implicates Jones, / To the slur of self-interest nobody owns; But each one must know at the back of his mind, / If his patriotism spells axes to grind.
– *Profiteers*
by Jessie Pope

Daddy, what did YOU do in the Great War

The others were all required to operate the controls. The driver, sitting to the right of the commander, was effectively there to make the tank go. Apart from the steering wheel, that was almost useless, he had no control whatever over turning, or swinging the tank to use the contemporary term. He controlled the primary gearbox, clutch and footbrake which acted on the transmission shaft along with the ignition and throttle controls. The commander operated the steering brakes and either man could work the differential lock which was above, between and behind them. The two extra men worked the secondary gearboxes at the back, on instruction from the driver who had to work the clutch at the same time.

"It was, according to the instruction book, possible to steer the tank by selecting a different ratio in each of the secondary gearboxes although experience soon proved that this would result in twisted gear shafts. Thus, except for slight deviations when the steering brakes were used, the standard procedure for steering was to halt the tank, lock the differential and take one track out of gear. First was then selected in the primary box and the other secondary box, the brake was then applied to the free track and the tank would swing in that direction."

By February 1917 the Marks II and III had gone to war incorporating only minor improvements over the Mark I, but by April the substantially-improved Mark IV entered service, protected by much better armour. The Mark IV also featured a vacuum-feed fuel system, a new cooling and ventilation system, an exhaust silencer and a rear-mounted external fuel tank. While the males had the same armament as the prototype, the females were armed with six machineguns (five Vickers and one Hotchkiss.) A total of 420 male and 595 female tanks were produced before the arrival in May 1918 of the Mark V, by far the best and most dramatically advanced version of this pioneering vehicle. The Mark V incorporated an entirely new epicyclic steering system designed by the former

Lieutenant, now Major, W.G. Wilson, as well as an extended hull to increase its trench-crossing capability. With enhanced power from a 150hp Ricardo engine, the Mark V was capable of a 4.6 mph maximum speed, compared to the 3.7 mph top speed of the earlier Marks. Production totalled 400 male and 632 female Mark Vs.

The armoured strike force of the British Army was forming in 1916 and the Army wisely elected to establish it as a new branch under the overall command of Ernest Swinton. Lieutenant-Colonel Hugh Elles, a Royal Engineers officer, was appointed field commander in France. Elles had been GHQ representative for tank development and policy .The new organization was initially called the Tank Detachment until June 1917 when it was redesignated the Tank Corps. It became the Royal Tank Corps in 1923, the award coming from King George V. Then, in 1939, the Royal Tank Corps was renamed the Royal Tank Regiment and became part of the Royal Armoured Corps, along with other units, mainly former cavalry regiments.

Elles put together a small staff of officers in 1916 who brought considerable intelligence, enthusiasm and foresight to the war front in France. Realizing the enormous potential of the tank weapon, Elles's key staff, including Captain G. Martel and Major J.F.C. Fuller, predicted the coming battles between opposing tank forces and other advanced tank tactics that were destined to change land warfare forever. It was Fuller who, in 1917, wrote of the tank, "It is, in fact, an armoured mechanical horse."

Brought to France under the cover of canvas sheets, the first British tanks entered battle against the Germans in September 1916. In his book, *Tanks In Battle*, Colonel H.C.B. Rogers describes the supplies that were carried into action in the British tanks: Rations for the first tank battle consisted of sixteen loaves of bread and about thirty tins of foodstuffs. The various types of stores included four spare Vickers machinegun barrels, one spare Vickers machinegun, one spare Hotchkiss machinegun barrel, two boxes of revolver ammunition, thirty-three thousand rounds of ammunition for the machineguns, a telephone instrument and 100 yards of cable on a drum, a signalling lamp, three signalling flags, two wire cutters, one spare drum of engine oil, one spare drum of gear oil, two small drums of grease, and three water cans. Added to this miscellaneous collection was all the equipment which was stripped off the eight inhabitants of the tank, so that there was not very much room to move about.

The training of the crews that went to war in these early tanks had been sub-standard and there had been no instruction in cooperation between the tanks and the infantry. The only point of agreement between the two arms was that the tanks ought to reach their first objective five minutes ahead of the infantry forces and that the primary task of the tanks was to destroy the enemy strongpoints which were preventing the advance of the infantry.

In their initial combat action, it was intended to deploy 49 British tanks, but only 32 were able to take part. Nine of these suffered breakdowns, five experienced "ditching" (becoming stuck in a trench or soft ground) and nine more couldn't keep up the pace, lagging well behind the infantry. But the remaining nine met their objective and inflicted severe losses on the German forces. While accomplishing less than had been hoped for, this first effort of the British tank force produced an important and unanticipated side effect. Those tanks which reached the enemy line made a powerful impression on the German troops facing them, causing many to bolt in fear even before the tanks had come into firing range.

The following passage from the book *Iron Fist* by Bryan Perrett, describes operational conditions for the crews of the early British tanks in France around the midpoint of the First World War: "Such intense heat was generated by the engine that the men wore as little as possible. The noise level, a

My Dear,
I must tell you about the *chic affaire* given by the dear Tank boys at Farnborough. A nice boy in horn spectacles I met at Bretts simply insisted on my coming. Quite *comme il faut*, don't you know. I was so disappointed the dear boys didn't play tennis in their red coats and bearskins, or whatever it is they wear, you know. That cat Jane was there, looking absolutely *demodée* in green georgette with sky blue undies and flesh coloured . . . I felt absolutely *risquée* drinking gin with the teeniest touch of pink angostura. When I had three I felt absolutely . . .

At dawn the ridge emerges massed and dun / In the wild purple of the glow'ring sun, / Smouldering through spouts of drifting smoke that shroud / The menacing scarred slope; and , one by one, / Tanks creep and topple forward to the wire.
– from *Attack* by Siegfried Sassoon

Daddy, what did YOU do in the great war?, a 1915 World War I poster by Savile Lumley.

Shrieking its message the flying death / Cursed the resisting air, / Then buried its nose by a battered church, / A skeleton gaunt and bare.

The brains of science, the money of fools / Had fashioned an iron slave Destined to kill, yet the futile end / Was a child's uprooted grave.
– *The Shell*
by Private H. Smalley Sarson

Well, how are things in Heaven? I wish you'd say Because I'd like to know that you're all right. / Tell me, have you found everlasting day, / Or been sucked in by everlasting night? / For when I shut my eyes your face shows plain; I hear you make some cheery old remark– / I can rebuild you in my brain, Though you've gone out patrolling in the dark.
– from *To Any Dead Officer*
by Siegfried Sassoon

above: A British Mark I tank with faked Russian lettering at the Foster's works in Lincoln. above right: 'Mother' in trials at Hatfield Park north of London in February 1916. right: A Mark II female.

compound of roaring engine, unsilenced exhaust on the early Marks, the thunder of tracks crossing the hull, weapons firing and the enemy's return fire striking the armour, made speech impossible and permanently damaged the hearing of some. The hard ride provided by the unsprung suspension faithfully mirrored every pitch and roll of the ground so that the gunners, unaware of what lay ahead, would suddenly find themselves thrown off their feet and, reaching out for support, sustain painful burns as they grabbed at machinery that verged on the red hot. Worst of all was the foul atmosphere, polluted by the fumes of leaking exhausts, hot oil, petrol and expended cordite. Brains starved of oxygen refused to function or produced symptoms of madness. One officer is known to have fired into a malfunctioning engine with his revolver, and some crews were reduced to the level of zombies, repeatedly mumbling the orders they had been given but physically unable to carry them out. Small wonder then, that after even a short spell in action, the men would collapse on the ground beside their vehicles gulping in air, incapable of movement for long periods.

"In addition, of course, there were the effects of the enemy's fire. Wherever this struck, small glowing flakes of metal would be flung off the inside of the armour, while bullet splash penetrated visors and joints in the plating; both could blind, although the majority of such wounds were minor though painful. Glass vision blocks became starred and were replaced by open slits, thereby increasing the risk, especially to the commander and driver. In an attempt to minimise this, leather crash helmets, slotted metal goggles and chain mail visors were issued, but these were quickly discarded in the suffocating heat of the vehicle's interior. The tanks of the day were not proof against field artillery so that any penetration was likely to result in a fierce petrol or ammunition fire followed by an explosion that would tear the vehicle apart. In such a situation the chances of

When the war is over and the KAISER'S out of print, I'm going to buy some tortoises and watch the beggars sprint; / When the war is over and the sword at last we sheathe, / I'm going to keep a jelly-fish and listen to it breathe.
– from *From a Full Heart*
by A.A. Milne

Madame, please,
You are requested kindly not to touch / Or take away the Company's property As souvenirs: you'll find we have on sale / A large variety, all guaranteed. / As I was saying, all is as it was, This is an unknown British officer, / The tunic having lately rotted off. Please follow me — this way . . .

the *path*, sir, *please*,
The ground which was secured at great expense The Company keeps absolutely untouched, / And in that dug-out (genuine) we provide Refreshments at a reasonable rate. / You are requested not to leave about / Paper, or gingerbeer bottles, or orange-peel, There are waste-paper baskets at the gate.
– from *High Wood*
by Philip Johnstone

Experimental Depot for Tanks, Dollis Hill, London, a painting by W.B. Adeney.

being able to evacuate a casualty through the awkward hatches were horribly remote.

"Despite these sobering facts, the crews willingly accepted both the conditions and the risks in the belief that they had a war-winning weapon."

One eyewitness, a British Army corporal, said they looked like giant toads. The spectre of nearly 400 enemy tanks emerging from the early morning ground fog and mists of Cambrai in north-eastern France on 20 November 1917 must have impressed all who saw it. After years of stalemate and staggering attrition this first use of massed tanks in warfare was the turning point. British armoured commanders had awakened to the possibilities of the tank when imaginatively and skilfully utilized.

For most of 1917 the Allies on the Western Front had been bogged down in their trenches, unable to breach the German defences. Now in November, the tank commanders saw an opportunity to break the cycle of despair and hopelessness that hung over the Allied armies. They proposed a massive tank raid to be launched against German positions near the town of Cambrai. They liked the prospects. The terrain of the attack was gently rolling, well-drained land. As their plan called for surprising the Germans with a fast and relatively quiet approach, there was to be no conventional softening-up artillery bombardment in advance of the raid. The commanders had intended that the great tank force would arrive quickly, inflict maximum damage and get out fast, having completed their task in three hours or less. They had presented their plan to Sir Douglas Haig, the British Commander-in-Chief on the Western Front, in August when he was incurring catastrophic losses fifty miles to the north of Cambrai in the swamps of Passchendale. At the time, the optimistic Haig was still looking for a victory and shelved the Cambrai idea. But by the autumn his Passchendale ambitions had sunk in the mud there and he was forced to accept the proposal of his tank men.

The plan called for the great mass of tanks to force a breakthrough between the two canals at Cambrai, capture the town itself as well as the higher ground surrounding the village of Flesquieres and the Bourlon Wood. They were then to roll on towards Valenciennes, 25 miles to the northeast. The tanks were carrying great bundles of brushwood which would be used to fill in the trenches that they would encounter when crossing the German defences of the Siegfried Line. It was intended that the tanks would advance line abreast while the accompanying infantry troops would follow in columns close behind to defend against close-quarter attacks.

Deception and diversion were employed by the British in the days leading up to the attack. Dummy tanks, smoke and gas were all used to fool the Germans, and the men and equipment that would be involved in the attack were moved up entirely by night and kept in hiding by day. All 381 tanks allocated for the attack advanced towards Cambrai along a six-mile front.

British planning and attention to detail had been thorough and fastidious, but they had failed to factor in the possibility of one of their own commanders, a General Harper of the 51st Highland Division, deviating from the plan. It seems that Harper had doubts about the ability of the new-fangled tanks to breach the Siegfried Line as quickly as the planners required. On the day of the attack Harper delayed sending his tanks and infantry troops forward until an hour after the rest of the force had left. The delay allowed German field artillery to be positioned with disastrous results for some tank crews. Five burnt-out tank hulls were found after the action. Elsewhere along the tank line, however, the armour and infantry had moved swiftly through the German lines, advancing five miles to Bourlon Wood by noon. It had been a brilliant achievement for the British tank crews.

WANTED SMART MEN FOR THE TANK CORPS, a poster of World War I by Alfred Leete.

For it's clang, bang, rattle, W'en the tanks go into battle, / And they plough their way across the tangled wire, / They are sighted to a fraction, When the guns get into action, An' the order of the day is rapid fire; / W'en the hour is zero Ev'ry man's a bloomin' 'ero, W'atsoever 'is religion or 'is nime, / You can bet yer bottom dollar / W'ether death or glory foller, / That the tanks will do their duty ev'ry time.
– from *A Song of the Tanks* by J. Dean Atkinson

Soon after Cambrai the Germans were devoting their whole energies to preparations for their own great offensive, which was launched in the following spring, and defensive measures of all kinds were secondary considerations for the time being. But when the three successive blows on the Somme, Lys, and the Aisne had come at length to an end, and were countered, with startling rapidity and effect, by the French and British attacks on 18th July and 8th August 1918, the enemy was aroused very roughly to a realisation of his peril and of the power of the weapon he had affected to despise. The 8th August, in particular, was entirely a tank victory— a greater and more brilliant Cambrai; and the astonishing collapse of the defence threw the Great General Staff into a panic from which it never was allowed to recover. From this date to the end a persistent refrain, rising at length to a frantic crescendo of warning and exhortation, runs through all the orders issued to the German armies, and the burden of it is tanks, tanks, and again tanks.
— from *The Tank in Action* by Captain D. G. Browne, MC

The push continued the next day with the British taking Flesquieres and advancing a further 1 1/2 miles. In the next nine days, they won and lost the village of Fontaine-Notre Dame and the surrounding area several times. Then, on 30 November, the Germans counterattacked. Like the British, they struck without the usual initial artillery bombardment, hiding behind heavy gas and smoke screens. The British troops, exhausted by their recent effort, were forced to retreat from the rapidly advancing fresh German forces and in just a few days had to relinquish all of their gains. In the action the Germans took 6,000 prisoners. Blame for the defeat fell on everyone except those actually responsible — the commanders. There was concern in Whitehall that pointing the finger at their Army commanders would crush the faith of the British people in their military leadership. Still, the British had learned the valuable lesson of how effective tanks and infantry could be when properly employed in concert.

The German offensive of March 1918 began on the 21st and saw the first appearance of their tanks in battle. Designed early in 1917, the A7V was much larger and heavier than the British heavy tank of the day. It weighed 33 tons and was operated by a crew of eighteen. The armament consisted of one forward-mounted 57mm gun (roughly equivalent to a six-pounder) and six machineguns positioned at the sides and rear. The maximum armour thickness was 30mm enabling the front of the tank to resist direct hits from field guns at long range, but the overhead armour was too thin to provide much protection. The fitting of the armour plating was such that the hull was very susceptible to bullet splash. Power came from two 150hp Daimler sleeve-valve engines. Sprung tracks allowed the vehicle to achieve 8 mph on smooth and level ground, a high speed for the time. However, the design and the low ground clearance resulted in relatively poor cross-country performance. The Germans built only fifteen A7Vs. In their initial venture into combat, four of the German tanks were used together with five captured British Mark IVs. One month later, thirteen A7Vs participated in the capture of Villers-Brettoneux and in this action enemy tanks had the same psychological effect on the British infantry as their tanks had had earlier on their German counterparts. Tanks broke the opposing lines.

Shortly after the German success at Villers-Brettoneux, the world's first tank-versus-tank action took place in the same neighbourhood. In the early morning light one male and two female Mark IVs were ordered forward to stem the German penetration. Though some of the British tank crew members had suffered from gas shelling, they all advanced and soon sighted one of the A7Vs. The machineguns of the two females were useless against the armour of the German tank and both were put out of action. But the male was able to manoeuvre for a flank shot and scored a hit causing the German tank to run up a steep embankment and overturn. Two more A7Vs then arrived and engaged the British tank which saw one off. The crew of the second A7V abandoned their tank and fled.

The Cambrai experience undoubtedly saved many lives, influencing the British attack of 8 August 1918, the battle of Amiens, in which 456 tanks finally broke the enemy lines. It was the decisive battle of the war, leading to the German surrender. The battle was launched along a thirteen-mile front. The three objectives were the Green Line, three miles from the start line, the Red Line, six miles from the start and in the centre of the front, and the Blue Line, eight miles from the start and in the centre. The attack was to begin at 4.20 a.m. with the tanks moving out 1,000 yards to the start line. A thick mist helped the British forces to achieve complete surprise and overrun the German forward defences.

The main attacks were to be delivered by the Canadian Corps on the right and the Australian Corps on the left, both of them being south of the Somme. North of the Somme, the Third Corps was to make a limited advance while covering the left flank. Before the Canadian Fifth Tank Battalion reached and crossed its Green Line objective it had suffered heavily, losing fifteen tanks. It lost another eleven tanks achieving the Red Line, leaving it only eight machines still operable. The Canadian Fourth Tank Battalion was advancing across firm ground and achieved the Green and Red Lines with ease. Heavy German artillery then took a great toll of the Fourth's tanks, leaving only eleven for the push on towards the Blue Line.

The Australian Corps, attacking with vehicles of the Fifth Tank Brigade, reached the Green Line by 7 a.m., the Red Line by 10 a.m. and they took the Blue Line an hour later. The tanks had eliminated German opposition up to the Red Line. After that, the Australian infantry poured through the weakened enemy defences and the tanks were unable to keep pace with them.

After the fighting, most tank crews were suffering the ill effects of having spent upwards of three hours buttoned up for action. With their guns firing, most of them suffered from headaches, high temperatures and even heart disturbances.

Though it was not immediately apparent, the Allies had won a great victory at Amiens, taking 22,000 German prisoners, and the German High Command realized that it had no more hope of winning the war. In the Reichstag, the German politicians heard from their military commanders that it was, above all, the tanks that had brought an end to their resistance against the Allies. That evening the downcast Kaiser said to one of his military commanders: "It is very strange that our men cannot get used to tanks." Major (now General) J.F.C. Fuller summed up the result: "The battle of Amiens was the strategic end of the war, a second Waterloo; the rest was minor tactics."

below: A Mark III male, driver training at Bovington Camp, in 1917.

The house is crammed: tier beyond tier they grin And cackle at the Show, while prancing ranks / Of harlots shrill the chorus, drunk with din; / 'We're sure the Kaiser loves our dear old Tanks!'

I'd like to see a Tank come down the stalls, / Lurching to rag-time tunes, or 'Home, sweet Home', / And there'd be no more jokes in Music-halls / To mock the riddled corpses round Bapaume.

'Blighters'
by Siegfried Sassoon

YPRES 1917

From the first introduction of tanks in the field, the conditions with which they had to contend had gone from bad to worse. Ypres was the climax. The tanks were sent by scores, and then by hundreds, to drown ineffectually in a morass, and the very existence of the corps was imperilled by this misusage. The whole countryside was waterlogged: reclaimed from the sea, for even Ypres once had been a port, its usefulness and habitability depended in normal times upon an intricate system of drainage, for whose upkeep the farmers were responsible, and for the neglect of which they were heavily fined. This drainage had now been destroyed, or had fallen into desuetude and decay, over the whole area about the front lines. During our reconnaissances in July the deplorable results were not at first apparent. The weather was fine, and the surface soil dry and crumbling: we walked, so far as it was safe, over what seemed to be solid earth covered with the usual coarse grass and weeds; and then, from observation- *continued on page 24*

continued on page 24

right: *Tanks Passing Along a Road in France*, a painting by W.B. Adeney

The following is an account of the third battle of Ypres in World War I. It is rare to come across a memoir of the great war that is as thoughtful, observant and evocative as this, from *The Tank Corps Journal* of 1921-22, attributed only to E. and M.D.

3.40 A.M. ON Y-Z NIGHT. An almost deathly silence spreads over the front, broken only by the occasional bark of an eighteen pounder or 4.5 howitzer. The crew of "Caledonian" sit inside their bus awaiting zero hour. Guns have been cleaned, "Spuds" fitted, petrol tank filled, and six brand new plugs are waiting to make 500 sparks a minute each as soon as called upon. A few sections of infantry pass the Tank at intervals, and their voices can be plainly heard from inside. "That's the stuff to gie 'em" and "I wouldn't go over in one of they things, I'm safer wi' me old tin 'at and 'ipe."

A whistle in the distance, a shower of golden rain from the front line, and with a crash that reverberates throughout the countryside, the barrage, the greatest barrage ever put up, breaks forth.

To those who have never heard a barrage before it comes as a revelation. A thousand grand pianos, ten million drums, and a forest of trees being split by an army of giants, mix these together, and a hurricane at sea for the shriek of the shells as they rush through the air, and you have a very passable imitation of a barrage.

The first of the Tanks has moved off, but "Caledonian" still waits; her job is to take the green line and, if all goes well the red line as well, a total distance of some eleven thousand yards. Her rendezvous is Zonnebeke on the Ypres-Roulers railway where the Boche is reported to be in force, and from where, in all probability, he will launch a desperate counter-attack.

4. a.m. A voice from outside the Tank shouts, "Start up, number four section," and a few sharp barks followed by the running purr of engines shows that all is in readiness for the advance. The

points in well-constructed trenches, peered out through our binoculars upon a barren and dun-coloured landscape, void of any sign of human life, its dreary skyline broken only by a few jagged stumps of trees. From this desolation clouds of dust shot up where our shells were falling. It was much the same as any other battlefield, to all appearances. But even then the duckboards under foot in the trenches were squelching upon water; and a few hours' rain dissolved the fallacious crust into a bottomless and evil-smelling paste of liquid mud. And the rain was the least offender. It was our own bombardment which finished the work of ruin, pulverised the ground beyond repair, destroyed what drainage there was left, and brought the water welling up within the shell-holes as fast as they were formed.
– from *The Tank in Action* by Captain D. G. Browne, MC

Ground gained was measured by the yard; casualties by the thousand.

British and Commonwealth soldiers called it "Wipers."

right: The Mark I female WE'RE ALL IN IT at the Somme, 1916.

first Tank moves slowly forward, followed by "Crocodile," "Carmarthen," "Calcium" and "Caledonian"; it is still almost dark and the drivers, their eyes smarting from the gas which they have passed through only a few hours before, find difficulty in following the track.

A message comes back from the front, "Blue line taken, very few casualties." "Caledonian's" crew stamp their feet and try to cheer themselves with this news while warming their hands on the exhaust pipes.

Day breaks and the barrage seems almost heavier than before.

Sssssssst—bang. An early balloon has spotted No. 4 section coming and has instructed an ever willing 77 millimeter field gun to try its luck. The Tanks, at this time, in passing down a partly sunken road in a straight line, are a fair mark and the first shot falls only a few yards ahead of "Celtic."

Sssssssst—bang. Between "Celtic" and "Crocodile" this time and near enough to be unpleasant. The crews begin to sit up and take notice, wondering where the next one will fall. They have not long to wait.

Sssssssst—bang. A cloud of smoke and dust goes up, hiding for the moment the two first Tanks from the view of the others. Another miss.

"Crocodile" calmly wags her tail and proceeds—a rather longer pause this time—Fritz must be ashamed of his bad shooting and is going to chuck his hand in. Not a bit of it, a shriek and a bang and the next shell has arrived, bursting under "Calcium's" sponson. "Caledonian's" crew hold their breath as they peep from out their reflectors. All to no purpose, however; as soon as the smoke has cleared "Calcium" is perceived to be holding her course and a surprised gunner looks out of the hatchway to see if "Caledonian" will be unluckier than the rest.

To "Caledonian's" driver it seemed that she took half an hour to cross the five yards dip where the enemy could spot her. Most of her crew were

imitating the action of a University cox, trying to increase her speed from 2 to 20 miles an hour. A muffled report from behind tells them that they are safe. The leading Tanks now begin to branch off across the shell hole desert. Eight are to be in the first wave, followed by five Tanks of No. 4 section as "moppers up." The sun is now well up, but a slight mist hangs over the ground, obscuring the view and blurring the periscopes and reflectors of the Tanks. The planes are flying low, swooping down to within twenty feet of the ground and sounding their "Klaxon" horns. In a few minutes "Caledonian" is hopelessly lost. The other Tanks of her section are gone right and left, and she has to find the remains of a railway embankment somewhere on her right, and steer a course between "Bill Cottage" and "Douglas Villa."

Both are probably non-existent after this morning's barrage, so it remains to find the embankment, which being about seven miles long and only half a mile away on the right, should not prove very difficult.

The going so far has been good, the best the driver has ever seen so close to the line; it seemed when studying the maps in La Lovie Wood that they would never reach the British front line, so broken did the ground look, but surely they cannot be far from it now, yet there is almost room for a horse and cart to drive between the shell holes.

Wire ahead. Is it British or German? A close inspection reveals the pointed tops to the corkscrews; they are German and the front line has been crossed unknowingly. On the right the railway looms up through the mist, only a hundred yards away, "Caledonian" is half a mile to the right of her course.

"Neutral left," shouts the driver, "left brake on, sir," and the Tank gradually swings to her new course. "Neutral right, two up left, two up right; we may as well get a move on while the good ground lasts." and again the Tank moves forward, this time about three miles an hour.

above: A German World War I film poster, *Die englischen Tanks bei Cambrai*. right: *The Ypres Salient at Night*, a painting by Paul Nash

Ten minutes of uneventful going brings "Bill Cottage" and "Douglas Villa" into view—two ruins standing about six feet high, their walls spattered with shrapnel and machinegun fire. The mopping up parties of the infantry can be plainly seen, dodging shells, dropping bombs into dug-outs lately occupied by the Hun, and gathering prisoners and souvenirs.

A red flare bursts out three hundred yards ahead, quickly followed by another and another, until there is a chain of them miles long.

This is the signal the second wave has been waiting for; the black line has been taken and No. 4 section's work has begun. No. 1 section should be ahead somewhere, but the only Tanks visible are those of No. 9 company returning from the black line. The rest of No. 7 company appears to be lost. Two Tanks on the right are badly ditched and "Caledonian" gives them a wide berth. One of their sergeants comes across to try and borrow "Caledonian's" unditching boom, but the crew are not to be had, they may need it themselves later. An officer comes along with the same purpose, but with no better result. "Keep your flaps shut when you get to the top of the hill," he shouts, "they're sniping and machinegunning pretty badly" and from the blood running down his face it can well be believed. Two hundred yards more and a warning smack on "Caledonian's" front plate tells the crew to shut all means of entry for bullets.

Bang, bang, bang, bang. The sergeant is firing his gun from the right front mounting. Bang, bang, bang. Two more join in. The driver, straining his eyes to the right, catches sight of a few grey figures dropping hurriedly into a trench; he must steer for that trench and have them if they haven't beat it down their dug-out. Tat, tat, tat, tat—a machinegun starts pattering on the steel side without much effect; another half minute, however, and someone at the back shouts for the first aid kit. "Who's hit?" "Percy." "Anything serious?" "No, only bullet splashes in the face."

In those days tank equipment was devised and issued on a lavish scale. One took over with the machine a vast assortment of instruments calculated to soften the asperities of a very cramped and uncomfortable mode of warfare, and calling to mind the fittings of H.M.S. *Mantelpiece*. If we had no zoetropes, excellent carriage clocks, mounted in heavy brass, were the perquisites in more senses than one of every tank commander. The number of these clocks destroyed by shell-fire was so abnormal in the Salient that after that deplorable campaign the issue was stopped, it being felt that the residue of timepieces in stock would serve a more useful purpose and lead a safer life in the numerous offices of Central Stores and Workshops at Erin. A haversack full of splints, shell- dressings, iodine, and other sinister medical comforts, quite passable continued on page 31

top right: A damaged Mark I male tank, but this turret is still operative. centre right: A German cartoon of World War I, 'And then they came – Tanks, Tanks, Tanks.' top far right: 'Hyacinth', a Mark I male at the Hindenburg Support Trench System, Cambrai, 20 November 1917. right: A Mark I male tank attacking at Thiepval on the Somme, September 1916.

Percy is quickly anointed with oicric acid and resumes his seat at the secondary gears. More bursts of fire against the Tank followed by vigorous replies from within. A lonely Boche hiding in a shell-hole attracts the driver's attention; the front flap opens a few inches, a revolver barks, and the Boche has paid the penalty of attempting to stop a Tank single handed. Crrrump—a five-nine drops ten yards ahead of "Caledonian" and shakes the ammunition boxes in their racks. An inferno of machinegun fire breaks out against the front and sides—there must be at least four firing at her. Bullet splinters fly all over the interior and the smell of burning paint mixes with that of hot steel and cordite fumes; the temperature is unbearable and the whole crew are pouring with perspiration. Hell—! A loud exclamation from the driver calls attention to the fact that he has been hit and requires the first aid bag. It is quickly passed along, but before he has finished swearing about his first "packet" a second bullet enters by way of the observation slit, and striking the driver again, this time in the leg, causing him to break out afresh. By the time he is tied up most of the mirrors in the observation slits are broken and he and the officer are constrained to keep their direction by means of the periscope, a difficult job, as all who have tried it know. Another loud exclamation, this time from the Tank Commander. A bullet has driven a rivet through the front plate and given him a thick lip; this followed almost immediately by another which completely closes one eye. A shell dressing is quickly applied and the advance continues.

The ground is now getting bad and it needs all the skill of the driver to prevent the Tank from becoming ditched.

Another fusillade breaks out against the sides, and the bullet splinters come in in such showers that the gunners, have perforce to leave their guns and protect themselves behind the ammunition racks.

The fire redoubles its energy and the second

28

binoculars, electric hand-lamps, signalling shutters, six periscopes, and an ingenious device like a pair of pantomime braces fitted with batteries, switches, and red and green lights, to be used in guiding tanks at night, were also among the treasures thrust upon us in a very open-handed manner. But this halcyon age did not endure for long. Vulgar considerations of waste and expenditure supervened. Before the end the whereabouts of every spanner and split-pin became a cause of acute worry to us all. It should be unnecessary to add that this era of suspicion brought with it a veritable spate of new Army Forms . . . continually superseding each other and never by any chance filled in correctly. We were already in possession of immense log-books, atrocities known as

far left: *Treat 'Em Rough*, World War I poster by August Hutaf depicting "Black Tom", mascot of the United States Tank Corps. centre, top and bottom: World War I posters. left: A portrait of Major General Hugh Elles by Sir William Orpen. Elles had the demanding task of creating an orderly, disciplined, effective fighting force from the chaos of the early British Royal Tank Corps. He became Master General of the Ordnance in 1934, responsible for the procurement of tanks.

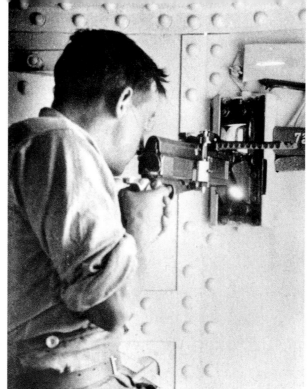

far left: A British tank park in France, 1918. left: The starboard Hotchkiss gunner of a Mark I male tank. below: The driver's position in a Mark I male.

battle history sheets, and pigeon-message forms. A fully equipped tank, in short, was a combination of a battleship, an ironmonger's shop, an optician's, a chemist's, a grocer's and a Government office. We only wanted a typewriter to round off the outfit.
— from *The Tank in Action* by Captain D. G. Browne, MC

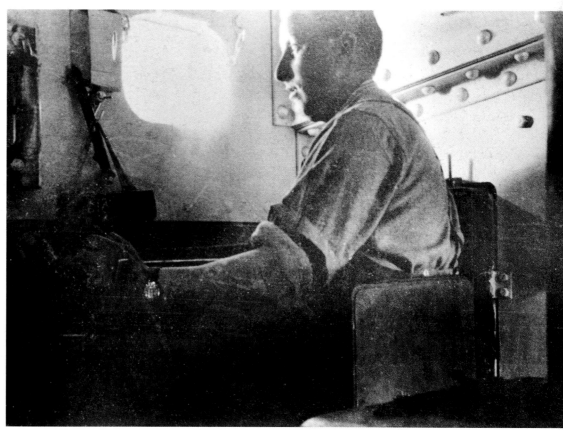

33

And now I'm drinking wine in France, / The helpless child of circumstance. Tomorrow will be loud with war, / How will I be accounted for?
– from *Soliloquy*
by Francis Ledwidge
Killed in action, 1917.

gunner is seen to be bleeding badly from the face. Rivets begin to drop out and the front driving flaps are only hanging by one or two, the bullet proof glass in the centre prism hole is entirely gone and two guns are out of action, ripped to shreds by the storm of bullets.

Two Boches loom up in the direction of Zonnebeke and the front gun is turned on them. A couple of barks and it stops, an armour piercing bullet from an enemy machinegun having jammed under the body cover.

"Spare gun up"—the damaged gun is quickly replaced and the firing recommences, this time with better luck. One of the Huns drops his gun and falls headlong and the other dives into a shell hole.

The ground is now very bad indeed and the tracks are continually slipping round without gripping. Altering direction to avoid getting ditched, a round concrete structure appears immediately ahead.

It has a slit about twelve inches deep, four feet from the ground, and through this peeps the nozzle of a machinegun. The left hand gunners at

1.   2.   3.   4.   5.

once open fire and the offending gun is quickly withdrawn.

To make sure of matters, however, the driver brings "Caledonian" alongside of the slit, completely preventing any fire from that quarter, and waits for the infantry to arrive and administer the *coup de grace* with a Mills bomb. This is soon done and "Caledonian" continues on her way rejoicing.

The driver, faint from the heat and loss of blood, suddenly perceives a large shell crater immediately ahead. "Neutral right," he shouts to the gearsman, but his wounded leg is unable to work the clutch so that the gears may be withdrawn, and the Tank creeps on towards the hole which is bound to ditch her. Percy struggles vainly at the gear handle, but is unable to make any impression; the driver, wounded in both hands, endeavours to pull out the primary gear handle, but finding all these efforts useless he shuts the throttle and stops the engine, leaving the Tank on the edge of the crater almost beyond the point of balance.

The enemy, seeing the Tank stop, direct more shell and machinegun fire on to it, and the interior becomes a perfect inferno.

The driver gives the order to start the engine up again. the engine starts with a roar, but it is useless for the driver to continue, with one leg and both arms out of action. The gunners carefully lift him down on to the floor of the Tank, and revive his spirits somewhat with rum and sal volatile.

The officer takes the driving seat and endeavours to pull the bus out of the hole, but without success, and he has to give up the job.

All the guns are now out of action and the ammunition boxes riddled with bullet splinters. The enemy fire has slackened somewhat, but it is still far from safe to leave the Tank. The fan having stopped, the heat inside is terrible, and even the unwounded feel it badly. Will the infantry never come up? To make matters worse an anti-Tank gun opens fire and "Caledonian's" crew begin to

give themselves up for lost.

But hark, another small gun speaks out, this time with a familiar clang about its voice. The third driver quickly hoists a periscope, and to the joy of all announces that "Crocodile" is only half a mile away and is firing at the anti-Tank gun. The infantry are now level with the Tank and the enemy fire begins to die down. At last it ceases altogether, and with a sigh of relief the three more seriously wounded members of the crew open the doors and roll out on to the ground. The fresh air acts like a tonic and the first driver so far recovers as to make an inspection of the outside.

Not a trace of paint to be seen on the front of the Tank, name all shot away, Lewis guns torn to shreds, periscopes punctured, and the whole of the crew stone deaf and mostly covered with dried blood.

The officer, somewhat dazed from the blow to his head, leads the way for the wounded, leaving the sergeant to take care of the remainder.

On the way they stop and try to hold conversation with "Crocodile," but without much effect owing to their deafness. The little party passed down towards the dressing station pursued by machinegun fire which they fortunately—being deaf—could not hear. On the way they picked up "Calcium's" driver wounded in the arm and also passed the dead body of poor old "Bunny," the gallant officer of "Carmarthen."

Exhausted, they reached a regimental aid post, and after having their wounds dressed were sent rejoicing on their way with a cup of coffee and a packet of "Players." Of the remainder of the crew, "Percy" was killed later in the day and Sergeant Richards was wounded, as also were two others, leaving only one of the crew of eight to return to his company to tell the story.

Sergeant Richards was afterwards awarded the Military Medal for his gallantry in remaining with "Percy" after he was wounded, and under heavy fire until the latter died.

far left: *Tank Corps*, a World War I painting by A.E. Haswell Miller. below: A World War I poster: *THE TANK is a travelling fortress that clears the way for our soldiers*.

'Good-morning; good-morning!' the General said
When we met him last week on our way to the line. / Now the soldiers he smiled at are most of 'em dead, / And we're cursing his staff for incompetent swine. / 'He's a cheery old card,' grunted Harry to Jack
As they slogged up to Arras with rifle and pack.

But he did for them both by his plan of attack.
– *The General*
by Siegfried Sassoon

GUDERIAN

right: General Heinz Guderian, the father of modern tank warfare and Germany's Panzer force.

PRIOR TO WORLD WAR I, a young German infantry officer named Heinz Wilhelm Guderian had chosen a technical role for himself with a telegraph battalion because he was particularly interested in the military uses of communications. With the coming of war Guderian was assigned to command a heavy wireless station linked to the cavalry. He was fascinated by the opportunities which were afforded by improvements in the wireless technology of the day. They would soon enable commanders to utilize radio communications wherever they were, in a command post, aboard an aircraft, or, once it had been invented, in a tank.

Guderian was born on 17 June 1888 at the Vistula River town of Kulm south of Gdansk (Danzig) in what is now Poland. Friedrich, his father, was a Senior Lieutenant in the 2nd Pomeranian Jaeger Battalion of the German army and his duties took the family to live in Colmar, Alsace and later to Saint-Avold. Heinz was sent off to boarding school and then to the Karlsruhe cadet school in Baden, where his teachers thought him a very serious boy, highly articulate and, at times, quite cold. He entered the army with a commission as a Second Lieutenant on 27 January 1908. He married Margarete Goerne on 1 October 1913 and they had two sons, both of whom fought with the Panzertruppen in World War II. Guderian's obvious promise won him various divisional and corps staff appointments and, near the end of World War I, attendance at a General Staff officer's course, where he was the youngest officer. The end of the war left him appalled by the catastrophic loss of life in the trenches. He focused on refining a tactical theory based on his belief that "only movement brings victory."

After the war, Guderian remained on active service and was eventually given a position on the staff of the Transport Troops Inspectorate. He had been brought in specifically to study the theoretical uses of motorized infantry in combat,

Lili Marlene is based on a German poem of World War I. The song was a favourite of German and British troops in the desert war in 1941 and, with the arrival of American forces in North Africa in 1943, its popularity was extended when the German-born actress Marlene Dietrich made it famous. The English version is not a direct translation of the German lyric.

Aus dem stillen Raume,
aus der Erde Grund,
Hebt mich, wie im Traume
dien verlieber Mund,
Wenn sich die spaeten
Nebel drehn, / Werd ich
bei der Laterne stehn,
Wie einst Lilli Marleen, wie
einst Lilli Marleen.
– from *Lilli Marleen*

Resting in a billet just behind the line, / Even tho' we're parted your lips are close to mine; / You wait where that lantern softly gleams, / Your sweet face seems to haunt my dreams, / My Lili of the lamplight, / My own Lili Marlene.
– from *Lili Marlene*

The Germans often accuse us of being low plagiarists when it comes to music, and that we cannot deny. Our musical geniuses at home never did get around to working up a good, honest, acceptable war song, and so they forced us to share *Lili Marlene* with the enemy. Even if we did get it from the krauts

but, as so often happens in military organizations, he was immediately reassigned to another task that was totally unrelated to either his experience or his interests. Disappointed by this unwanted turn in his career, he devoted his spare time to studying the theory of mechanized warfare with particular attention to the writings of the tank pioneer, Major General J.F.C. Fuller, and military theorist Sir Basil Liddell-Hart. It was Liddell-Hart who, after serving in World War I, developed the concept of mechanized warfare to replace the bitter static warfare he had experienced. Fuller and Liddell-Hart's ideas about tank tactics, together with his own theories, formed the basis of what was to be Heinz Guderian's immense contribution to the evolution of armoured war.

The peace treaty of Versailles following World War I stipulated that Germany would not be permitted to develop an effective army. It forbade Germany the possession or construction of armoured vehicles, tanks or any similar equipment which might be employed in war. Britain and other nations continued to experiment with tanks and other armoured weapons, but with little real fervour. The German Army, though, was becoming infused with the mechanized warfare doctrine of another genius, General Hans von Seekt, who would also contribute enormously to the reform and reorganization of the Army. Determined to pursue their burgeoning interest in tanks and armour, the Germans worked out a secret arrangement with the Soviets in 1928, for their common use of a test facility near the Volga river. They shared ideas, technology and some small tanks that the Russians had acquired, including the British Vickers-Loyds.

Through the 1920s and early '30s Germany paid lip service to the armament restrictions that had been imposed on her by the victors of the Great War. But behind the scenes she continued to experiment and work towards the development of an armoured capability. Heinz Guderian,

meanwhile, was active on the lecture circuit, spreading his gospel on the uses and implications of armour, motorized infantry and aircraft in future conflicts. In Britain great strides were being made in the area of radio communications for use in tanks and armoured vehicles and there was no keener observer of these developments than Guderian, who would one day become known as "the Father of the Panzer Force".

By early 1934, with Adolf Hitler now the Chancellor of Germany, the Daimler-Benz company was well along in the design and construction of a promising tank prototype, the PzKw (Panzerkampfwagen)1. By early February 1935 Hitler had visited the secret German Army ordnance testing ground at Kummersdorf and witnessed trials of the new tank; his widely reported comment: "That's what I need. That's what I want to have." The inexpensive light tank was indeed just what he needed; an impressive new weapon that could be had in great numbers if production could somehow be achieved in spite of the serious rubber and fuel shortages and the small scale of steel production in Germany. The optimistic Führer immediately authorized the creation of three panzer divisions.

In the autumn of 1935 Colonel Guderian was made chief of staff of the new German armoured force. His ideas about armoured warfare technique, tactics and equipment found great favour with Hitler and his command was receiving much of the equipment and materials it requested, largely at the expense of the other army organizations which were forced to do without. Even with this favoured treatment, however, Guderian was not able to get the tracked armoured vehicles he thought essential to his philosophy, which required the ability to move motorized infantry overland in concert with his tanks.

From the early years of his military career, through the early years of World War II, Heinz Guderian sought out and capitalized on every opportunity to expand his knowledge and experience of mechanized warfare. His imaginative, far-sighted concepts placed him in the forefront of thinking about future tank warfare. Unlike some armoured warfare specialists, Guderian was a hands-on type; an activist who believed in leading from the front. He played a key role in the design, development and manufacture of his tanks, contributing to the main design features of the PzKpfw III and PzKpfw IV types (the former intended for attacking soft targets with a short, large-calibre cannon, and the latter with a long gun for tank-killing). He took an aggressive interest in all aspects of the tanks his panzers would take to war.

In 1936 Guderian attained the rank of General and in 1937 his book *Achtung—Panzer!* was published. Over the years comment about the book among military historians has ranged widely. Len Deighton thought it: "Hastily written and rather bland . . . contributed little to the theory of tank warfare but clearly established its author as a supporter of Hitler." Liddell-Hart, in contrast, believed the book to be " . . . of great interest as a self-exposition of the specialist mind and how it works. He had far more imagination than most specialists, but it was exercised almost entirely within the bounds of his professional subject, and burning enthusiasm increased the intensity of his concentration." Paul Harris was even more enthusiastic: "*Achtung—Panzer!* is one of the most significant military books of the twentieth century. Guderian distilled into it about fifteen years' study of the development of mechanized warfare from its origins in the First World War until 1937. He sought to demonstrate that only by the intelligent use of armoured formations could Germany achieve swift and decisive victories in future wars, and avoid the ruinous attrition experienced in 1914-18. Although a number of conservative senior officers were sceptical of Guderian's message, by the outbreak of the Second World War it had

gained a good deal of acceptance. The panzer (armoured) divisions became the cutting edge of the German Army in its spectacular victories of 1939-42".

The book certainly impressed Adolf Hitler who, in February 1938, promoted Guderian to Lieutenant-General, appointing him to command the world's first armoured corps. The new position would provide a showcase for the capabilities of his armoured units when, in 1939, they were required to perform as the lead force in the *Anschluss*, Hitler's annexation of Austria. But the impression of ruthless efficiency given to Europe and the world by their role in the bloodless takeover of Austria was a false one, in reality. Guderian's armoured units suffered from insufficient supplies and an ill-conceived logistics organization. His petrol-engined tanks only managed to keep rolling by taking on fuel from service stations along the invasion route. The tank breakdown rate was reported to be at least 30 per cent. Food and ammunition were in critically short supply and the experience caused Guderian to rethink and rebuild his entire supply system.

Hitler had intended that his panzers would roll into Poland early on 26 August 1939, but he cancelled the attack at the last minute on the chance that something positive might yet come from his diplomatic manoeuvring with Britain, which had guaranteed Poland's integrity. Lacking acceptable progress, he rescheduled his Polish adventure. The panzers were alerted on 31 August and the German armoured divisions were moved up to forward positions, ready for the attack.

Heinz Guderian: "On the 1st of September at 04.45 hrs. the whole corps moved simultaneously over the frontier. There was a thick ground mist at first which prevented the air force from giving us any support. I accompanied the 3rd Panzer Brigade, in the first wave, as far as the area north of Zempelburg where the preliminary fighting took

it's a beautiful song, and the only redeeming thing is the rumour kicking around that 'Lili' is an ancient French song, stolen by the Germans. It may not be true, but we like to believe it.

'Lili' got a couple of artillerymen in trouble in France. They were singing it at a bar the day after this particular town had been taken. Some local partisans came over and told them to shut the hell up. The guys understood, apologized, and bought drinks all around.
– Bill Mauldin, World War II cartoonist

place. Unfortunately the heavy artillery of the 3rd Panzer Division felt itself compelled to fire into the mist, despite having received precise orders not to do so. The first shell landed 50 yards ahead of my command vehicle, the second 50 yards behind it. I reckoned that the next one was bound to be a direct hit and ordered my driver to turn about and drive off. The unaccustomed noise had made him nervous, however, and he drove straight into a ditch at full speed. The front axle of the half-tracked vehicle was bent so that the steering mechanism was put out of action. This marked the end of my drive. I made my way to my corps command post, procured myself a fresh vehicle and had a word with the over-eager artillerymen. Incidentally it may be noted that I was the first corps commander ever to use armoured command vehicles in order to accompany tanks on to the battlefield. They were equipped with radio, so that I was able to keep in constant touch with my corps headquarters and with the divisions under my command."

Guderian again: "Messages from the 2nd (Motorized) Infantry Division stated that their attack on the Polish wire entanglements had bogged down. All three infantry regiments had made a frontal attack. The division was now without reserves. I ordered that the regiment on the left be withdrawn during the night and moved to the right wing, from where it was to advance next day behind the 3rd Panzer Division and make an encircling movement in the direction of Tuchel.

"The 20th (Motorized) Division had taken Konitz with some difficulty, but had not advanced any appreciable distance beyond that town. It was ordered to continue its attack on the next day.

"During the night the nervousness of the first day of battle made itself felt more than once. Shortly after midnight the 2nd (Motorized) Division informed me that they were being compelled to withdraw by Polish cavalry. I was speechless for a moment; when I regained the use of my voice

left: PzKpfw III German medium tanks halted on a rail line in Greece. The Panzer III was one of the best all-round tanks of World War II.

41

below: A PzKpfw V Panther 'D' in Italy, 1944. The Panthers made their combat debut at Kursk, the biggest tank battle in history, in July 1943. While impressive, they were not present in sufficient numbers to make a difference in the outcome, and were not then ready to perform to their full capability.

I asked the divisional commander if he had ever heard of Pomeranian grenadiers being broken by hostile cavalry. He replied that he had not and now assured me that he could hold his positions. I decided all the same that I must visit this division the next morning. At about five o'clock I found the divisional staff still all at sea. I placed myself at the head of the regiment which had been withdrawn during the night and led it personally as far as the crossing of the Kamionka to the north of Gross-Klonia, where I sent it off in the direction of Tuchel. The 2nd (Motorized) Division's attack now began to make rapid progress. The panic of the first day's fighting was past."

Guderian was famously the creator of the theory of "blitzkrieg" or lightning war. The main way in which tanks were used in the latter part of World War I—to try and force a hole through the enemy line—had made him realize the validity of his own notion: a powerful, well-supported armoured force is best utilized in a high-speed, long-ranging push deep into enemy territory, achieving rapid, sustainable gains while wreaking maximum confusion, chaos and panic as it travels. He believed in versatility and adaptability in combat, cherishing the radio capability that enabled these qualities. His watchwords were *mobility* and *velocity*. In his book, *The Other Side of the Hill*, Basil Liddell-Hart said of Guderian: "Sixty per cent of what the German Panzer forces became was due to him. Ambitious, brave, a heart for his soldiers who liked and trusted him; rash as a man, quick in decisions, strict with officers, real personality, therefore many enemies. Blunt, even to Hitler. As a trainer—good;

thorough; progressive. If you suggest revolutionary ideas, he will say in 95% of cases: 'Yes,' at once."

Guderian: "On the 5th of September our corps had a surprise visit from Adolf Hitler. I met him near Plevno on the Tuchel-Schwetz road, got into his car and drove with him along the line of our previous advance. We passed the destroyed Polish artillery, went through Schwetz, and then, following closely behind our encircling troops, drove to Graudenz where he stopped and gazed for some time at the blown bridges over the Vistula. At the sight of the smashed artillery regiment, Hitler had asked me: 'Our dive bombers did that?' When I replied, 'No, our panzers!' he was plainly astonished. During the drive we discussed at first the course of events in my corps area. Hitler asked about casualties. I gave him the latest figures that I had received, some 150 dead and 700 wounded for all the four divisions under my command during the Battle of the Corridor. He was amazed at the smallness of these figures and contrasted them with the casualties of his own old regiment, the *List* Regiment, during the First World War: on the first day of battle that one regiment alone had lost more than 2,000 dead and wounded. I was able to show him that the smallness of our casualties in this battle against a tough and courageous enemy was primarily due to the effectiveness of our tanks. Tanks are a life-saving weapon. The men's belief in the superiority of their armoured equipment had been greatly strengthened by their successes in the Corridor. The enemy had suffered the total destruction of between two and three infantry divisions and one cavalry brigade. Thousands of prisoners and hundreds of guns had fallen into our hands.

"Our conversation turned on technical matters. Hitler wanted to know what had proved particularly satisfactory about our tanks and what was still in need of improvement. I told him that the most important thing now was to hasten the delivery of Panzers III and IV to the fighting troops

and to increase the production of these tanks. For their further development their present speed was sufficient, but they needed to be more heavily armoured, particularly in front; the range and power of penetration of their guns also needed to be increased, which would mean longer barrels and a shell with a heavier charge. This applied equally to our anti-tank guns.

"With a word of recognition for the troops' achievements Hitler left us as dusk was falling and returned to his headquarters.

"On the 6th of September the corps staff and the advance guards of the divisions crossed the Vistula. Corps headquarters was set up in Finckenstein, in the very beautiful castle that belonged to Count Dohna-Finckenstein and which Frederick the Great had given to his minister, Count von Finckenstein. Napoleon had twice used this castle as his headquarters. The emperor first came there in 1807, when he took the war against Prussia and Russia over the Vistula and into East Prussia. After crossing the poor and monotonous Tuchel Heath, Napoleon exclaimed at the sight of the castle: *'Enfin un château!'* His feelings are understandable. It was there that he had planned his advance towards Preussisch-Eylau. A mark of his presence was still to be seen in the scratches left by his spurs on the wooden floor. He was there for the second time before the Russian campaign of 1812; he spent a few weeks in the castle in the company of the beautiful Countess Walewska.

"I slept in the room that had been Napoleon's."

With the end of the European war in May 1945, Heinz Guderian surrendered to a U.S. Army unit and became a prisoner of war. While the Russians wanted to him to face trial at Nuremberg, the Western Allies did not concur. Guderian spent two years in West German prisons and was finally released in 1948. Thereafter, he wrote his memoirs and other works at his home in Schwangau bei Fussen, where he died on 14 May 1954.

I met her paddling down the road, / A vast primeval sort of toad, / And while I planned a swift retreat She snorted, roared, and stamped her feet, / And sprinted up a twelve-foot bank; / Whereat a voice cried, "Good old Tank!"

She paused and wagged her armoured tail, / There was a "Jonah" in the "Whale," / Since from her ribs a face looked out; Her "skipper" hailed me with a shout, / "Come on and watch my beauty eat A batch of houses down the street!"

It was pure joy to see her crunch / A sugar factory for lunch; / She was a "peach" at chewing trees— / The Germans shuddered at her sneeze— / And when she leant against a wall / It shortly wasn't there at all.

I stroked the faithful creature's head; / "What gives her greatest bliss?" I said. / Her skipper glibly answered, "Tanks are crazed about Abdullas . . . Thanks! / She waddled off— and on the air / Arose Abdulla's fragrance rare!

– *The Ways of Tanks* from an Abdulla cigarettes ad in the 2 November 1918 issue of *The Sphere*

LIGHTNING WAR

You were given the choice between war and dishonour. You chose dishonour and you will have war.
— Winston Churchill, in response to Prime Minister Neville Chamberlain's Munich agreement with Adolf Hitler of 29 September 1938

right: A German Panzer III in France, 1940.

NO ONE is certain about the exact origin of the word *blitzkrieg* (lightning war). As defined by the *American Heritage Dictionary of the English Language*, it means: A swift, sudden military offensive, usually by combined air and mobile land forces. Credit for coining it has gone variously to *Time* magazine, Adolf Hitler, Sir Basil Liddell-Hart and others. Whatever the origin, historians generally agree that the concept itself is Prussian.

"In this year, 1929, I became convinced that tanks working on their own or in conjunction with infantry could never achieve decisive importance. My historical studies, the exercises carried out in England and our own experiments with mock-ups had persuaded me that tanks would never be able to produce their full effect until the other weapons on whose support they must inevitably rely were brought up to their standard of speed and cross-country performance. In such a formation of all arms, the tanks must play the primary role, the other weapons being subordinated to the requirements of the armour. It would be wrong to include tanks in infantry divisions: what was needed were armoured divisions which would include all the supporting arms needed to allow the tanks to fight with full effect.
— from *Panzer Leader*
by Heinz Guderian

"In a few words then, the whole future of warfare appears to me to lie in the employment of mobile armies, relatively small but of high quality and rendered distinctly more effective by the addition of aircraft, and in the simultaneous mobilization of the whole defence force, be it to feed the attack or for home defence."
— General Hans von Seeckt, German Army

While it was the vision of von Seeckt that led to the birth of the panzer division; it was Heinz Guderian who conceived and fully realized the blitzkrieg tactic. In the 1930s majority opinion in the German Army held that the tank, while a useful weapon, was not a decisive one. Many senior officers opposed the development of a massive panzer capability which they saw as a threat to their cavalry arm. But Adolf Hitler himself, having experienced and been traumatized by the terrible stalemate warfare of World War I, conveyed his belief in the blitzkrieg concept when he told the audience at the 1935 Nuremberg Party Rally: "I shouldn't negotiate for months beforehand and make lengthy preparations, but—as I have always done throughout my life—I should suddenly, like a flash of lightning in the night, hurl myself upon the enemy." The blitzkrieg approach to warfare brought advantages that Hitler quickly appreciated. He liked the economies afforded through the use of brief and decisive military actions and he needed such speedy and relatively low-cost victories to convince the German people that his aggressive foreign policy would bring results.

Guderian later described his own vision of how a blitzkrieg action might develop: "One night the doors of aeroplane hangars and army garages will be flung back, motors will be tuned up, and squadrons will swing into movement. The first sudden blow may capture important industrial and raw-material districts or destroy them by air attack so they can take no part in war production. Enemy governmental and military centres may be crippled and his transport system disorganized. In any case, the first strategic surprise attack will penetrate more or less deep into enemy territory according to the distances to be covered and the amount of resistance met with.

"The first wave of air and mechanized attack will be followed up by motorized infantry divisions. They will be carried to the verge of the occupied territory and hold it, thereby freeing the mobile units for another blow. In the meantime the attacker will be raising a mass army. He has the

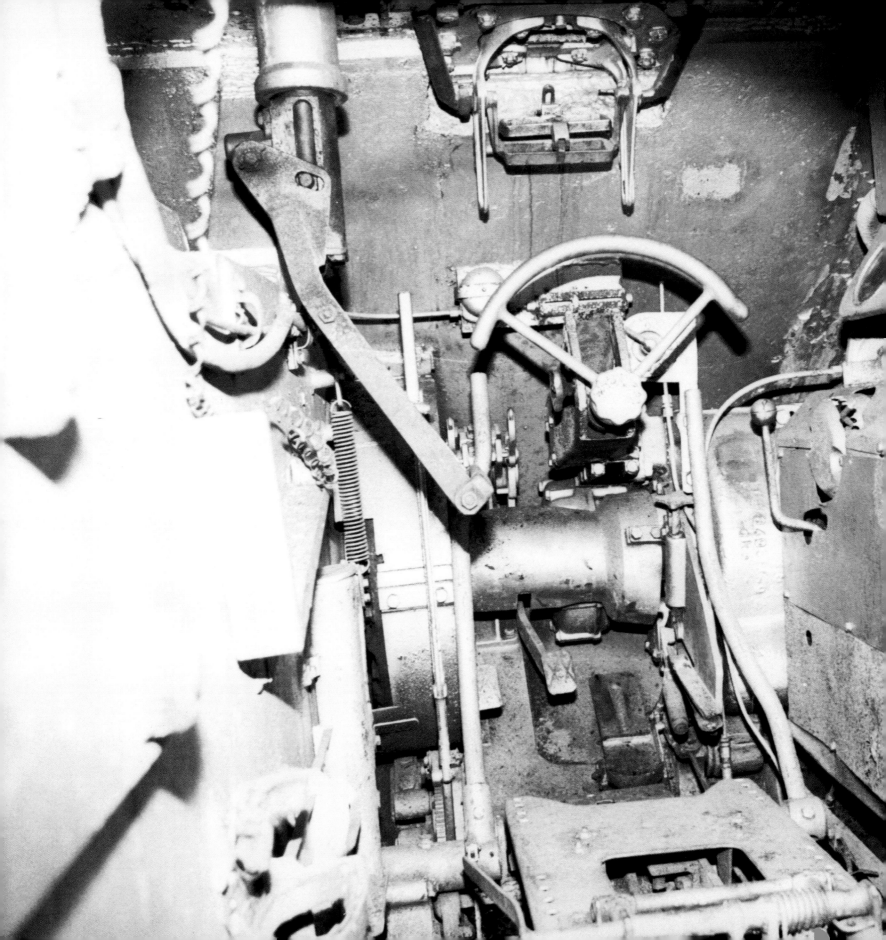

choice of territory and time for his next big blow, and he will then bring up the weapons intended for breaking down all resistance and bursting through the enemy lines. He will do his best to launch the great blow suddenly so as to take the enemy by surprise, rapidly concentrating his mobile troops and hurling his air force at the enemy. The armoured divisions will no longer stop when the first objectives have been reached; on the contrary, utilizing their speed and radius of action to the full they will do their utmost to complete the breakthrough into the enemy lines of communication. Blow after blow will be launched ceaselessly in order to roll up the enemy front and carry the attack as far as possible into enemy territory. The air force will attack the enemy reserves and prevent their intervention."

Two days after German forces crashed into Poland on 1 September 1939 in the start of the *Fall Weiss* (Case White) campaign, Britain and France declared war on Germany. By May 1940 Hitler and his war planners had devised and were on the brink of implementing a grand scheme for the conquest of Western Europe. The plan called for a spectacular coordinated strike: an amazing blitzkrieg combining massive armoured power, infantry, paratroops, dive-bombers, surprise, speed and deception.

German Army Group B, comprising 30 Wehrmacht divisions, was positioned along a 200-mile front-line facing Belgium and Holland. It would be their job to push through the low countries in a four-pronged attack. But this effort was essentially diversionary. German planners expected the British and French to immediately move the bulk of their best divisions northward and come to the aid of the Dutch and Belgians mainly along the Dyle River in Belgium.

To the south Army Group A, the massive main force of 45 German armour and motorized infantry divisions, waited near the Rhine. When the call

The tank seemed to be momentarily stuck. Its treads spun, digging into the soft clay, and its machineguns waved erratically back and forth. It was the first German tank Noah had seen, and as he watched it he felt almost hypnotized. It was so large, so impregnable, so full of malice . . . . Now, he felt, there is nothing to be done. He was despairing and relieved at the same time. Now, there was nothing more that could be done. The tank took everything out of his hands, all decisions, all responsibilities . . .
– from *The Young Lions* by Irwin Shaw

left: Interior and driver's position in a PzKpfw IV German tank, this example a late-model with anti- bazooka plates and a high-velocity 75mm gun.

left: An experimental
PzKpfw Panzer III. The III
was operated by a crew
of five, had a 50mm gun
and a range of 112
miles (180 km).

21 January 1944
High Command of the
Armed Forces (Operations
Staff)
I order as follows:
1. Commanders-in-Chief,
Commanding Generals,
and Divisional
Commanders are
personally responsible to
me for reporting in good
time:
a. Every decision to carry
out an operational
movement.
b. Every attack planned in
Divisional strength and
upwards which does not
conform with the general
directives laid down by the
High Command.
c. Every offensive action in
quiet sectors of the front,
over and above normal
shock troop activities, which
is calculated to draw the
enemy's attention to the
sector.
d. Every plan for disengaging
or withdrawing forces.
e. Every plan for
surrendering a position, a
local strong point, or a
fortress.
They must ensure that I
have time to intervene in
this decision if I think fit,
and that my counter-orders
can reach the front line
troops in time.
2. Commanders-in-Chief,
Commanding Generals, and
Divisional Commanders, the
Chiefs of the General Staffs,
and each individual officer of
the General Staff, or officers
continued on page 52

continued on page 52

right: 'One Hundred Per
Cent', by Frank Reynolds.

came it would be their task to break through a gap between the Maginot and Dyle lines, through the forests of the Ardennes and then race across France to the English Channel. Once there, they were to turn northward in support of Army Group B, to surround and entrap as many as one million Allied soldiers. That accomplished, the Germans would then be able to concentrate their efforts in occupying all of France, their campaign was known as *Fall Gelb* (Case Yellow). Finally, the role of German Army Group C, a 19-division force, would be one of keeping the defenders of the Maginot line fortifications busy having to respond to a persistent series of attacks and feints.

André Maginot was Defence Minister of France in 1930 when his government started work on an 87-mile-long system of underground fortifications against any future threat from their German neighbours. Seven years and $200 million later, the massive project neared completion and was named in Maginot's honour.

Constructed in defensive layers, the line was fronted with tank trap obstacles which lay ahead of a network of pillboxes protected by barbed wire. Behind these were gun emplacements set in ten-foot-thick concrete walls. These were supported by anti-tank guns from 37mm to 135mm and machine-guns. Gigantic underground forts were located every three to five miles along the line. They were constructed with several levels, each had elevators, casemates, shell hoists, sleeping quarters, a command post, a guard room, a hospital, munitions magazines, stores, a telephone exchange, a power plant and a network of connecting tunnels all fitted with protective steel doors. These forts were sunk to a depth of 100 feet. Each was manned by up to 1200 personnel.

The French believed that the formidable Maginot Line fortifications of the Franco-German frontier would deter any future German assault or require the Germans to approach France through the Low Countries. Towards the Franco-Belgian border, the Maginot Line dwindled into a smattering of small defensive elements known as the Little Maginot. An important French industrial region lay just behind this relatively weak defence. The Belgian border, however, was strongly defended and the Allies believed (just as Hitler was sure they would) that their best option in the event of German attack would be to move a large force of troops quickly into Belgium when the Germans made their move.

Hitler had wanted to begin his western assault before the worst of the 1939-40 winter set in, but was persuaded by his meteorologists and others that it would be prudent to wait until the spring. In preparation for the attack he ordered the readying of a special panzer corps whose task would be an assault on the city of Sedan, the strategically important link between the Maginot and Little Maginot lines.

General Erich von Manstein, Chief of Staff to German Army Group A, the organization given the task of hitting Sedan, believed adamantly that those in the German General Staff who thought of the Ardennes as impenetrable and utterly unsuited for tank warfare were wrong. He was certain that the forest offered excellent opportunities for the panzers, with its good roads and many wide fields. The forest areas themselves, he thought, provided ideal camouflage cover for the German armoured forces against aerial reconnaissance observation. But Manstein, with Guderian in complete agreement, also felt that Hitler's idea of committing a single panzer corps to the Ardennes attack was folly and would probably result in a World War I-style stalemate. Manstein and Guderian were convinced that the primary emphasis needed to be on the destruction of the Allied forces in one swift and decisive panzer strike, which could only be achieved through employment of the bulk of Army Group A.

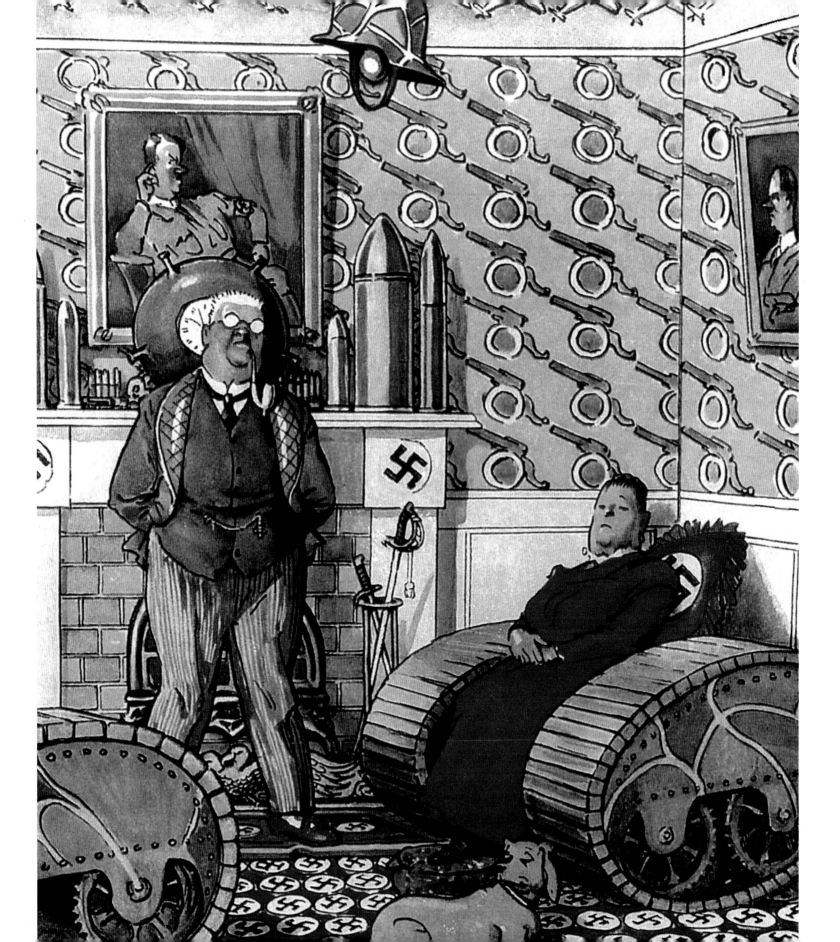

employed on General Staffs, are responsible to me that every report made to me either directly, or through the normal channels, should contain nothing but the unvarnished truth. In future, I shall impose draconian punishment on any attempt at concealment, whether deliberate or arising from carelessness or oversight. 3. I must point out that the maintenance of signals communications, particularly in heavy fighting and critical situations, is a prerequisite for the conduct of the battle. All officers commanding troops are responsible to me for ensuring that these communications both to higher headquarters and to subordinate commanders, are not broken and for seeing that, by exhausting every means and engaging themselves personally, permanent communications in every case are ensured with the commanders above and below.
– Adolf Hitler

Guderian: ". . . a conference took place attended by the army and army group commanders of Army Group A, accompanied by General von Kleist and myself, in the Reich Chancellery. Hitler was there. Each of us generals outlined what his task was and how he intended to carry it out. I was the last to speak. My task was as follows: on the day ordered I would cross the Luxembourg frontier, drive through southern Belgium towards Sedan, cross the Meuse and establish a bridgehead on the far side so that the infantry corps following behind could get across. I explained briefly that my corps would advance through Luxembourg and Southern Belgium in three columns; I reckoned on reaching the Belgian frontier posts on the first day and I hoped to break through them on that same day; on the second day I would advance as far as Neufchâteau; on the third day I would reach Bouillon and cross the Semois; on the fourth day I would arrive at the Meuse; on the fifth day I would cross it. By the evening of the fifth day I hoped to have established a bridgehead on the far bank. Hitler asked: 'And then what are you going to do?' He was the first person who had thought to ask me this vital question. I replied: 'Unless I receive orders to the contrary, I intend on the next day to continue my advance westwards. The supreme leadership must decide whether my objective is to be Amiens or Paris. In my opinion the correct course is to drive past Amiens to the English Channel.' Hitler nodded and said nothing more. Only General Busch, who commanded the Sixteenth Army on my left, cried out: 'Well, I don't think you'll cross the river in the first place!' Hitler, the tension visible in his face, looked at me to see what I would reply. I said: 'There's no need for you to do so, in any case.' Hitler made no comment.

"I never received any further orders as to what I was to do once the bridgehead over the Meuse was captured. All my decisions, until I reached the Atlantic seaboard at Abbéville, were taken by me and me alone. The Supreme Command's influence on my actions was merely restrictive throughout."

Hitler finally agreed to Manstein's approach after the General brilliantly articulated it to him at a High Command dinner. Greatly impressed with the new plan, the German leader immersed himself in a process of refining it with his generals and, on 24 February, declared it ready for implementation in May.

There were ten divisions of the British Expeditionary Force near the Franco-Belgian border in April 1940, about 400,000 men, and just one tank brigade. The Belgians were trying to remain neutral, while the French were boasting confidently that they would beat the Germans when they came and British Prime Minister Neville Chamberlain was talking about "Herr Hitler" having missed his best chance at a western offensive by not striking right after Poland had fallen.

At dawn on 10 May 1940 the first elements of a German army of more than two million men began to move on Holland, Luxembourg and Belgium. Great masses of tanks and infantry spearheaded the campaign to secure the whole of Western Europe. It was the final day of the so-called Phony War and the day that Winston Churchill became the new British Prime Minister.

Aircraft of the Royal Air Force and the French Armée de l'Air rose from French airfields to attack the German columns but did little real damage to the advancing enemy. Everywhere the Germans went, their panzers coursed through the opposition, with little apparent effort, except at Rotterdam where determined Dutch resistance held firm. Hitler then ordered a massive air strike on the port city, starting major fires which destroyed nearly 650 acres in the main section. 800 citizens died and more than 75,000 were left homeless. The Dutch forces surrendered after holding out for five days against the enemy assault.

Just north of Liége lay the largest and most heavily fortified example of Belgium's modern defences, Eben Emael. Positioned near where the Albert Canal merged with the Meuse River, the fort housed a 1,500-man garrison and was defended by two 120mm guns and sixteen 75mm guns capable of covering all approaches to the site—except from above. Before daybreak on the 10th, hundreds of German airborne troops landed near the fort, some of them on the roof of the structure. Their mission included the placing of explosive charges in ventilators and gun slits, in addition to hollow-charge demolition explosives specially devised to bust the three-foot-thick concrete walls and spread a deadly inferno through the interior and galleries. The fires were supplemented by flame throwers fired into the gunports. By 7 a.m. the fort had effectively been neutralized and by mid-day on the 11th, the garrison was forced to surrender.

The Allied forces rushed north to position themselves on the Meuse and Dyle rivers, ready to face the German onslaught. Gathered there were a combined force of 37 British, French and Belgian divisions. The Allies, in particular the French, were aware of the enemy activity in the Ardennes, but were confident that the Germans would require a minimum of ten days to make their way through the heavily-wooded region. They further believed that the real defensive test would come at the Meuse, which they were quite sure they could hold, having prepared the banks with hundreds of dugouts and, behind them, artillery positions. German armoured elements, however, had little trouble with the minefields near the German-Belgian frontier in the night of 9-10 May, nor with Allied troops in the zone. In only two days seven German armoured divisions reached a point on the Meuse near Sedan.

By the morning of 13 May little remained of the vaunted French defences on the Meuse. German armour didn't need to fire a shot. Their easy access to the river, which they immediately began crossing on pontoon bridges they brought with them, had been made possible by their air force whose low-level bombers and Stuka dive-bombers had ceaselessly pounded the French defenders. General Guderian led the armoured units crossing the Meuse and wrote of the event: "On the far bank of the river I found the efficient and brave commander of the 1st Rifle Regiment, Lieutenant-Colonel Balck, with his staff. He hailed me with the cheerful cry: 'Pleasure boating on the Meuse is forbidden!' I had in fact coined the phrase myself during the training we had had for this operation, since the attitude of some of the younger officers had struck me as too light-hearted. I now realized that they had judged the situation correctly."

The slower French tanks were no match for the German armour at the Meuse, with the panzers destroying more than 50 in just two hours. German anti-aircraft defences performed effectively, downing 268 of the 474 RAF aircraft in France by 14 May.

Guderian: "Once again to the 1st Panzer Division, where I found the divisional commander accompanied by his first general staff officer, Major Wenck; I asked him whether his whole division could be turned westwards or whether a flank guard should be left facing south on the east bank of the Ardennes Canal. Wenck saw fit to interject a somewhat slangy expression of mine 'Klotzen, nicht Kleckern' [a phrase which might be roughly translated as 'Boot 'em, don't spatter 'em'], and that really answered my question. 1st and 2nd Panzer Divisions received orders immediately to change direction with all their forces, to cross the Ardennes Canal, and to head west with the objective of breaking clear through the French defences. That I might co-ordinate the movements of the two divisions I next went to the command post of the 2nd Panzer Division, which was in the Château Rocan, on the heights above Donchéry. From that vantage point a good view could be obtained over

You'd think, to hear some people talk, / That lads go West with sobs and curses, / And sullen faces white as chalk, / Hankering for wreaths and tombs and hearses. / But they've been taught the way to do it Like Christian soldiers; not with haste / And shuddering groans; but passing through it / With due regard for decent taste.
– from *How to Die* by Siegfried Sassoon

the ground across which 2nd Panzer Division had advanced and attacked on the 13th and 14th of May. I was surprised that the French long-range artillery in the Maginot Line and its westerly extension had not laid down heavier fire and caused us more trouble during our advance. At this moment, as I looked at the ground we had come over, the success of our attack struck me as almost a miracle."

Having crossed the Meuse, the great mass of German armour was able to fan out as it raced west. Many dispirited French troops were cluttering the roads being used by the panzers. Some recalled the derisive shouts from German tankers: "Drop your rifles and get the hell out of here—we don't have time to take you prisoner."

Guderian: "I was pleased to have retained my freedom of movement when, early on the 16th of May, I went to the headquarters of the 1st Panzer Division. I drove through Vendresse to Omont. The situation at the front was not yet clear. All that was known was that there had been heavy fighting during the night in the neighbourhood of Bouvellemont. So on to Bouvellemont. In the main street of the burning village I found the regimental commander, Lieutenant-Colonel Balck, and let him describe the events of the previous night to me. The troops were over-tired, having had no real rest since the 9th of May. Ammunition was running low. The men in the front line were falling asleep in their slit trenches. Balck himself, in wind jacket and with a knotty stick in his hand, told me that the capture of the village had only succeeded because, when his officers complained against the continuation of the attack, he had replied: 'In that case I'll take the place on my own!' and had moved off. His men had thereupon followed him. His dirty face and his red-rimmed eyes showed that he had spent a hard day and a sleepless night. For his doings on that day he was to receive the Knight's Cross. His opponents—a good Norman infantry division and a brigade of Spahis—had fought bravely. The enemy's machineguns were still firing

into the village street, but for some time now there had been no artillery fire and Balck shared my opinion that resistance was almost over.

"Now on the previous day we had captured a French order, originating if I am not mistaken from General Gamelin himself, which contained the words: 'The torrent of German tanks must finally be stopped!' This order had strengthened me in my conviction that the attack must be pressed forward with all possible strength, since the defensive capabilities of the French was [sic] obviously causing their high command serious anxiety. This was no time for hesitancy, still less for calling a halt.

"I sent for the troops by companies and read them the captured order, making plain its significance and the importance of continuing the attack at once. I thanked them for their achievements to date and told them that they must now strike with all their power to complete our victory. I then ordered them to return to their vehicles and to continue the advance."

As Guderian's tank forces advanced rapidly westward, higher-ranking German officers feared that his swift pace was laying his force open to the possibility of being cut off and trapped by the Allies as he continued to outrun his infantry units. Twice in the first few days after the breakthrough, they ordered his advance halted to allow the infantry time to catch up with the tanks. Guderian clearly disagreed and lobbied heatedly for the freedom to maintain his pace towards the coast. Incredibly, 71 German divisions were on the march westward, ten of them armoured.

Guderian: "After our splendid success on the 16th of May and the simultaneous victory won by XLI Army Corps, it did not occur to me that my superiors could possibly still hold the same view as before, nor that they would now be satisfied with simply holding the bridgehead we had established across the Meuse while awaiting the arrival of the infantry corps. I was completely filled with the ideas that I had expressed during our conference with

Hitler in March, that is to say to complete our break-through and not stop until we had reached the English Channel. It certainly never occurred to me that Hitler himself, who had approved the boldest aspects of the Manstein plan and had not uttered a word against my proposals concerning exploitation of the breakthrough, would now be the one to be frightened by his own temerity and would order our advance to be stopped at once. Here I was making a great mistake, as I was to discover on the following morning.

"Early on the 17th of May I received a message from the Panzer Group: the advance was to be halted at once and I was personally to report to General von Kleist, who would come to see me at my airstrip at 07.00 hrs. He was there punctually and, without even wishing me a good morning, began in very violent terms to berate me for having disobeyed orders. He did not see fit to waste a word of praise on the performance of the troops. When the first storm was passed, and he had stopped to draw breath, I asked that I might be relieved of my command. General von Kleist was momentarily taken aback, but then he nodded and ordered me to hand over my command to the most senior general of my corps. And that was the end of our conversation. I returned to my corps headquarters and asked General Veiel to come to see me, that I might hand over to him.

"I then sent a message to Army Group von Rundstedt by wireless in which I said that after I had handed over my command at noon I would be flying to Army Group headquarters to make a report on what had happened. I received an answer almost at once: I was to remain at my headquarters and await the arrival of Colonel-General List, who was in command of the Twelfth Army that was following behind us and who had been instructed to clear this matter up. Until the arrival of Colonel-General List all units were to be ordered to remain where they were. Major Wenck, who came to receive these orders, was shot at by a

French tank while returning to his division and was wounded in the foot. General Veiel now appeared and I explained the situation to him. Early that afternoon Colonel-General List arrived and asked me at once what on earth was going on here. Acting on instructions from Colonel-General von Rundstedt he informed me that I would not resign my command and explained that the order to halt the advance came from the Army High Command (the *OKH*) and therefore must be obeyed. He quite understood my reasons, however, for wishing to go on with the advance and therefore, with the Army Group's approval, he ordered: 'Reconnaissance in force to be carried out. Corps headquarters must in all circumstances remain where it is, so that it may be easily reached.' This was at least something, and I was grateful to Colonel-General List for what he had done. I asked him to clear up the misunderstanding between General von Kleist and myself. Then I set the 'reconnaissance in force' in motion. Corps headquarters remained at its old location in Soize; a wire was laid from there to my advanced headquarters, so that I need not communicate with my staff by wireless and my orders could therefore not be monitored by the wireless intercept units of the *OKH* and the *OKW*.

"On the 19th of May we crossed the old Somme battlefield of the First World War. Until now we had been advancing north of the Aisne, the Serre and the Somme, and those rivers had served to guard our open left flank, which was also covered by reconnaissance troops, anti-tank units and combat engineers. The danger from this flank was slight; we knew about the French 4th Armoured Division, a new formation under General de Gaulle, which had been reported on the 16th of May and had first appeared, as already stated, at Montcornet. During the next few days de Gaulle stayed with us and on the 19th a few of his tanks succeeded in penetrating to within a mile of my advanced headquarters in Holnon wood. The headquarters had only some

The European war will be an industrial war of aircraft, tanks and movement.
– Dwight D. Eisenhower, while an aide to General Douglas MacArthur in the Philippines

above: Food ration stamps issued to civilians by the United States government during World War II.

Glowed through the violet petal of the sky / Like a death's-head the calm summer moon / And all the distance echoed with owl-cry.

Hissing the white waves of grass unsealed / Peer of moon on metal, hidden men, / As the wind foamed deeply through the field.

Rooted to soil, remote and faint as stars, / Looking to neither side, they lay all night Sunken in the murmurous seas of grass.

No flare burned upwards: never sound was shed But lulling cries of owls beyond the world / As wind and moon played softly with the dead.
–*After Night Offensive*
by James Farrar,
killed in action, 1944

right: High-speed mobility in the form of a German Army Zundapp motorcycle and sidecar operating near Smolensk, Russia in July 1941.

20mm. anti-aircraft guns for protection, and I passed a few uncomfortable hours until at last the threatening visitors moved off in another direction. Also we were aware of the existence of a French reserve army, some eight infantry divisions strong, which was being set up in the Paris area. We did not imagine that General Frére would advance against us so long as we kept on moving ourselves. According to the basic French formula, he would wait until he had exact information about his enemy's position before doing anything. So we had to keep him guessing; this could best be done by continuing to push on."

The German lightning strike was producing better results than even Hitler had expected. Guderian's panzers had reached Abbeville and Amiens by 20 May and nearly one million Allied troops were isolated in the north by the panzer units racing to the Channel coast. The best elements of the British and French armies, and all of the Belgian army, were cut off and could not be resupplied except through a few of the Channel ports.

In the last days of the blitzkrieg on France, she was also subjected to a short but noteworthy procession of staggeringly inept generals in top command roles. Elderly, exhausted and essentially devoid of any practical ideas for turning back the invaders, this little parade contributed nothing but more confusion to the sad situation, all soon lost their will, the plot and finally, the fight.

As the end approached for the Allied forces in France, the BEF's Commander, Lord Gort, managed to launch an armoured attack aimed at reinforcing the Allied headquarters position at Arras. Gort threw two divisions and 74 tanks into the action and had the support of 60 French tanks. The effort caught Rommel's 7th Panzer Division by surprise and gave him a brief fright. But he quickly rallied, and soon had Gort's force reeling from a counterattack with artillery, anti-tank guns and, ultimately, his powerful tank force. Forty Allied tanks were destroyed against a German loss of twelve. The advance of the panzers

continued unabated to the French coast. With the end of May came the end of the Battle of France and the most powerful and impressive armoured sweep the world had ever seen.

Trapped at the French seaside town of Dunkirk, 338,000 troops mostly from the British Expeditionary Force, along with some French and Belgian units, now faced likely annihilation at the hands of the German invaders. Field Marshal von Rundstedt sat behind the town with his five Army Group A armoured divisions, poised to destroy the massive Allied congregation which was gathered mainly on or near the beaches. He certainly had the firepower and the will to complete the task, but it was not to be. Rundstedt: "If I had had my way the English would not have got off so lightly at Dunkirk. But my hands were tied by direct orders from Hitler himself. While the English were clambering onto the ships off the beaches, I was kept uselessly outside the port unable to move. I recommended to the Supreme Command that my five Panzer divisions be immediately sent into the town and thereby completely destroy the retreating English. But I received definite orders from the Führer that under no circumstances was I to attack . . ."

It seems that Hitler believed that his panzers had been severely strained in their race across France. He dared not risk them in a direct assault over the difficult terrain around Dunkirk when he needed to deploy them against the remaining French armies to the south. So he gave the job of wiping out the beach-bound BEF to Hermann Goering's Luftwaffe which he felt could easily destroy the enemy forces by bombing them. His misjudgement allowed most of the British troops to be evacuated from the beaches when the Royal Navy, together with an improvised fleet of vessels including coasters, paddle steamers, fishing boats, colliers, yachts and other craft, managed to rescue them. British losses during the evacuation amounted to 68,111 killed, wounded or taken prisoner.

CHARIOTS OF FIRE

IN NOVEMBER 1919, British Tank Corps Captain G. le Q. Martel wrote a paper in which he prophesied the use and evolution of tanks to come: "In any case the tanks will be of such great importance that future great wars are almost sure to start with a duel between the tank armies of the respective sides." Martel believed that the primary role of the tank army was the destruction of the enemy's tanks. He envisioned such advances as half-inch-thick armour, a quick-firing gun, and a tank capable of a 20 mph speed.

Following the First World War, France, like most nations, was fed up with war and all things related to it. She was left with a huge surplus of weapons and equipment and had little interest in the development and purchase of expensive new arms. The French posture in the 1920s was one of defence; protecting her borders. Her remaining 3,000 obsolete Renault FT tanks formed the core of France's arsenal and nothing new would be added to it for many years. But with the signing of the Lucarno Pact on 1 December 1925, one provision of which required Britain, France and Germany to aid one another in the event of an aggression against one of them, some attitudes changed. Though the treaty was intended to minimize the liklihood of conflict between these nations, it also caused the British and French to fear being out of the research and development loop of new weaponry and thus, disadvantaged and threatened. Instead of armoured vehicle development, however, the French government took the opposite view and invested heavily in frontier fortification, the Maginot Line. The British government, secure in the belief that major war was not in prospect in the foreseeable future, continued to use up their supply of surplus tanks. They had already disbanded their Tank Design Establishment in 1922.

While France's advocacy of a fixed defence priority still prevailed, there was agreement that

At the beginning of August 2002 the British Ministry of Defence was fielding questions from the press about the state of readiness of some of its principal equipment. One example, the Challenger 2 main battle tank, was shown to have particular deficiencies when operating in the extreme conditions of the Omani desert exercises conducted during 2001. In Exercise Saif Sareea, the tanks were unable to tolerate the talcum powdery sand they churned up, breaking down after fewer than four hours of operation. The dusty sand blocked the engines of the Challengers, which were not designed for desert service. In an effort to economize, British Army officials had earlier decided against fitting the tanks with desertised air filters and special skirts to keep out the sand. At the end of the exercises, only 50 per cent of the Challengers were still operable. The rest faced months of costly repairs.

left: The Challenger 2 main battle tank entered service with the British Army in 1998.

below: The interior of Little Willie, the modified version of the first tank in the world, Britain's Number One Lincoln Machine. Little Willie underwent trials at Burton Park, England in December 1915. right: British Mark II tanks at the World War I Battle of Arras in April 1917.

You can't say civilization don't advance. In every war they kill you in a new way.
– Will Rogers

the infantry must be given the close support of tanks, this in spite of acceptance that current French tanks were too slow and thus vulnerable to anti-tank weapons. Work now began to develop heavier tank armour. Concentration was on medium and heavy defensive tanks in the run-up to the Second World War. Examples include the Char B1 heavy tank, which served with the French Army from 1936 until the fall of France in 1940, and the Char SOMUA S-35 medium tank. With good mobility and sufficient firepower, the S-35 was a capable opponent for most German tanks in the Battle of France. Its main drawback was that, in addition to command duties, the commander was required to load, aim and fire the 47mm gun. Many S-35s were operated by the Germans on the Russian front.

The Americans came away from the First World War with nearly 600 tanks (128 British heavies and 450 Renaults which had been built in the United States), nearly all of them unused in the war. The

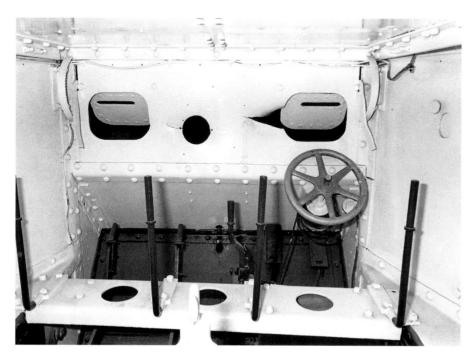

Tank Corps of the U.S. Army had few personnel and was significantly underfunded. In 1920 the Congress altered the National Defense Act and put the Army's tanks in the infantry. Almost no one there wanted to see tax money spent on weapons of war and, in 1921, a mere token budget was allocated to operate America's tanks. There was virtually no interest in the views of those in the military who wrote and spoke of the importance of tanks in the nation's future. The mood was isolationist. But by the mid-1930s American industry was at work on the Stuart, a light tank which would be used in North Africa by the British Eighth Army, and the M3 Grant/Lee medium, which would also serve with the British, as well as the American, Canadian and Russian armies.

The principal American tank of World War II was the M4 Sherman medium. The Sherman, like nearly all the tanks of the Western Allies, did not compare well with German tanks of the period. Early M4s were known for exploding and/or burning when hit by anti-tank rounds, but the problem was fixed in many of the tanks when improved ammunition stowage and the use of water-jacket surrounds for the 75mm ammunition were employed. While the Sherman was certainly not the equal of the German Tiger or Panther tanks, it ultimately prevailed by being available in ever-increasing numbers. A total, in all variants, of 49,230 Shermans were produced.

By 1924, Captain Heinz Guderian had become a leading proponent of the tank in Germany. Two years earlier, Germany and Russia began a secret collaboration to construct, test and evaluate a wide range of prototype tank designs, many of them based largely on the designs of the British Vickers company. Both the Russians and the Germans made rapid and significant progress as they took advantage of readily obtainable information about British tank technology. The Russians were keenly interested in the work of Vickers and that of the

Dear Nephew,
Although I am now growing old, I think I may truthfully say that I do not consider myself too old to learn. Your letter about the camp was most interesting and I was not a bit bored by the "technical details". There are lots of things the I would like to ask you about. Why shouldn't we learn from each other? You spoke about the shell of the six-pounder guns. What a little shell it must be if the gun itself weighs only six lbs.! Could you get me one of the empty shell-cases? I will get Tom to make it into a thimble for me. If you could get two—but perhaps this is asking too much!—I might get them made into earrings. Try not to disappoint me. Your affectionate aunt.
— from *The Tank Corps Journal* Vol. III 1921-22

left: The French Renault FT 17 of World War I.

American tank designer J. Walter Christie who, by 1928, had developed an impressive nine-ton tank capable of 30 mph. In the early '30s, Vickers and Christie ideas formed the basis of Russia's burgeoning new tank force. By 1932, they had built 3300 mainly Vickers-derived tanks and were well along in development of a Christie-type which was suitably modified for the Russian terrain and conditions.

With Adolf Hitler's accession to power in 1933, Germany's "tank school" pact with Russia was cancelled. Utilizing what they had learned about tanks with the Russians, the Germans then secretly went to work on design and construction of their own tanks and aircraft at facilities in Germany. Their initial efforts impressed Hitler who became convinced that the new German tanks would give him the means to create the Panzer divisions which would allow him to develop the blitzkrieg war tactic. Guderian wanted "to make a breakthrough and roll up the enemy front in order to exploit the characteristics of the tank in co-

left: The mass production of the 28-ton M3 medium tank was the original purpose of the Chrysler Tank Arsenal in World War II. The facility was more than five city blocks long and two blocks wide, occupying 700,000 square feet. The one-mile test track, winding over 40 acres, permitted a 75-mile test run for each tank. During the war the arsenal employed up to 10,000 workers. below: General Bernard Montgomery, commander of the British Eighth Army in his Grant command tank at Alamein.

far right: Interior of a British Crusader III at the Tank Museum, Dorset, England. above: The Crusader III was the final production model of the series and arrived in the North African desert in time for the Alamein action in 1942. While appreciated for its speed, both its armour and armament were insufficient and the tank was essentially obsolete by the end of the Western Desert campaign. right: The burnt hull of a knocked-out Crusader I in the Western Desert.

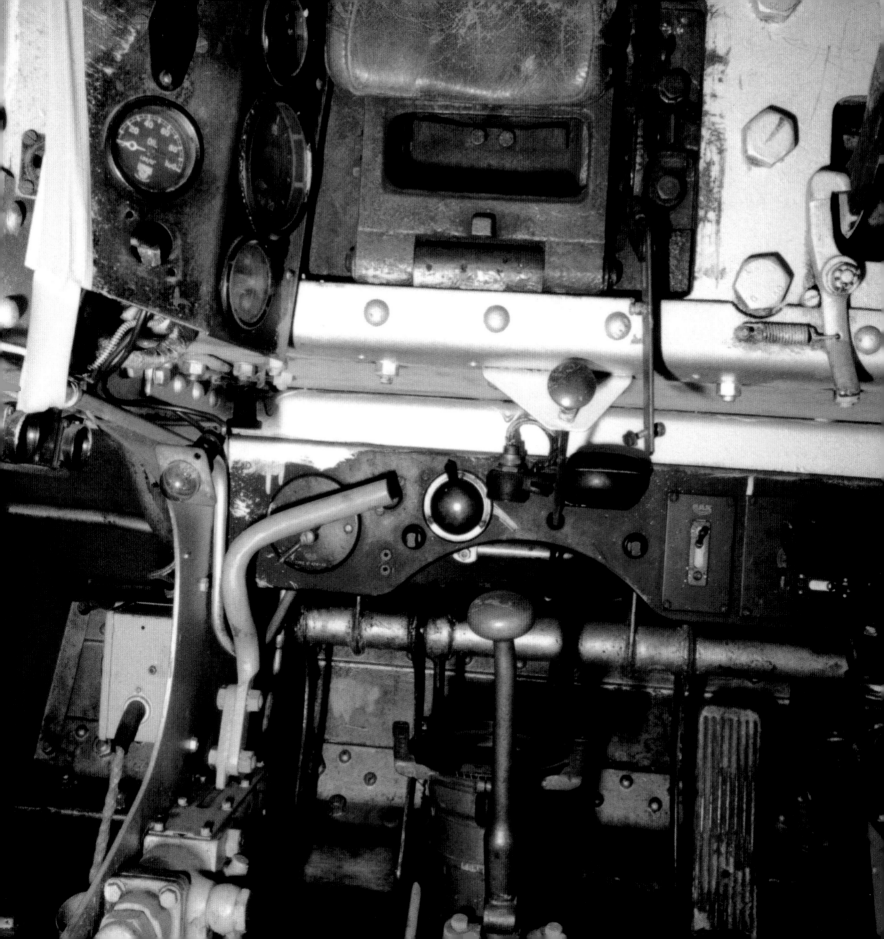

operation with other weapons." He intended his Panzer divisions to be thoroughly capable of operating in any European terrain. But the needs of Hermann Goering's air force took top priority in German industrial resources and manpower. Germany's allocation of industry was also hampered by an extremely limited supply of the raw materials used in tank manufacture, most of which had to be imported.   By 1934 the Mark II light tank, mounting a 20mm gun, and the Mark IV medium with a 75mm gun, were in work. By 1936

the Mark III medium tank with a 37mm gun was ready, but supply and production problems meant that by September 1939 when World War II began, the Germans could field just over 200 Mark IVs and fewer than 100 Mark IIIs.

From its combat introduction in the summer of 1942 near Leningrad, the German PzKpfw VI Tiger was, for a long period, the most powerful and formidable tank in the world. While not successful initially, and somewhat handicapped by its great weight and mechanical complexity, the Tiger, with

preceding spread and left: The M4 assembly line at the massive Chrysler Detroit Tank Arsenal in World War II. centre: A Bill Mauldin cartoon from his 1944 book *Up Front*: 'I'd rather dig. A movin' foxhole attracks th' eye.' bottom: An M4 instrument panel.

71

right: The British A22 Churchill infantry tank, this example, an AVRE (Armoured Vehicle Royal Engineers) towing another Churchill on a tracked recovery vehicle. 5,600 Churchills were produced in World War II. below: A 1930s toy tank.

I, the Tank, am a symbol of the unity of the nation. I was made to be used by soldiers in the battle, but not as they willed, but in accordance with the plans of generals. I was made by the workers in a great Midland city, but they only put me together. I am the child of many brains. I am fashioned from many parts made on divers great machines in many works that represented great masses of capital, and in order that I and my brothers might get ready for war in sufficient numbers, organising and managing capacity on a vast scale was required, and I, more than any other single factor in the war, brought victory!
– from a speech by Sir Auckland Geddes, president of the British Board of Trade in 1920

its 88mm gun and its maximum 4.33 inch armour, was an awesome package and was greatly feared by Allied crews of the inferior Sherman. The German tanks of World War II consistently outgunned the tanks of the Western Allies, though the Shermans were often able to outmanoevre the heavier Tiger to attack it from the rear.

The Tiger's worthy successor was the PzKpfw VI Tiger II, King or Royal Tiger. It was the most powerful, heaviest and best-armoured tank of the war and was designed to dominate on the battlefield. Built by Henschel, a single King Tiger was capable of engaging and destroying many enemy tanks while suffering little damage itself. If not the most reliable or manoevrable armoured fighting vehicle, the King was the most impressive German tank of the era.

A series of tanks called "cruisers" resulted from a prewar concept of the British Army requiring two distinct types of tank, one being the cruiser, a weapon for the cavalry to use in open warfare, and the other, a heavy support tank for the infantry. Originally, cruisers were meant to be light and fast tanks capable of a cavalry-type pursuit. The cruisers included the Mk IV, and adaptation of an American Christie design, the A9 Mk 1, a medium designed for tank-to-tank combat and operated by the British Army between 1938 and 1941, the Crusader, a heavy cruiser which saw extensive service in the Western Desert of North Africa, the Valentine which was actually a combination armoured cruiser and infantry tank, the Cromwell, another heavy cruiser, and the last of the cruisers, the Comet.

Like many tanks of the prewar and early war periods, the Crusader went into production well before its teething problems had been identified and resolved. Its combat debut was Operation *Battleaxe*, June 1941 in the Western Desert where it served through the entire desert war. Mechanical failure caused many Crusaders to be

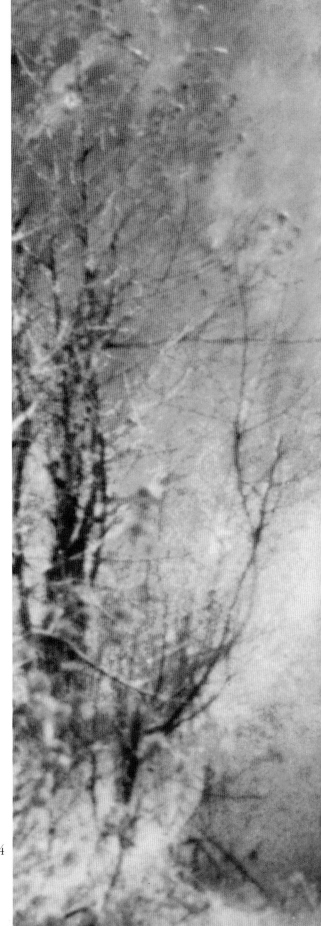

right: Soviet T-62, the first main battle tank to be armed with a smoothbore gun. It fired a variety of fin-stabilized ammunition. above: U.S. Marines behind an M26 Pershing firing on enemy troops during the Korean War.

captured by the Germans, many more than were knocked out by battle damage. Like most of the cruisers, it also suffered from inadequate armament and insufficient armour.

The Churchill was an important and long-lived infantry tank of World War II which was designed to replace the Matilda II. It was built by Vauxhall Motors. Like the Crusader, the Churchill had been rushed into production and the early marks had plenty of problems. In its first year the tank became known for unreliability, a label which in later marks was undeserved. Many Churchill variants were built, including an armoured recovery vehicle, a flamethrower, a mine-clearer, and an AVRE (Armoured Vehicle Royal Engineers). Churchills served in the British Army from 1941 to 1952.

The best tank of World War II was the Russian T-34 medium. Simple in concept, design and construction, fast and with a good range, the T-34 first greeted the German invaders at Grondno in

A line-up of modern main battle tanks at Bovington Camp, Dorset, England. From left to right: The British Chieftain and the Challenger 1, the American M1 Abrams, the British Vickers Challenger 2 and the German Leopard II.

below: The General Dynamics M1A1 Abrams is a tank of the 1980s which will continue in U.S. service well into the 21st century. The Abrams performed brilliantly in the 1990-91 Persian Gulf War, destroying more than 2,000 Russian-made Iraqi tanks without a single U.S. combat loss. The M1A1 is armed with a 120mm gun, a 12.7mm machinegun and two 7.62mm machineguns. It is protected by armour of rolled homogenous steel with composite arrays and is operated by a four-man crew.

Belorussia on 22 June 1941, shocking them with its great capability and performance. To counter the threat posed by the T-34, the Germans began work on their own copy of the tank, but in time elected to develop the Panther which they based heavily on characteristics of the T-34. The most innovative of these was the sloped, shaped and inclined armour which proved more resistant to shell penetration than that of previous tank designs. Production of the T-34

continued into the 1950s.

In the protracted Cold War era after World War II, most Western main battle tanks were technically superior to most of those of the Russians. The Russians always mounted a big gun, from the T-54 main battle tank of 1947 with its 100mm weapon, and the T-10 heavy of 1957 with a 122mm gun, to the T-55 MBT of 1960 with a 100mm gun. But it was not until the introduction of the T-62 MBT in

1963 that a Soviet tank was armed with a gun able to fire armour-piercing (fin-stabilized) discarding sabot rounds as well as HEAT and HE rounds. The first numerically significant Western tank capable of firing the APFSDS was the Israeli version of the American M47 medium of 1952. Other NATO nation tanks with APDS as well as HEAT or HESH firing capability include the British Conqueror heavy of 1956, the Chieftain MBT of 1967, the French AMX-32 of 1979, and the more highly evolved systems of the Leclerc MBT of 1990, the German Leopard II MBT of 1980, the Israeli Merkava MBT of 1980 and the American M1A1 and M1A2 Abrams MBT of 1985. Major advances in range-finding capability, ranging machineguns, integrated fire-control systems and explosive reactive armour first appeared on the British Centurion main battle tank of the early 1950s. The first important full-solution ballistic computer coupled to a laser range-finder was mounted in the U.S. M60A2 MBT of 1971.

The view from inside a tank, as one cannot repeat too often, is restricted and misleading. Once we had crossed our front line, the few miserable tree-clumps which we had studied from a distance might appear very different near at hand. They might have been destroyed, or we might fail to see them at all. The one unmistakable landmark, Kitchener's Wood—a plantation, still in fair condition, some 700 yards in length—was actually out of sight until we had climbed out of some dead ground at the foot of the ridge; and with the dust and smoke of the battle the first hour after dawn was certain to be dark and confusing. As our compasses were thoroughly unreliable, there was a danger of losing direction at the very start. A few tanks, indeed, quite excusably did so. And throughout the day, all over a battlefield whose utter bewildering sameness no words can express, there was much groping and guessing and general uncertainty. One of G Battalion's tanks wandered right across two corps' fronts. But on the whole our lengthy and sedulous coaching was very triumphantly vindicated: routes were maintained and objectives reached with surprising accuracy and punctuality. Delays in most cases were due to the appalling state of the ground, some tanks having to be unditched two or three times before they got into action at all.
— on the battle at Ypres, from *The Tank in Action* by Captain D. G. Browne, MC

THERE WERE MORE than 22,000 tanks in the Soviet arsenal by 22 June 1941 when the German invasion of Russia began. At that time the Soviets had more tanks than all the other armies in the world put together — and four times as many as the Germans. But the majority of this armour was obsolete and the Germans knew it. What they didn't know was that their Russian enemy had tested and made operational two new and significantly better tanks in the KV heavy and T-34 medium, and that some of these new tanks were already serving in front-line units. Both were externally well-designed, excellent fighting vehicles that mounted a heavy gun and were protected by thick armour. They did, however, have shortcomings. They were essentially simple, low-technology weapons with little mechanical assistance for the crews, poor habitability and vision and a high mechanical breakdown rate. Still, the T-34 cruised through World War II, finishing with very high marks, and is often referred to by experts as the best tank of the war.

Like the Japanese attack on the U.S. battleships moored in Pearl Harbor on 7 December 1941, the German Panzer divisions surprised the Russians on a Sunday morning, overrunning the enemy positions and swiftly advancing considerable distances before the Soviets could react. The surprise worked well for the German invaders. Even with the overwhelming number of tanks in the Soviet inventory, only 25 per cent were in good working order, and most of their tank officers and men had little experience driving and operating their vehicles. Their units were in the process of being reformed and spare parts and equipment were in short supply.

   While the Soviets were unprepared for the fight, the Germans were split over the approach they should take. Heinz Guderian, Erich von Manstein and the other German generals strongly favoured applying powerful military force to destroy the Red Army, while Hitler and others thought it essential

BARBAROSSA

In the eight hours of the Battle of Prochorovka, the Germans lost 400 tanks and 10,000 men. They called it The Death Ride.

left: Captured by German troops in Russia during 1941, this T-34 has seen better days. below: General Heinz Guderian in his armoured command car.

below: A Russian T-34, among the best tanks of World War II, in firing position. right: 1943 Russian poster, *GERMAN TANKS WON'T GET THROUGH HERE*, by N. Shukov.

to paralyse Russia's government by seizing political and economic objectives. Hitler finally stipulated "the destruction of the Red Army in western Russia by deep penetrations of armoured spearheads".

At the start, the fast-paced Panzer attacks seemed to provoke only slow (though courageous), poorly coordinated responses by the Soviet armour. The Panzer generals knew that it was vital to maintain momentum in their attacks; to keep up pressure on the opposition through quick thrusts followed by bold encirclements of the enemy forces. Manstein: "The farther a single Panzer corps . . . ventured into the depths of the Russian hinterland, the greater the hazards became. Against this it may be said that the safety of a tank formation operating in the enemy's rear largely depends on its ability to keep moving. Once it comes to a halt

it will immediately be assailed from all sides by the enemy's reserves."

When the German attack began, the Panzers were able to race through the stunned Soviet tank and artillery units, leaving them crushed in their wake. But the seemingly superior Panzer forces were, like any army, heavily dependent on continuing re-supply of fuel, rations and munitions. The progress and security afforded by their momentum could only be assured if the enemy could be kept from interfering with German supply routes. That crucial momentum could also be lost if the rains came and mired the supply trucks in Russian mud.

The Germans may have had initial advantages in momentum and better organization, but in their early encounters with the KV heavy tank, and later with the T-34, they found to their cost, what a formidable threat the 76mm gun could be. While these Soviet tanks were able to lie back beyond 1,000 yards and penetrate the thickest German armour with the 76mm rounds, German tanks had to fire from within 200 yards to kill a KV or a T-34.

For a while the Panzers continued to have their way with the enemy armoured units, destroying Soviet tanks with an ease they would never again know in the campaign. For now, they faced only a relative handful of the KVs and T-34s. German forces were benefitting from superior training, leadership, organization, co-ordination and, not least, highly effective aerial reconnaissance. They invariably knew in advance of any Soviet armoured attack, the strength and position of the enemy force.

The Soviets seemed incapable of putting all the necessary elements together to counter the Panzers effectively, much less grabbing and holding the initiative. They were weakened by inadequate training and incompetent leadership and their tank crews, inept in the handling and operation of their vehicles, had a lot to worry about. They were plagued with frequent mechanical breakdowns due in part to the negligent way they handled the machines. Their tactics were often unsophisticated and at times naive; their shooting accuracy was uneven at best and there were too few KVs and T-34s available to make an appreciable difference.

In the Pacific war, American navy pilots would refer to the great aerial engagement of 19 June 1944 as 'The Marianas Turkey Shoot.' On that day, the Japanese lost 378 aircraft while the U.S. Navy lost but 29. It is perhaps fair to compare the experience of the German Panzers from the onset of their campaign, through December when Soviet losses totalled more than 15,000 tanks and one million men, to the 'Turkey Shoot.'

In spite of the successes achieved by the Panzers to this point, the Germans were awakening to a new reality. As impressive as their gains had been, with Heinz Guderian's units pushing more than 400 miles in 25 days from Brest Litovsk to Smolensk, the Germans were incurring losses 50 per cent greater than in their earlier campaigns. Guderian was experiencing tank repair and resupply problems similar to those of Rommel in the desert war and, after two and a half months of fighting, the spectacularly successful blitzkrieg tactic of the previous two years was coming up short. The advance of the Panzers was slowing visibly, and as the horrific winter arrived, the tanks of both sides were less and less effective, imposing ever greater demands on the infantry elements to consolidate the gains made by their tank units and to fend off any enemy tank action.

Moscow remained the prize that Hitler demanded and expected to be his by late October. Now the exhausted German armour units were required to behave as though fresh and still vigorous. They were asked to mount a new campaign towards the Russian capital and, to their credit, they did manage a sizeable offensive with Guderian's armies making gains between Sevsk and Bryansk and at Vyazma, before becoming bogged down on their new front. And then the rains came. The already

НЕМЕЦКИЙ ТАНК ЗДЕСЬ НЕ ПРОЙДЕТ

What happens to a Russian, or to a Czech, does not interest me in the slightest. What the nations can offer in the way of good blood of our type we will take, if necessary by kidnapping their children and raising them here with us. Whether nations live in prosperity or starve to death interests me only in so far as we need them as slaves for our *Kultur*: otherwise, it is of no interest to me. Whether ten thousand Russian females fall down from exhaustion while digging an anti-tank ditch interests me only in so far as the anti-tank ditch for Germany is finished.
– Heinrich Himmler, October 1943

J. Kugies served as a panzer platoon leader and tank commander in the Balkans and on the Russian Front in World War II. "At Tilsit in East Prussia I led a section of five tanks. In the lead tank we were only able to advance at about 12 to 14 km/h over the soft, marshy roads. Our riflemen marched ahead of us in a wide front to deal with any resistance that I could not break through. Just behind the Russian-Latvian frontier, we encountered Soviet soldiers. Our section had been ordered to halt, but, due to my defective wireless set, I did not receive the order in our tank and continued to drive on alone. The road soon became blocked by Soviet trucks and my driver had to take us through open terrain. He couldn't stop because of the marshy ground. The Russian truck convoy was escorted by many of their tanks and, before they could turn their turrets toward me I began to fire on them. Their aiming was bad and I managed to shoot nine of them out of action. With their tanks burning, and the crews fleeing, I was then able to destroy an anti-aircraft battery and an continued on page 87

above right: German tanks carrying troops in Russia during 1941. below right: The burning hulk of a Russian (U.S.-built) M3 tank

inadequate road surfaces in the region were turned into quagmires as rain fell with an intensity normally associated with the tropics. Meanwhile, General Georgi Zhukov, Russia's most successful and powerful military commander of the war, tried in vain to build his armour and crews and develop them into a force capable of performing on a par with the German armour. The incessant rains (and ensuing mud) kept the Germans from advancing beyond a position 150 miles from Moscow and this delay enabled General Zhukov to reinforce his own armour units and continue to fight a delaying action, adding significantly to the Germans' problems. While they persisted in their plodding, uneven movement towards the enemy capital, the Germans had clearly lost most of their earlier momentum and, within sight of Moscow, they could go no further. It was then that the weather worsened dramatically and a deep, unyielding freeze set in, paralyzing the now battle-weary tanks of the Panzers where they sat. The grease in guns froze as did the oil in the vehicles. The glue-like mud now froze and had to be chipped from the tanks and vehicles with pickaxes.

What Zhukov had going for him at this point was the small but highly effective T-34 and KV tank force, which, in fact, had been outperforming the German tanks in the appalling conditions thus far. But he didn't have nearly enough of them to overwhelm the opposition. He also had a large and effective, efficiently-placed concentration of anti-tank obstacles giving him a substantial capability for defending Moscow and its environs. As the winter (the worst in 140 years) wore on, the Germans suffered terribly in the numbing cold and the clogging, sucking mud that appeared to reduce all effort and movement, human and mechanical, to slow motion. The Soviets seemed somehow more fit and better able to cope with the brutal conditions. As the snows and bitter cold intensified, the normally impeccable serviceability

and performance standards of the German forces and their equipment began to slip. They had come to Russia with the expectation of fighting a relatively brief summer campaign and were ill-prepared for the extremes of winter in the region. They were kitted in summer-weight uniforms and their tanks and other vehicles were not properly winterized. Frozen engine blocks were common; frostbite, trench foot, shock and exposure brought their men suffering and death on an awesome scale. Their units were achieving less each day, their early success pattern was but a memory and their commanders were rapidly losing faith in and respect for the directions coming to them from Berlin.

Still, the Germans managed a recovery of sorts, though not to the point of really regaining the offensive momentum. By spring they had somehow effected a partial resupply, repair and re-organization to the extent that they could now readily repel every Soviet penetration and immediately hit back with short, swift tank and infantry assaults which, while not gaining them much, served to hold their positions for the most part. This became German standard operating procedure for most of their remaining operations on the Russian Front.

For both sides, the effective use of tanks was essential to success in the Russian campaign. Tanks could provide the ability to penetrate the enemy front line, bring vital support to one's over-extended infantry and powerfully defend against penetrations by the enemy forces. The Germans were losing in the contest to field, fight and maintain tanks in this unrelenting, unforgiving situation. By early 1943, the German Panzer force in the Soviet Union was in bad shape. Deteriorating morale and operational inefficiencies, confusion and indecision at the manufacturing, supply and command levels were to blame. In terms of their equipment, the Germans were forced to continue their reliance on the PzKpfw III and IV tanks, of which the III was utterly outclassed by the Soviet T-34, a fact not lost on the Panzer commanders in the field. They strongly urged their superiors to prevail upon the German Ordnance Office to quickly design and build a copy of the T-34 for their use in the East. But Ordnance Office designers scoffed at that approach to a new and capable rival for the Soviet tank and set about planning a new design of their own, the 45-ton general purpose Panther.

Hitler's armies had reached the outskirts of Moscow and Leningrad in their most successful push of Operation Barbarossa in 1941. By the summer of 1942 the Führer's primary goal was the Caucasus oilfields which he hoped to capture and thus deprive the Russians of their main fuel supply. To achieve this aim, the German Sixth Army had been directed to capture and occupy Stalingrad and, in so doing, isolate and neutralize this key enemy communications and manufacturing centre in southern Russia.

The determination to defend Stalingrad was total and not to be questioned. Every Russian soldier was ordered "Not one step backwards" by Josef Stalin. Waged between August 1942 and February 1943, the Battle of Stalingrad was the major Soviet victory of World War II and proved to be the turning point in the war. Hitler himself sealed the fate of his Caucasus campaign in July when he diverted much of the army intended to occupy the oilfields, to the already futile struggle at Stalingrad. General Zhukov meanwhile had amassed a force of nearly a million men which attacked and encircled the German troops in a pincer movement on 19 November. The Germans ran out of food and ammunition and were freezing. In the battle 70,000 German soldiers died and 91,000 became prisoners. Near the end of the fight Hitler's commander there, General Friedrich von Paulus, was asked by the Russians to surrender. He had been forbidden by the Führer to attempt to break out of the encirclement and now was urged by Hitler not to be taken alive. On 2 February he gave himself up to the Russians. The German advance in the south was halted and thereafter the Russians were virtually always on the offensive and on the move towards Berlin.

In the belief that the Soviet victory at Stalingrad might have been some kind of aberration, the Germans struggled to recover, regroup and plan a new offensive for May 1943. It was to be called

artillery position. I crossed a bridge and then closed my hatch-cover to prevent any enemy shells from coming in. By this time, my cannon ammunition supply was exhausted and I could only shoot with my machine-gun. We now stayed where we were, alone, for about thirty minutes until our following tanks reached us. After such a dangerous situation, we all had a sip of vodka which, unfortunately, was warm for having been under our gear. Later, we learned that the tanks behind us had stopped often, as ordered, on the marshy ground. They incurred many losses.

While trying to aid a German infantry-reconnaissance patrol which was fighting in a lost cause on 13 August 1941 at the Luga bridgehead, I was wounded. I was nearly out of ammunition and a Russian machinegun was only five metres ahead of us. I ordered us forward to try and save the reconnaissance patrol. Standing in the hatch, I was pointing in the direction of the Russian machinegun, which was

left: With smoke from burning houses near the front line behind them, a group of No. 8 Panzer Division crewmen in a brief time out of war. Tank commander Johannes Kugies is at the far left in the white scarf.

now firing at us. I was shot three times through my right hand and forefinger and got a graze on the side of my head. My cap was torn to pieces but I was hardly bleeding. As I sank into the tank, I was fired on from a nearby house. I was hit in the right shoulder by splinters and my uniform jacket was torn up. My chief took me

below: Russian troops riding captured German tanks in 1941. right: Russian anti-tank troops in action against a passing panzer.

Operation *Zitadelle* (Citadel) and entailed a mighty effort to encircle and destroy the five Soviet armies in the area of the Kursk salient between Orel and Belgorod.

The Battle of Kursk would be the greatest tank battle in history. A win here would buy time for the Germans to gather new strength and perhaps retake the offensive on the Eastern Front, as well as slowing the progress of the Soviets.

The Russian victory at Stalingrad was no fluke. They would be ready for the enemy at Kursk and would, in fact, receive a gift from Hitler in the form of an extra two months to prepare and set their defences for the coming attack. The German leader had become so enamoured of what he believed would be his new superweapon, the PanzerKampfWagen V — Panther — that, when it

was not yet ready for battle by May, Hitler elected to postpone *Zitadelle* until July.

The Panther was the brainchild of Dr Ferdinand Porsche, an automotive designer greatly admired by the Führer. It would be, he assured Hitler, superior to the T-34, but in the spring of 1943 it had problems typical of a complex new mechanism, and they had to be worked through. Eventually, it would become one of the great tanks of the war, but not in time for Kursk. And in the interim, Hitler and Porsche strove to advance development of new self-propelled tank-destroyers (*Jagdpanzer*); as well as self-propelled infantry-support guns (*Stürmgeschütze*). Hitler saw in these new weapons a relatively quick means of expanding his armoured capability and possibly re-acquiring the momentum he sought in the East. Dr Porsche's

contribution to this effort was a re-designed version of the Tiger tank, to be known on the Front as the "Elefant." It was actually called the Ferdinand. This mammoth tank destroyer resembled an oversize Jagdpanzer and was armed with a 100mm L70 gun in a fixed mounting. Like the Jagdpanzer, it came with a whole range of drawbacks including poor crew habitability, a narrow field of fire, no secondary armament and the complex, costly production techniques usually associated with a tank. Ninety Ferdinands were built by Krupp and were less than successful in their combat debut. But their cousin, the Tiger, being manufactured by Henschel, showed extremely well in its initial action at Leningrad in late 1942. That performance led to a standardization of both the Krupp and Henschel vehicles in which the 88mm L71 gun was fitted.

All of this effort and expense on Jagdpanzers would actually result in less armour (fewer tanks) rather than the expansion that Hitler had wanted, with Germany's motorized infantry and Waffen SS units reaping the benefit of increased armoured capability while the key Panzer divisions suffered a quantitative reduction in tank strength . . . on the road to Kursk.

At the Kursk salient the Soviets had prepared for their visitors with "Germanic efficiency" and attention to detail. They had established seven defensive lines, laid millions of mines, built an imposing network of anti-tank ditches and dug-in anti-tank strongpoints. At an assembly point nearly 200 miles behind the front line they had a massive 850-tank force in waiting, the Fifth Guards Tank Army, should it be required. All participating units had been reorganized, manned and re-equipped to full strength or beyond. They were ready for the Germans when the assault began at 7 a.m. on 5 July.

Soviet Intelligence was working well prior to the attack and the German troops found themselves subjected to an intense bombardment in their assembly areas during the evening of 4/5 July.

What followed was a chaotic mixture of tank-versus-tank and hand-to-hand combat lasting for several days. The German Ninth Army on the north flank of the salient went at the Soviets each day with greater intensity, manpower and tank strength until, by 12 July, they had spent their wad and been defeated by the excellent enemy defences. The Soviet defenders were then able to capitalize on the German failure and move onto the offensive themselves.

The 48th Panzer Korps was operating on the southern end of the salient. They were the first major armoured formation to field the PzKpfw V Panther and it was an inauspicious start for the highly-touted new tank. Breakdowns were commonplace and crews found their vehicles regularly becoming stuck in the soft, wet ground and the Germans were reminded of their famous reference to the Sherman tanks operated in the desert war by the British—"Tommy Cookers"—as the Panthers showed an alarming tendency to catch fire when hit.

Things appeared to improve for the Germans on the southern flank by 11 July when they prepared to engage in the most massive tank battle ever. The "field" was a land-bridge between the rivers Don and Psel at a place called Prochorovka. It was there that the Germans would try to break the Soviet lines and gain access to the open region beyond. It would be the climactic engagement of *Zitadelle* at what would later be remembered as the "gully of death".

What happened at Prochorovka on 12 July 1943 has been the subject of many books, film and television documentaries. Historians have disagreed about the facts, with wildly varying versions being rendered over the years. The majority, however, generally adhere to the following.

Something between 500 and 700 German tanks, many of them *Panzerkampfwagen* VI Tigers mounted with 88mm cannon and *Panzerkampfwagen* V Panthers with their 75mm guns, rumbled out

immediately to the doctor at a nearby field unit where my wounds were bandaged. I was then flown by JU-52 aircraft to a field hospital near Dünaburg followed by a two-day train trip to a military hospital in Germany. I always remember hearing infantrymen say to us again and again: "I wouldn't like to go in your deathboxes", and we always answered: "And we don't like to walk."

below: A German Panzer III in flames on the Russian Front. right: The uncomplicated Russian T-34, armed with a high-velocity 85mm gun, was a reliable performer in all conditions and terrain and its sloped armour helped to deflect German projectiles.

The panzer tankers were forced to run their engines for fifteen minutes every four hours in the horrific Soviet winter, increasing their fuel consumption and putting additional strain on their beleaguered supply system. Running them that way made it impossible to keep their positions secret.

towards the Soviet line at just before noon. They were unaware that the 850 tanks of the Fifth Guards Tank Army had been moved up during the night of 11/12 July to meet the anticipated assault. When the German tanks encountered the hundreds of more agile T-34 mediums of the Soviets, it resembled a free-for-all, in which the T-34s brought chaos and confusion to the German armoured units by driving directly into their midst. This close-in tactic effectively neutralized the formidable 88mm guns of the Tigers. The Soviets then went on to outmanoeuvre the enemy armour, destroying 400 German tanks, including nearly 100 Tigers and many Panthers. It seems probable that Soviet tank losses for the day amounted to many more than the 400 admitted to by Lieutenant-General Pavel Rotmistrov, commander of the Fifth Guards Tank Army, possibly as many as 650. But at the end of the day, the Soviets prevailed and held the battleground.

The next day Hitler uncharacteristically ordered

his principal commanders, Field Marshals Guenther von Kluge and Erich von Manstein, to cancel the operation and begin an immediate withdrawl from the area. Manstein resisted but was overruled. *Zitadelle* had been an unmitigated defeat and an absolute disaster for the Germans. Their offensive against the Soviets was finished.

Some historians claim that as many as 6,000 tanks, 4,000 aircraft and two million fighting men were involved in the Battle of Kursk. Others state that far fewer tanks actually participated and that only fifteen Tigers and no Panthers were still in action by the 12 July battle at Prochorovka. German and Soviet official reports and press accounts also vary greatly. Here are a few examples.

SOVIET INFORMATION BUREAU, MOSCOW: Wednesday, 14 July 1943
In the past twelve hours, German assault activity has slackened further with the Red Army increasingly seizing the initiative. Since yesterday evening, German attacks around Byelgorod too have decreased in force. General Rokossovsky, on the other hand, has sent new reserves to the front and is attacking in almost all sectors. The panzer spearheads which the Germans drove into the Soviet positions in the first days of the offensive are shrivelling, and the initiative is gradually passing over to the Red Army.

WEHRMACHT HIGH COMMAND: Thursday, 15 July 1943
The heavy fighting on the Eastern Front is continuing despite the deteriorating weather. We defeated another enemy force in a concentrated attack near Byelgorod, and counterattacks renewed by enemy forces weaker than on previous days have been repulsed with heavy losses to them. East and north of Orel, the enemy continued his attacks Wednesday, with the support of tanks and ground-attack aircraft. Attempts by the Soviets to break through German positions have failed under heavy casualties. We immediately mounted

counterattacks which are progressing successfully. Along the entire sector of this large-scale battle, we destroyed 336 more Soviet tanks on Wednesday, and our air force shot down 70 enemy planes.

SOVIET INFORMATION BUREAU, MOSCOW: Thursday, 15 July 1943
The following special communiqué was published this evening: Our troops have now gone on the offensive against the German troops to the north and east of Orel. Our offensive was launched in two directions: southward from the area north of Orel, and westwards from the area east of Orel. North of Orel, our troops have penetrated a 38-kilometre-wide stretch of strongly fortified German defensive positions and have advanced 43 kilometres in a period of three days. Large numbers of enemy fortifications have been destroyed.

On 2 February 1943 German Field Marshal Friedrich von Paulus surrendered the entire Sixth Army to General Zhukov. Twenty German divisions had been anhilated with 1,500 tanks lost in Germany's greatest battlefield defeat of the war. The morale of her panzers would not recover.

EL ALAMEIN

WHEN ONE THINKS of El Alamein, it is with visions of a mighty clash in which two vast World War II tank armies, the British and Commonwealth forces versus the Deutsches Afrika Korps and its Italian partners, engage somewhere in the desert wastes of Egypt back in 1942. It was Erwin " Desert Fox" Rommel against Bernard "Monty" Montgomery. It was M4 Sherman tanks with 75mm guns and armour-piercing shot, Crusaders, Stuarts, Grants and Matilda mine-clearing flails against the German Panzer IIIs and IVs and a lot of obsolete Italian armour. But equally, it was deprivation, debilitating heat and crippling, blinding sandstorms whose grit clogged every pore and every mechanical seam, frequently rendering men and machines useless.

The British called the wind *khamsin*, Arabic for "the hot wind that blows out of the Sahara". The wind could raise the temperature by up to 35°F. in just a few hours. It is said that Bedouin tribal law permitted a husband to kill his wife after five days of such conditions. For the soldiers of both sides, the stinging sand clouds reduced visibility to zero and made breathing difficult through their makeshift sand masks. Odd electrical disturbances caused compasses to misbehave wildly, while the hurricane-force gusts often overturned vehicles and uprooted telephone poles.

To call conditions for soldiers in the Western Desert harsh is to understate them tenfold. When either Allied or Axis troops reached a place where they were required to dig in and establish a position, they frequently found themselves unable to make an impression on limestone underlying the thin sheet of sand. Their only option was to lie still in their exposed positions under the sweltering sun, hoping that they would not be observed and draw enemy fire. By day they were prey to attack from swarms of black flies and at nightfall, when the temperature plummeted, they suffered an opposite misery to that of the day.

In the rectangle of desert 500 miles long and 150 miles wide where most of the campaign was fought, the coastline was relatively fertile, but inland the inhospitable wastes supported little more than prickly camel's thorn, vipers and scorpions. The only human life in the area was a handful of nomadic Bedouin tribesmen. Water, that most precious resource, was scarce and was only available at widely spaced cisterns or through the drilling of deep wells. But the greatest torment of the soldier was probably the powdery sand that irritated and inflamed the eyes, ruined rifle breeches, penetrated tents, covered food and equipment and minimized visibility.

As correspondent in Egypt for the London *Daily Express*, Australian writer Alan Moorehead reported the desert conflict: "Each truck or tank was as individual as a destroyer, and each squadron of tanks or guns made great sweeps across the desert as a battle-squadron at sea will vanish over the horizon . . . . When you made contact with the enemy you manoeuvred about him for a place to strike, much as two fleets will steam into position for action . . . . There was no front line . . . . Always the essential governing principle was that desert forces must be mobile . . . . We hunted men, not land, as a warship will hunt another warship, and care nothing for the sea on which the action is fought. Always the desert set the pace, made the direction and planned the design. The desert offered colours in browns, yellows and grays. The army accordingly took these colours for its camouflage. There were practically no roads. The army shod its vehicles with huge balloon tyres and did without roads. Nothing except an occasional bird moved quickly in the desert. The army for ordinary purposes accepted a pace of five or six miles an hour. The desert gave water reluctantly, and often then it was brackish. The army cut its men—generals and privates—down to a gallon of water a day when they were in forward positions. We did not try to make the desert livable, nor did we seek to subdue it. We found the life of the desert primitive and nomadic, and primitively and nomadically the army lived and went to war."

The green Nile irrigates a barren region, / All the coarse palms are ankle-deep in sand; / No love roots deep, though easy loves are legion: / The heart's as hot and hungry as the hand.
– from *Egypt*
by G. S. Fraser

We ploughed the sand with shell and burning bomb And found few bones there where we left our own Bleached by the drifting detritus of stone, / Bright in their busy many-fingered tomb.
– from *Eighth Army*
by T. W. Ramsey

left: A German panzer crew in North Africa during 1942.

There are flowers now, they
say, at Alamein; / Yes, flowers
in the minefields now. / So
those that come to view that
vacant scene Where death
remains and agony has been
Will find the lilies grow—
Flowers, and nothing that we
know.

It will become a staid historic
name, / That crazy sea of
sand! Like Troy or Agincourt
its single fame Will be the
garland for our brow, our
claim, / On us a fleck of glory
to the end: And there our
dead will keep their holy
ground.
– from *El Alamein*
by John Jarmain
killed in action, 1944

The Suez Canal is a 103-mile channel which
crosses the Isthmus of Suez in Egypt and links the
Red Sea and Gulf of Suez with the Mediterranean
Sea. The canal was built under the supervision of
Ferdinand de Lesseps and opened in November
1869. In 1875 it came under British control and in
1879 the British Prime Minister Benjamin Disraeli
purchased the shares in the canal held by the
Khedive of Egypt. This assured Britain's ongoing
and increasing interest in that country, which she
helped to modernize and develop as a
protectorate. In 1922 Britain recognized Egypt as
an independent ally. The canal was essential to
Britain's trade and it was in her vital interest to
keep it open and protected. In World War I the
Turks tried to attack the canal and were decisively
beaten back by British troops. By the 1930s the
presence of an Italian army in neighbouring Libya,
in support of its Fascist régime's determination to
seize the canal, posed an obvious threat in the
event of war. In 1936, an Anglo-Egyptian treaty was
signed with Britain agreeing to defend the canal

until such future time as the Egyptians would be in
a position to do so.

After Italy entered the war in spring 1940 the
British forces in the Middle East were under the
stewardship of General Sir Achibald Wavell. Some
historians refer to Wavell as being highly
competent but one of the unluckiest British
commanders of the war. He always seemed to
take command in a theatre just prior to the worst
of defeats and then get the bad publicity for it. He
was deliberate and determined to plan his
operations well and act only when he believed his
men and equipment were absolutely sufficient to
the task. He considered the comments, criticism
and advice coming to him from the British Prime
Minister Winston Churchill by the fall of 1940 to
be "barracking", a form of heckling, and realized
that the PM was losing confidence in him. Still, he
was determined not to attack the Italians until he
felt that his preparations were complete.

Wavell was planning a five-day raid halting at

Buq Buq, 25 miles west of Sidi Barrani. He meant to accomplish three things: to test the mettle of the Italians in actual battle rather than in mere skirmishes, to take a few thousand prisoners and, most importantly, to hit the Italians decisively before the Germans could intervene in Libya. The British could field 30,000 men, a mix of Englishmen, Cameron Highlanders, Ulstermen, Sikhs and Hindus, against an Italian force of 80,000.

Just three days after the attack had begun on 9 December, 39,000 Italian soldiers had surrendered or been captured by Wavell's forces. He was amazed and Churchill was tickled pink. Wavell had not intended a major action but now it seemed to have a momentum of its own, and the major port of Tobruk was to be the next British objective. At the same time, the German advance on Greece (to rescue their Italian allies after Mussolini's failed invasion effort) was of great concern to Churchill and Wavell chose that moment to send a message to the PM questioning British policy towards Greece: ". . . nothing we can do from here is likely to be in time to stop the German advance if really intended." Churchill fired back: "Nothing must hamper capture of Tobruk but thereafter all operations in Libya are subordinated to aiding Greece. We expect and require prompt and active compliance with our decisions."

The Libyan harbour and fortress of Tobruk was captured by the British, along with 25,000 Italian prisoners, on 22 January 1941.

Hitler had become aware of Erwin Rommel in 1937 with the publication of Rommel's book *Infanterie Greift an* (The Infantry Attacks), a widely acclaimed work. In it he explained his aggressive tactical ideas which had evolved from his WWI experiences. The Führer was most impressed and began to follow Rommel's career with great interest. When Germany invaded Poland in the late summer of 1939, he made Rommel commander of the Führer's Headquarters (*Führerhauptquartier*).

Born in Heidenheim in southern Germany on 15 November 1891, Erwin Johannes Eugen Rommel was the son of a mathematics teacher. He entered the German Army in 1910 and made a name for himself in the World War I offensive to the Piave River in 1917, for which he was awarded the *Pour le Mérite*.

Rommel was well aware of the conservatism among Hitler's General Staff officers and the gulf it had created between them and their leader. He frequently found himself agreeing with Hitler and opposing the views of the Staff, which continued to enhance Hitler's opinion of him. With the end of the Polish campaign, Rommel asked that he be given command of a Panzer Division, and, overruling the objections of his Generals, Hitler was pleased to grant the request. In February 1940 Rommel took charge of the 7th Panzer Division, which was then being formed at Bad Godesberg and quickly organized their efficient and demanding training programme. His efforts resulted in the best performance by any Panzer formation during the invasion of France in May. Hitler showed his pleasure by giving Rommel the first Knights Cross to be awarded to a divisional commander in the campaign. Rommel extended his reputation for bold, aggressive methods when he drove his division to the Channel coast and on to Cherbourg at the amazing pace of 40 to 50 miles a day, to take the surrender of the French garrison there. His performance in France, however, while dramatic, did not impress his detractors in the High Command. They felt that he was inclined to act impulsively rather than with considered judgement, that he failed to cover his flanks or provide proper logistical support for his spearheads, that he was ego-driven and rarely willing to acknowledge the accomplishments of others, and, not incidentally,

With grey arm twisted over a green face / The dust of passing trucks swirls over him, / Lying by the roadside in his proper place, / For he has crossed the ultimate far rim / That hides from us the valley of the dead. / He lies like used equipment thrown aside, / Of which our swift advance can take no heed, / Roses, triumphal cars—but this one died.

Once war memorials, pitiful attempt / In some vague way regretfully to atone For those lost futures that the dead had dreamt, Covered the land with their lamenting stone— / But in our hearts we bear a heavier load: / The bodies of the dead beside the road.
– *War Dead*
by Gavin Ewart

The American Sherman was the most successful Allied tank of World War II. More than 40,000 were built between 1942 and 1946. It first went into action in the desert war at El Alamein.

In World War II the British 7th Armoured Division called themselves the 'Desert Rats' after the jerboa, a small desert rodent. They adopted the animal as their divisional emblem. Ultimately, the name Desert Rats came to be used to describe the entire British Eighth Army. In February 1943, Winston Churchill said of the Eighth Army: "When the war is over it will be enough for a man to say, 'I marched and fought with the Desert Army.'"

right: In Tunisia, British soldiers rush from a German PzKpfw III tank on which they have just planted an explosive charge.

they resented his special relationship with Hitler.

Rommel was propelled by nerve, self-confidence, ego and will. He understood the importance of using his resources to apply and maintain pressure on the enemy, as well as the value of psychological warfare techniques. He was a great improviser and enjoyed involving himself in the minutiae of his planning. He was, for the most part, an inspiring leader who knew how to bluff and deceive his enemy and give the impression of having a more powerful and threatening force than he actually had. He was skillful and quite intuitive, able to get into the mind of an enemy commander and sense the man's interpretation of Rommel's intentions.

In North Africa Rommel's aggressive, audacious exploits earned him the nickname "The Desert Fox" and he soon became a kind of legendary figure credited by many on both sides of the conflict with being superhuman. The British were plainly in awe of his blitzkrieg tactics and, for a time, when a British soldier performed a duty particularly well, his fellow troopers would refer to him as "doing a Rommel".

"We have a very daring and skillful opponent against us, and, may I say across the havoc of war, a great general" said Prime Minister Winston Churchill of Rommel in an address to the House of Commons in 1942.

Late in 1941 Rommel is known to have been sitting in a Libyan farmhouse while an artist was painting his portrait. At one point the area came under attack by British bombers and two bombs fell quite near the farmhouse, making a lot of noise and causing many broken windows and much dust and falling plaster. Undisturbed by the event, Rommel continued to pose, but the fearful artist hesitated in his work as a second wave of bombers approached and the local flak guns roared into action. Rommel, so the story goes, quietly asked the artist if the raid was bothering him. The man

I was given a job in the Officer's Mess. We were told to get the place tidied up as there were some important people coming to dinner. We found out later that it was to be General Montgomery and some other high-ranking officers. The officer in charge of the Mess had heard from one of the lads that I was the best scrounger in the Company, so he sent for me. He asked me to take the cook with me and go scrounge something special for the dinner. The cook and I borrowed a jeep and travelled about three miles out into the desert where we found a big white house with big letters painted on it that said: OUT OF BOUNDS TO ALL ALLIED FORCES. Never mind. The cook and I knocked on the door and an old man came to ask what we wanted. We asked him if he had any chickens to sell us and he invited us into the house. He said he would be back shortly. In this big room there was a large and highly-polished table about twenty feet long and four feet wide. There were a dozen naked women sitting at the table. The *continued on page 101*

continued on page 101

In *Crusaders*, a painting by David Shepard, tanks of the British 5 Royal Tank Regiment roll past a burning Panzer III.

replied: "No, Herr General."
"Then carry on, carry on," said Rommel.

In his grand scheme Hitler considered North Africa a low-priority theatre, but did not want to see his Axis partner Italy pushed out of the region. Field Marshall Heinrich von Brauchitsch, Rommel's immediate superior, informed the General that his new role was to be strictly defensive and that, for the time being, Germany would not be able to provide suffcent additional forces to drive the British from their present position in the eastern Libyan province of Cyrenaica. Rommel was, however, promised a fully-equipped panzer division by the end of May. But he expected the British to move against his army as early as February and quickly began work on one of his greatest ruses. "It was my belief that if the British could detect no opposition they would probably continue their advance, but that if they saw they were going to have to fight another battle they would first wait to build up supplies. With the time thus gained I hoped to build up our own strength until we were eventually strong enough to withstand the enemy attack." To enable his forces to appear as strong as possible and to induce the maximum caution in the British, Rommel ordered a workshop to make dummy tanks of wood and canvas and mount them on Volkswagen chassis. The task was completed by 17 February and Rommel, pleased with the result, awaited his enemy.

The British, however, did not come. Their main focus, and much of Wavell's army, had been shifted to Greece where they began landing on 4 March. That effort reduced British defences in eastern Libya to a bare minimum. It was not until late March that Wavell refocused on these defences, "when it was rather too late", and realized with dismay that he had utterly overestimated the protection afforded by the escarpment south of Benghazi. "When I actually went out and saw the escarpment, I realized

below: The inspiring, spirited, tough-minded British Prime Minister Winston Churchill. Here he inspects a 'Tommy gun' in July 1941.

Before Alamein there were almost no victories. After it, there were almost no defeats.
– Winston Churchill

Churchill mobilised the English language, and sent it into battle.
– Edward R. Murrow

that it could be ascended almost anywhere and was no protection." He had thought the escarpment would be an effective barrier against tanks. At the end of February Wavell had made a dubious appointment, naming Lieutenant General Philip Neame to be commander in Cyrenaica. He may have had second thoughts about his choice almost immediately when he learned of Neame's tactical dispositions, declaring them to be "just crazy" and ordering a prompt redeployment.

Rommel, Wavell still believed, would not be able to mount an attack before May. The German had, in fact, been ordered by Brauchitsch in a Berlin meeting on or about 20 March to do nothing before the end of May, but Rommel had other plans. On 24 March, he launched a dawn attack of tanks and armoured cars on El Agheila, and employing for the first time his "Cardboard Division" of Volkswagen-mounted dummy tanks which, together with his real armour, created huge clouds of dust. The ruse worked like a charm and the British garrison at El Agheila quickly withdrew 30 miles to Mersa Brega in the northeast. On learning of the attack and the lack of a British counter-attack, Churchill cabled Wavell on 26 March: "I presume you are only waiting for the tortoise to stick his head out far enough before chopping it off." On 30 March, Wavell told Neame not to be overly concerned about the enemy: "I do not believe he can make any big effort for at least another month." Rommel hit Mersa Brega the next day. His reconnaissance reports showed that the fleeing British force were still on the move northward and not stopping to establish defensive positions. Although under instructions not to open a major offensive before the end of May, Rommel could not resist. Neame's soldiers were in full retreat, 500 miles in a week. The panic and confusion that Rommel had hoped to create in Neame's command had been achieved. Some British troops were referring to their flight as "The Benghazi Handicap" and "The

Tobruk Derby".

On 2 April, Wavell visited the front to evaluate the situation: "I soon realized that Neame had lost control." Rommel, meanwhile, was busy justifying the contravention of his orders. "It was becoming increasingly clear that the enemy believed us to be far stronger than we actually were, a belief that it was essential to maintain, by keeping up the appearance of a large-scale offensive."

By 7 April Rommel had become obsessed with Tobruk. His men required 1,500 tons of water and food per day and Tobruk, the only suitable port in Cyrenaica east of Benghazi, was his only practical means of supply. The British were well-established there, however, and were busily reinforcing their defences in anticipation of Rommel's attentions, which he soon offered with reckless abandon. On 14 April his tanks blasted into Tobruk, directly into a trap set for them. He lost seventeen tanks in the action. In the British force at Tobruk, Rommel was up against Major-General Leslie Morshead, a 51-year-old Australian known by his troops as "Ming the Merciless" after a character in the Flash Gordon comic strip. On the approach of Rommel's armour, Morshead informed his staff: "If we have to get out we shall fight our way out. There'll be no Dunkirk here. There is to be no surrender and no retreat."

For the 35,000 British, Anzac and Indian defenders of Tobruk, waiting for Rommel meant putting up with endless dysentery, lice, sand fleas, sunburn and boredom. The thrust-and-parry action continued and by late April, Churchill was insisting that Wavell mount a counter-offensive. Wavell's response: "Action before mid-June is out of the question." Churchill was angry and Wavell decided to act with Operation *Brevity*, a limited effort to establish a launch position for the main offensive to come. *Brevity* opened on 15 May. By 27 May the Germans had driven Wavell's forces from Halfaya Pass, an important cut in the escarpment which led onto the Libyan plateau. *Brevity* had failed.

The British had been thrown out of Greece at the end of April, had taken refuge in Crete to regroup and were now under a considerable German threat there. And Churchill continued to badger Wavell to get on with the major offensive against Rommel, whom the Prime Minister believed was gaining strength by the day. At the same time, Wavell was having to fight campaigns in the Axis-puppet states of Syria and Iraq. Still, on 15 June he managed to launch Operation *Battleaxe*, the long-awaited Cyrenaica main offensive.

For *Battleaxe*, a reinforced infantry brigade with one and a half squadrons of tanks was to retake Halfaya Pass, while another infantry and armoured brigade formation was to move on the German position at Fort Capuzzo. Yet another reinforced armoured brigade was to sweep wide to the west towards Sidi Azeiz to protect the British units from Axis forces in the area of Sidi Omar. The Germans under the command of Captain Wilhelm Bach, had been ordered to let the enemy tanks come on into the pass at Halfaya. There they waited, concealed in emplacements all along the cliffside, with 88mm guns that fired 22-pound shells capable of putting holes twelve inches in diameter in Matilda tanks at a one-mile range. In five failed attempts to punch their way through the pass (which British troops thereafter called Hell Fire Pass), the British force lost eleven of their twelve leading tanks.

Thanks to the initiative of Major General F.W. Messervy, commander of the 4th Indian Division, the rest of the British forces in the pass were withdrawn, saving them from almost certain destruction by Rommel's army. In the disastrous operation, the British had lost 90 tanks, 30 aircraft and 1,000 men. Morale among British troops in the desert war was at an all-time low. To Wavell's admission of defeat, "Am very sorry for failure of *Battleaxe*", the reaction of the Permanent Under-Secretary to the Foreign Office, Sir Alexander Cadogan was succinct: "The German Army simply has better generals. Wavell and such like are no good against them. It is like putting me up to play Bobby Jones over 36 holes." On the morning of 22 June a message arrived for General Wavell from the Prime Minister: "I have come to the conclusion that public interest will best be served by appointment of General Auchinleck to relieve you in command of armies of Middle East."

The 57-year-old General Sir Claude Auchinleck was known to his troops in the British Middle Eastern Forces as "The Auk". It was an affectionate and respectful reference to a quick-thinking leader who had a good grasp of both tactical and strategic problems; a man they believed was certainly a match for Rommel. But Auchinleck had one major shortcoming; he was a poor judge of men when selecting his subordinate commanders, a flaw he compounded with misplaced loyalty and a stubborn refusal to deal with his failed choices. In Auchinleck, Churchill had a commander who carried out a war of manoeuvre against the Axis forces, continually attacking and destroying the Italian units. Rommel was then required to use his German forces to fill in the gaps, further draining his own limited manpower. However, Churchill was impatient with Auchinleck, feeling that the General was not making progress against the enemy at the necessary pace.

For several months after Operation *Battleaxe*, relative calm prevailed in the Western Desert. For both sides it was a monotonous period of waiting, watching the enemy across the front and suffering in the intense heat of the high summer and autumn sun. The miserable rations of the German troops, fatty sausage, tinned sardines in oil, and black bread, was surpassed in appeal only slightly by that of the British with their corned beef, hard tack biscuits and ration packs. It was a time of discomfort for all, of resupply and reinforcement for some elements, and of quiet reflection.

cook and I stood there with our eyes popping out and, after a while, the old man came back carrying a dozen chickens. We showed him a bag of tea that we had brought with us and he agreed to take the tea in exchange for the chickens. He also offered us two of the naked women so they could come with us and work as servants. We told him that we could not accept the women as the Army would not allow that, and we left.

When we got back to camp we explained about the chickens and the two women the old man had offered, and the Mess officer laughed and said we should have brought the women with us. At seven that evening General Montgomery and the other officers arrived. After their meal, the General and the Mess Officer came into the cook house and thanked the cook and everybody for an excellent dinner, shaking hands with us all.
– J. Ellison, Royal Tank Regiment, World War II

Battle is the most magnificent competition in which a human being can indulge. It brings out all that is best; it removes all that is base. All men are afraid in battle. The coward is the one who lets his fear overcome his sense of duty. Duty is the essence of manhood.
– General George S. Patton

On 21 June 1942, after a four-day siege, the Germans recaptured Tobruk and with it 33,000 British troops. By late June, Rommel was positioned to drive on to Cairo and Suez. His forces had shoved the British back to the Egyptian border and were threatening Britain's position in the eastern Mediterranean. If Rommel could take Suez he would have a clear path to the oil fields of the Middle East and would then be able to link up with German units in Russia. The British Eighth Army, under Auchinleck, had managed to make a stand at the small coastal town of El Alamein in early July. Alamein was the last defensive position on the western desert front from which the British could hold Alexandria and the Nile Delta. It lay on a 40-mile stretch of sand between the Mediterranean Sea and the salt marshes of the great impassable Qattara Depression. There is a coastal road and a railway line running along the ledges which are bounded on the sea side by salt lagoons. In places the rocky subsoil breaks through the thin sand layer and then ends abruptly in a sheer cliff down to the Depression. To the south of the Qattara is the great Sand Sea. The British position then, was vulnerable only to frontal attack. There the British and German forces had engaged in a clash now known as the First Alamein, in which the Germans were fought to a standstill.

Now Churchill moved to break Rommel in the desert war. He sacked Auchinleck and said later: "Firing Auchinleck was like killing a magnificent stag." He then appointed General Sir Harold Alexander in overall command and Montgomery to take charge of the Eighth Army. In Monty he had a man he did not like, but one he believed could get the job done.

General Bernard Law Montgomery was a professional soldier who also had served in World War I. After Alamein, Monty would go on to Italy and later to command land forces in the Normandy invasion of 1944. Born in 1887, the son of a bishop, he was a bible-reading teetotaler. Dogmatic, brusque, overbearing and uncompromising,

Montgomery was a natural leader who had excelled at sports in school. In the army his superior officers grudgingly gave him their recommendations for promotion though they found him excessively opinionated and often erratic. By his own admission, he was difficult to get along with: "I am a bit of a cad. One has to be a bit of a cad to succeed in the Army."

He seems to have carefully cultivated the image of an eccentric, but underneath it all he was undoubtedly a competent military professional who was gifted with the ability to inspire and command the loyalty and obedience of his soldiers. He was small and thin and quite ruthless. He nearly always wore a Royal Tank Regiment beret, a pullover sweater and khaki trousers. He had no experience commanding large formations of armour, but, unlike the earlier British commanders in the desert war, he seemed to be constantly visiting his frontline units, encouraging them and exuding confidence: "We will finish with Rommel once and for all."

The United States and Britain had agreed that the first American troops to go into action in the west should land in the French territories of Northwest Africa in autumn 1942. The idea was to put Rommel in a vice—to squeeze him between the two Allied armies—and the schedule called for an early-November starting date. Unlike Wavell and Auchinleck, Montgomery was able to take command at a point when everything he required for victory was coming together . . . air supremacy, strategy and resources. His Eighth Army was quickly becoming a far stronger force than that of his enemy. Monty now had nearly 200,000 men, 2,300 guns, 500 planes and more than 1,000 tanks. Importantly, many of his tanks were new American Shermans which were capable of destroying the German anti-tank guns at a considerable distance. In the Sherman the British had much more of a chance against the German Panzer IV than in their

LIBYA
Help them finish the jo

News of Field Marshal Sir Bernard Montgomery having invited his prisoner of war, General Wilhelm von Thoma, Field Commander of the Afrika Korps, to dine with him in his GHQ trailer in North Africa shocked and infuriated many Britons. But Prime Minister Winston Churchill reacted: "I sympathize with General von Thoma. Defeated, humiliated, in captivity, and . . . dinner with Montgomery."

left: A PzKpfw III panzer of German Lieutenant General Erwin Rommel's Afrika Korps. above: A British home front poster of World War II.

To the German troops in the desert war, the M-4 Sherman tanks were referred to as "Tommy-cookers" due to the propensity of the tank to catch fire when hit.

Nothing delights me as I sit
In this pestiferous clime;
Mosquitoes plague me and
the horrid / Sand-flies make
raids upon my forehead; / I
hit and curse and wildly hit,
And miss them every time.

Nothing delights me,
nothing does; / There
cannot be much bliss
Where all the animals
created / Seem only
differentiated / Between
the brutes that fly and buzz
And those that crawl and
hiss.
– from *Somewhere East of Suez*
by H.W. Berry

The American Grant tank mounted a 37mm gun in a turret and a 75mm gun in a sponson. By May 1942, the British Eighth Army was operating 167 Grants in the North African desert war. The 75mm gun of the Grant could fire both armour-piercing shot and high-explosive shells and was capable of penetrating the armour of German tanks at ranges up to 850 yards.

older British Valentines and Matildas.

Rommel's final attempt to break through the British lines in an effort to reach the Nile Valley was the Battle of Alam Halfa. It was Montgomery's first combat operation in the desert after taking command of the Eighth Army. It would prove a difficult and tense engagement for them both. On 31 August the German attacked with a powerful tank force along the Qattara Depression. He planned to veer north just behind the Alam Halfa Ridge. However, his force was delayed making its way through British minefields, which alerted Montgomery in time to make preparations and take countermeasures. Now Rommel's flanks were threatened by the British 7th and 10th Armoured Divisions and he was forced to make his turn earlier than intended, at the Ridge itself, which was lined with heavy British defences. It was there that the battle was fought. It continued until 2 September when, desperately short of fuel and supplies, Rommel was forced to break off the attack and retreat behind his own lines. The reality of his weakening force (only 203 tanks remaining against 767 British) meant he had to withdraw to regroup. The problem of resupply and re-equipping his armoured units was hampering his ability to prepare for the decisive battle that both sides knew was coming. In typical Rommel style, he discarded his offensive mode and went on the defence. With his remaining 100,000 soldiers he set out to establish a 40-mile defensive front along the Miteirya Ridge to block the space between the coast at El Alamein and the Qattara Depression. He constructed an elaborate five-mile-deep complex of minefields which he called "The Devil's Gardens". The minefields were designed with pathways intended to lure the enemy into the danger areas. They were planted with half a million mines, including Tellers which withstood the weight of a man but exploded under that of a tank or other vehicle,

as well as S-mines—deadly anti-personnel devices which, when tripped by a man, would jump into the air and explode at waist height.

To counter the minefield hazard, Montgomery could rely on British ingenuity in the form of the Baron, a tank comprised of an obsolete Matilda hull to which had been fitted a flail which rotated lashing chains well ahead of the tank to detonate mines as the vehicle moved through the field. In addition to his Baron fleet, he had 500 mine detectors. The newly-invented device would emit a high-pitched siren-like whine when swept over metal. He also borrowed an idea from his adversary and had an entire fake army base constructed near the southern part of the front. It included cardboard trucks, storage dumps, vehicles and a railway . . . all phoney and all in addition to an actual camouflaged base built by his men on the north end of the front.

Then there was luck. Rommel's had been rather bad recently and was getting worse, while Monty's seemed to be improving. The Desert Fox was having trouble with his blood pressure and in September he became ill with jaundice. It required proper treatment and for that he had to return to Vienna. This was a break for Montgomery and so was the codebreaking activity at Bletchley Park in the English midlands where German Enigma machine messages were being decrypted. The resulting product was called Ultra and one such message indicated that Rommel's immediate replacement was to be Lieutenant General Georg Stumme, a man with command experience on the Russian Front, but none in desert warfare.

Nigel Hamilton, in his book, *The Full Monty*, on the General's preparation for the decisive clash: "Monty's battle plan for Alamein was scripted five weeks in advance. Major William Mather remembered the moment. It was September 13, 1942—six days after the end of Alam Halfa. 'It was like a hen giving birth. He walked backwards and forwards on the sands of Burg el-Arab all day, like Napoleon with his head down, his hands behind his back. And he came back into his caravan and in about four hours he wrote the whole Operation Order for Alamein. That was it.' "

The British codename for the great Alamein offensive was Operation *Lightfoot*. The operation began under bright moonlight at 9.40 on the night of 23 October. For five hours the thunder of more than 1,000 British guns reverberated across the wastes. The night sky was lit by the brilliant flashes. The screaming of the shells was a sound that would never be forgotten by the combatants. The next noise the Germans heard was the rumble and squeal of many tanks crawling through the minefields to make routes which were carefully marked by the Allied sappers. They did well, but it was inevitable that most of the large mined area would remain uncleared. The

below: British Royal engineers dismantle a captured German tank in the Western Desert of North Africa, May 1941.

In defeat, unbeatable; in victory, unbearable.
– Winston Churchill, on Field Marshal Sir Bernard Montgomery

طبـــرق ٢٦
OBRUK 26

top: A postage stamp of the Grenadine Islands commemorating the Allied landings at Anzio that were made possible by the successful campaign in North Africa. above: A road sign now in the collections of the Tank Museum, Dorset, England. right: German Afrika Korps commander Lieutenant General Erwin Rommel, known as the "Desert Fox", seen here wearing a pair of captured British sun goggles in 1942. far right: General Bernard L. Montgomery, the British commander who, in the three months following El Alamein, drove Rommel's forces back across 1400 miles of North African desert. Painting by Sir Oswald H. J. Birley.

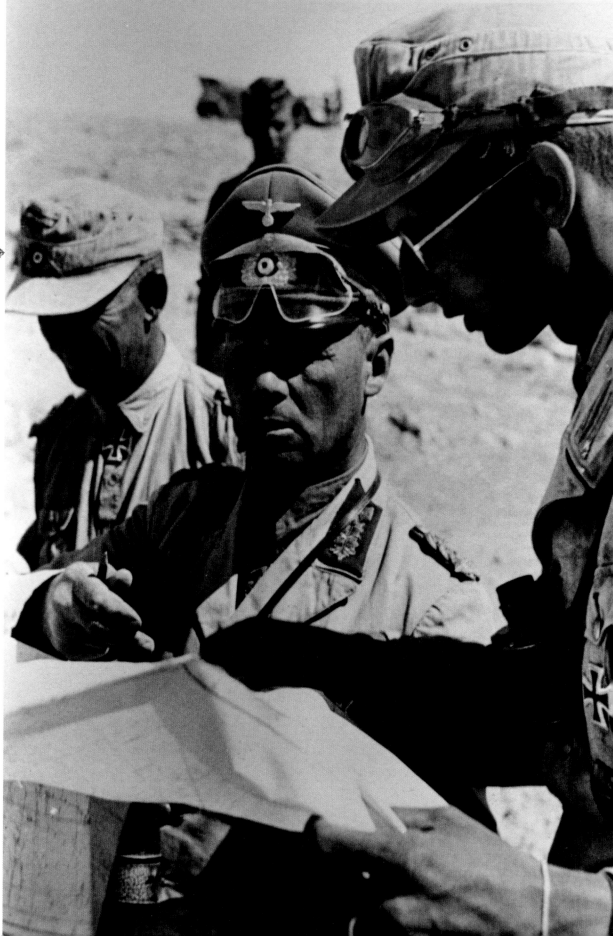

British units were advancing in two widely-separated formations. A main force of tanks and infantry was moving foward on a four-mile front near the coast while a secondary force was creating a diversionary attack well to the south. Again, Nigel Hamilton: "The courage of the infantry at Alamein would go down in history as almost 10,000 assault troops advanced through uncleared minefields and stormed the Axis outposts. The fighting was merciless—no quarter being given, lest taking prisoners slow down the rate of advance. It was brutal, surgical—and deadly, the wounded being left where they lay."

British progress through the minefields was slow and arduous. Their vehicles and armour were easy targets for the Germans in the first two days. But by the time Stumme's forces began a counterattack, they were facing a formidable array of British armour. They managed to slow the advance of Montgomery's force, but in the process the 15th Panzer Division lost 75 per cent of its tanks by the end of the second day of *Lightfoot.* During the second day the car carrying Stumme was hit by shell fire and the general was blown from it. Days later he was found there, dead of an apparent heart attack. In the evening of 24 October, Hitler telephoned Rommel to inform him that things were not going well at Alamein and that no one seemed to know what had happened to Stumme. The Führer asked Rommel if he was fit enough to take charge again in North Africa. Rommel headed for Alamein the following day.

Four times over the next two days German and Italian tanks attempted to assault a British position on the small hill called Kidney Ridge. When they tried a fifth time they became the target of British planes which dropped bombs on them for two hours, forcing the Germans to withdraw. Both sides now seemed stalled, unable to advance their positions. To break the stalemate, Montgomery quickly devised a new

plan which he named *Supercharge*. He redirected his forces northward and then implemented the plan, a new assault from Kidney Ridge in the evening of 2 November. This time the British armour was truly ensnared in the enemy minefields and suffered mightily under the German guns, losing a further 200 tanks.

Now the stalemate situation was critical for both the British and German forces. Rommel's army was hemmed in along the 40-mile corridor between the Mediterranean and the Qattara Depression. He was again in charge, but saw no other option than immediate retreat. His enemy seemed to have an inexhaustible supply of soldiers, artillery and swift new tanks. He had, perhaps, half as many personnel and only 55 tanks remaining. He ordered a retreat, but the order was countermanded by Hitler: "Yield not a metre of ground. Your enemy, despite his superiority, must also be at the end of his strength." The situation was bad enough for both sides that Montgomery, ordinarily supremely confident, was having second thoughts about his chances of defeating Rommel. Both Monty and Churchill were extremely concerned about the possibility of Rommel's army surviving to resist the Allied invasion scheduled to begin in just four days.

Actually, the British force still had more than 600 tanks, even after incurring losses to the Germans at a rate of four to one. The sheer magnitude of Allied arms was crushing the German effort.

Finally, in the early morning of 4 November, units of the 5th Indian Division and the 51st Highlanders achieved a breakthrough for the British when they forced a gap between Rommel's Afrika Korps and the Italian forces. Rommel's situation now became truly desperate with the probability that the British would be able to cut off the retreat that he knew he must attempt. Hitler finally relented and allowed Rommel to pull out of the battle, but the German's troubles were far from over. He bitterly resented Hitler's earlier "victory or death" order

which had compelled him to keep his men fighting 24 hours longer than he should have. Now in full retreat, his army had only ten tanks remaining and was forced to fight a series of rearguard actions, gradually giving up Sidi Barrani, Tobruk and Benghazi—all of the towns they had taken in better times. His soldiers, staff cars and tanks had clogged the coastal road for two days while Allied planes strafed them and Montgomery's forces pursued them. That pursuit lasted six weeks as Rommel struggled to bring his depleted force all the way back to the German supply base at Tripoli. Montgomery's vehicles were mired in the mud when a sudden, unusually heavy desert rainstorm struck, delaying them. Rommel was trying to bring his remaining forces all the way back to Tunisia and link up there with other German forces in order to re-engage with the British and with the Americans who had by now landed in French North Africa.

When Allied forces reached and entered Tripoli on 23 January, Rommel and what remained of the Afrika Korps had made their getaway by sea, but not before destroying Tripoli's port facilities. In the Battle of El Alamein, Montgomery had lost 13,500 men; Rommel lost 50,000. The British lost 500 tanks but of them only 150 were not repairable. The Germans lost 450 tanks.

Allied invasion troops had successfully made their landings in Algeria and Morocco in November and in April 1943 the two Allied forces linked and prepared to move up into the European continent via the scenic southern route, through Italy. By 13 May the last Axis soldier in Tunisia had surrendered; the Allies had taken 275,000 prisoners. Rommel and 700 other German soldiers had escaped.

The following excerpt is from a letter by Montgomery to Major General A.H. Gatehouse, head of the British Ministry of Supply Mission in Washington, D.C. on 18 September 1943: "The Eighth Army thanks from the bottom of its

General Montgomery was a very hard and strict person. When he gave an order you had to jump to it. He was the best general we had for the job. From Alamein to Tunis, he would predict that he would be in such-and-such a place in two days time and you could bet your boots that he would be there.
— J. Ellison, Royal Tank Regiment, World War II

Donald Chidson was a member of the British 4th Tank Regiment in North Africa in World War II. Commanding his troop in an attack during the breakout from Tobruk on 22 November 1941, he ordered his tank to move well beyond their objective, to give his accompanying infantry maximum support. His tank came under heavy shell fire and was shortly halted and immobilised. Even so, Lieutenant Chidson and his crew continued to fight, bringing substantial fire on the enemy forces. He radioed his squadron reconnaissance officer, arranging to bring fire onto the enemy positions ahead of his tank. He "ably and coolly directed this fire" read the citation for his MC, "from his tank despite continuous enemy fire directed upon it". Chidson kept on fighting and directing fire on the enemy until help arrived and the tank was towed away for repair. The following day, Lt. Chidson's tank again closed on enemy forces and was again heavily shelled and this time attacked with Molotov cocktails. His driver was seriously burnt. With that Chidson scrambled from the tank in a fury, attacking the nearby enemy troops with his revolver, whereupon several of them surrendered to him. For his actions Lt. Chidson was granted the award of an immediate Military Cross.

heart the Army Ordnance Department and all those factories and the men and women who work in them for what they have done. It wishes them the very best of luck in the future. Wherever we fight in the future our gratitude towards them will ever be fresh in our minds. May it ever remain so both while this war lasts; and afterwards when the United Nations together bring peace and order into being."

left: British Army Lieutenant Donald Chidson. above left: A burning Panzer III. below: The burnt-out wreck of a Panzer III which had been destroyed by British gunners.

NORMANDY

Hard pounding this,
gentlemen.
– Wellington

Britain's Queen Elizabeth
chats with a soldier of an
armoured division prior
to the D-Day landings.
below: The 88mm gun
of a German PzKpfw VI
Tiger, an awesome tank
which outclassed its
opponents in the final
years of World War II.

"SOLDIERS, SAILORS AND AIRMEN of the Allied Expeditionary Force! You are about to embark upon the Great Crusade, toward which we have striven these many months. The eyes of the world are upon you. The hopes and prayers of liberty-loving people everywhere march with you. In company with our brave allies and brothers-in-arms on other fronts, you will bring about the destruction of the German war machine, the elimination of Nazi tyranny over the oppressed peoples of Europe, and security for ourselves in a free world.

Your task will not be an easy one. Your enemy is well trained, well equipped and battle-hardened. He will fight savagely.

But this is the year 1944! Much has happened since the Nazi triumphs of 1940-41. The United Nations have inflicted upon the Germans great defeats, in open battle, man-to-man. Our air offensive has seriously reduced their strength in the air and their capacity to wage war on the ground. Our home fronts have given us an overwhelming superiority in weapons and munitions of war, and placed at our disposal great reserves of trained fighting men. The tide has turned! The free men of the world are marching together to victory!

I have full confidence in your courage, devotion to duty and skill in battle. We will accept nothing less than full victory!

Good Luck! And let us all beseech the blessing of Almighty God upon this great and noble undertaking."
– Dwight D. Eisenhower, Supreme Allied Commander, Europe

"Two kinds of people are staying on this beach, the dead and those who are going to die—now let's get the hell out of here."
– Colonel George A. Taylor, Commander, U.S. 16th Infantry Regiment

Since the U.S. entered the war in December 1941, the Allies had struggled desperately to prepare the way for a long-awaited second front, an invasion of the European continent, to liberate the nations under Nazi occupation. Hitler had been seeing to the fortification of much of Europe, including the massive Atlantic Wall stretching from Denmark to the Spanish frontier. But it was still an incomplete barrier, with many gaps, in the summer of 1944 when Allied preparations for the invasion were finally ready. The Germans had other concerns in their efforts to maintain control over Europe in 1944, not least being the ever-increasing activity of resistance organizations, saboteurs and spies in France, Holland, Norway, Poland, Albania, Greece and Yugoslavia. The German satellite states of Hungary and Rumania were restless and engaged in secret contacts with the West. And across the English Channel, in the ports of Falmouth, Dartmouth, Weymouth, Portsmouth and Newhaven, ships, planes, tanks, trucks, ammunition, weapons, food, fuel and all manner of supplies had been assembled in staggering numbers, together with more than 1.5 million Americans, 1.75 million Britons and 150,000 Commonwealth and European troops, most of them fresh and well trained, ready to take part in the greatest invasion of all time. Wags suggested that, with the weight of all that equipment, it was only the barrage balloons that were holding England up and keeping her from sinking.

At a conference at Cairo late in 1943, Churchill and Roosevelt had agreed that France would be the venue for the Allied assault on the continent and that the entire operation would be under the command of American General Dwight David Eisenhower who, in January 1944, was named Supreme Commander, Allied Expeditionary Force (SHAEF). Ike, as he was commonly known, had graduated from West Point in 1915 and had made his reputation as a military strategist and co-ordinator of Allied forces in the North African invasions of 1942. Initially, the land forces would

I know that all of us correspondents have tried time and again to describe to you what this weird hedgerow fighting in northwestern France has been like. But I'm going to go over it once more, for we've been in it two months and some of us feel that this is the two months that broke the German Army in the west.

This type of fighting is always in small groups, so let's take as an example one company of men. Let's say they are working forward on both sides of a country lane, and this company is responsible for clearing the two fields on either side of the road as it advances. That means you have only about one platoon to a field. And with the company's understrength from casualties, you might have no more than twenty-five or thirty men in a field.

Over here the fields are usually not more than fifty yards across and a couple of hundred yards long. They may have grain in them, or apple trees, but mostly they are just pastures of green grass, full of beautiful cows. The fields are surrounded on all sides by immense hedgerows which consist of an ancient earthen bank, waist-high, all matted with roots, and out of which grow weeds, bushes, and trees up to twenty feet high.

The Germans have used these barriers well. They

right: Inside a German gun casemate near Longue-sur-Mer. below: Omaha Beach, near Coleville, Normandy. far right: Rowe Road, dedicated to Private J.T. Rowe, killed in action on 6 June 1944.

be commanded by British General Bernard Montgomery. The coming operation was to be called *Overlord* and was scheduled for May, depending upon readiness and the weather. The first day of the operation would forever be known as D-Day.

Eisenhower and his staff were headquartered at Southwick Park near Portsmouth on the south coast of England. There they developed the plan for *Overlord,* including logistics, determining that a sixty-mile stretch of beaches on the Cotentin Peninsula of Normandy would be the landing area for the assault. While the area lacked sufficient port facilities, was often subject to heavy surf conditions and was much farther from the British embarkation ports than, say, the Pas de Calais coast, it did have certain advantages. It was relatively close to Cherbourg and the Brittany ports. It was less strongly fortified than the Pas de Calais (much the most likely site for a landing) and its beaches had relatively few cliffs, a minimum of clay and depressions, and were fairly well-suited to the landing of troops and equipment and their quick deployment inland. The solution to the lack of port facilites would come in the form of two immense pre-fabricated concrete harbours called Mulberries, which were towed to the landing area. Other ingenious ideas were devised and perfected to support the landings, including PLUTO (pipeline under the ocean), a flexible pipe system capable of pumping a million tons of fuel a day from England to France, SWISS ROLL and CARPET LAYER, armoured vehicles for laying an articificial road surface from the surf across the beach, and flail tanks which used chains on rotating drums to beat the ground and clear paths through minefields. There were the multi-purpose AVREs (Armoured Vehicle Royal Engineers) which were converted British Churchill tanks whose tasks included the carriage of sappers to take out pillboxes and other targets at close range, bringing in portable bridges for the use of

other tanks, and carrying fascines, as in World War I at Cambrai, to fill in ditches.

The Germans were quite aware that the invasion was coming, but could only guess about the date and location of the landings. Allied deception plans included an assault on Norway from Scotland, and landings on the Pas de Calais from ports in the southeast of England.

In addition to the German fortifications, Field Marshal Erwin Rommel had hurriedly prepared a formidable set of obstacles which the Allied troops and landing craft would have to negotiate. They included steel "hedgehogs" to hole the inbound landing craft, iron frames, and wooden stakes set at an angle.

At Omaha, the most difficult, dangerous and heavily defended of the landing beaches, 100-foot cliffs were backed by a pebble bank, dunes and a 200-yard salt marsh that abutted an escarpment. The salt marsh was heavily mined and criss-crossed with anti-tank ditches. The Atlantic Wall defences in the area of Omaha included eight large gun emplacements, 35 pillboxes, 18 anti-tank guns and 85 machineguns. 75mm and 88mm guns were positioned in three-foot-thick concrete emplacements in the cliffs at both ends of the beach. And, unknown to the Allies, the Germans had brought up eight battalions of battle-seasoned troops to defend Omaha. Rommel believed that the first twenty-four hours of the invasion would be decisive. But Field Marshal Gerd von Rundstedt, whom Hitler had brought from retirement to run the German forces in the West, had no confidence in the effectiveness of the Atlantic Wall defences at holding back the Allies, much preferring to maintain substantial reserves inland in order to make a fight at a location favourable to his force. But it was Rommel to whom Hitler had turned to make the extensive shoreline fortifications work. Rommel knew well the ability of Allied air power to interdict German communications. He was certain that, unless the Germans savagely repelled the Allies at

put snipers in the trees. They dig deep trenches behind the hedgerows and cover them with timber, so that it is almost impossible for artillery to get at them. Sometimes they will prop up machineguns with strings attached, so they can fire over the hedge without getting out of their holes. They even cut a section of the hedgerow and hide a big gun or a tank in it, covering it with brush. Also they tunnel under the hedgerows from the back and make the opening on the forward side just large enough to stick a machinegun through. But mostly the hedgerow pattern is this: a heavy machinegun hidden at each end of the field and infantrymen hidden all along the hedgerow with rifles and machine pistols.

Now it's up to us to dig them out of there. It's a slow and cautious business, and there is nothing very dashing about

above left: SS-Standartenführer Kurt Meyer of the 12 SS-Panzer Division conferring with Generalfeldmarschall Gerd von Rundstedt. above centre: SS-Hauptsturmführer Michael Wittmann resting on the gun of his Tiger. above far right: Wittman's burnt-out Tiger near Cintheaux where he was killed on 8 August 1944.

the point of the landings, they were lost.

The one thing that Rommel, von Rundstedt and Montgomery all agreed upon was that in the end, the great operation in Normandy would be settled by tanks.

The landings were set for 5 June, but unfavourable weather conditions caused a delay of 24 hours. Finally, Eisenhower got what he wanted to hear from his chief meteorologist and, at 4.15 a.m. on 5 June, declared the invasion on for the 6th. He later told his driver, Kay Summersby: "D-Day is on. Nothing can stop us now."

Lord Louis Mountbatten had stated the conditions for success in such an invasion effort. "First, get ashore against no matter what opposition. Second, having got ashore, stay ashore no matter what the weather conditions. Third, stop the enemy from building up his forces against you quicker than you can. Otherwise, he'll throw you back into the sea."

The ships that had brought the Allied troops to Normandy lay as much as twelve miles off the

French coast at 3 a.m. on 6 June when the men descended into the landing craft that would bring them in to the beaches. A four-foot swell was being whipped up by an 18-knot breeze. Many of the invaders would be miserable with seasickness before they reached the beach. Of 29 amphibious DD (duplex-drive) canvas-sided "swimming" tanks launched from assault ships when still four miles from Omaha beach, 21 sank immediately with the

loss of nearly all the crews. Three more were lost before reaching the beach, two of them to enemy action. Only two made it to the shore.

Many of the tank crews struggling to make the landing beaches that day were lost as their tanks were destroyed or crippled by mines, hung up on the myriad German obstacles or bogged down in the sucking sand.

Omaha was carnage. From 6.36 a.m., when the first Americans entered the surf from their landing craft, to 11 a.m., when things finally began to go their way and U.S. infantry soldiers were climbing the hill, crossing the plateau and swelling the numbers of their companions already engaged in house-to-house fighting in the village of Coleville behind Omaha, the beach had become littered with bodies, parts of bodies, and wounded. Men were struggling to clear the area of tanks, vehicles and equipment, hopelessly backed-up and crowding the limited space to the water's edge.

Those who survived the landings, the subsequent battles inland and the remaining campaign against the Germans would forever remember 6 June as the longest day of their lives. By the end of that day more than 155,000 Allied troops had come ashore across the five invasion beaches, Utah, Omaha, Gold, Juno and Sword, and 80 square miles of France were in Allied hands. All five landing beaches were secured at a cost of 2,500 lives. The British and Canadians at Gold, Juno and Sword, and the Americans at Utah, having had a far easier time on their sands than the men at Omaha, were now advancing inland. Within the first few days after D-Day it was apparent, to some Germans at least, that all hope of driving the Allies back into the sea had gone. "From June 9 on, the initiative lay with the Allies. The first phase of the invasion ended with an obvious military, political and psychological success for the Allies," wrote Lieutenant General Hans Speidel, Rommel's Chief of Staff. Adolf Hitler's reaction to the predicament

it. Our men don't go across the open fields in dramatic charges such as you see in the movies. They did at first, but they learned better. They go in tiny groups, a squad or less, moving yards apart and sticking close to the the hedgerows on either side of the field. They creep a few yards, squat, wait, then creep again.

If you could be right up there between the Germans and the Americans you wouldn't see very many men at any one time—just a few here and there, always trying to keep hidden. But you would hear an awful lot of noise.

Our men were taught in training not to fire until they saw something to fire at. But that hasn't worked in this country, because you see so little. So the alternative is to keep shooting constantly at the hedgerows. That pins the Germans in their holes while we sneak up on them.

The attacking squads sneak up the sides of the hedgerows while the rest of the platoon stay back in their own hedgerow and keep the forward hedge saturated with bullets. They shoot rifle grenades too, and a mortar squad a little farther back keeps lobbing mortar shells over onto the Germans. The little advance groups get up to the far ends of the hedgerows at the corners *continued on page 121*

"O God, thou knowest how busy we must be today; if we forget Thee, do not Thou forget us; for Christ's sake. Amen."
— Sir Jacob Astley at Edgehill, during the English Civil War

above: A German pillbox on the Normandy coast. above right: The helmet of a German soldier, recovered near Omaha Beach. right: West of Omaha Beach, Pointe du Hoc from the bomb-cratered plateau above it.

of his forces in Normandy was, "Hold at all costs." With the Normandy beachheads secured, General Eisenhower and his commanders concentrated on the next phase of the operation which included the capture of Cherbourg and the preparations for the Allied advance into France. But first they had to break out of the *bocage*, a patchwork quilt of tiny fields divided by tall, thick, impassable hedgerows that sat on broad-based six-foot-high banks, and were criss-crossed with a tangle of narrow lanes, east and west of the beachheads—not a good place for tanks. Initially, the Americans tried a combination of fighter bombers, artillery fire and planted explosives to blast gaps through the embanked hedgerows for their tanks, but they soon developed a better method. Salvaging metal elements from the German beach obstacles, they created a type of plough which they welded to the front of some tanks and were then able to cut through the thick hedge banks.

The Tigers and Panthers of the German armoured forces performed optimally when positioned to stand and fight at a range of 1,000 yards or more from their targets. Certainly, the Germans did not want to engage the Churchills, Cromwells and Shermans of the Allies in the area of the *bocage*, where firing ranges would be more like 200 to 400 yards. These Allied tanks were clearly inferior to the Tigers and Panthers in their armour and armament, but the Allies knew that this German advantage would be minimized if the fighting took place in the *bocage*. The Germans knew that the best place for the sort of tank battle they wanted was on the large open plain south of Caen.

In their fine book, *The Battle for Normandy*, Eversleigh Belfield and H. Essame provide the following account of a British tank crew's experience in the campaign: "To crash straight across country ignoring the easy route, taking in Churchillian [tank] strides small woods, buildings, hills, valleys, sunken roads and, worst of all, those

steep high banks which divide up the Norman *bocage* like the ridges on a monstrous waffle; this was something for which we were not quite prepared by our training in the Dukeries.

"There was no luxury and little comfort about the Churchills, save when driven slowly along a road: in the small fields of Normandy among the cider orchards, every move during the hot summer brought showers of small hard sour apples cascading into the turrets through the commanders' open hatches; after a few days there might be enough to jam the turret.

"Five men in close proximity, three in the turret and two below in the driving compartment, all in a thick metal oven, soon produced a foul smell: humanity, apples, cordite and heat. Noise: the perpetual 'mush' through the earphones twenty-four hours each day, and through it the machinery noises, the engine as a background, with the whine of the turret trainer and the thud and rattle of the guns an accompaniment. The surge of power as the tank rose up to the crest of a bank; the pause at the top while the driver, covered with sweat and dust and unable to see, tried to balance his forty tons before the bone-jarring crash down into the field beyond, with every loose thing taking life and crashing round inside the turret. Men, boxes of machinegun ammunition, shell-cases—and always those small hard apples.

"The skill of the driver, and indeed of all those men in the crew, was remarkable: the operator struggling to keep the wireless on net and the guns loaded: the gunner with eyes always at the telescope however much the turret revolved and crashed around him; the hot stoppages in the machineguns; the commander, with his head only above the hatches, choked with dust, not quite standing, not quite sitting during all those long Normandy days: always the wireless pounding at his eardrums.

"After dark was the time for maintenance, when the 3-ton trucks from the echelon came up with

below: A Sherman tank memorial in Normandy. bottom: Major-General Percy Hobart was the originator of some of the most innovative tank-based vehicle concepts of World War II. These included the Churchill Crocodile flame-thrower, the Churchill bridgelayer, the Sherman Crab chain-flail mine-clearing tank and the Sherman DD (Duplex Drive) amphibious tank.

petrol, ammunition and food; then the guns had to be cleaned and all repairs finished before first light and stand-to. Thanks to the tanks, repairs were not many, but crews could not go on very long without a rest."

Hitler's armoured strength was positioned to take full advantage of the ideal tank terrain near Caen. Montgomery's overview of the situation called for his armoured units to engage the panzers near Caen at the east end of the bridgehead and wear them down prior to hitting them with a surprise attack out of the *bocage* to the west by American armoured units.

Cherbourg was taken on 27 June by the U.S. VII Corps under command of General Joe Collins. With Montgomery's British and Canadian troops holding their position at Caen, Eisenhower ordered the controversial Lieutenant-General George S. Patton Jr., who had commanded U.S. troops in North Africa and Sicily and was the highest-ranking armoured commander in the invasion force, to take his forces south and east, to surround the bulk of the German army. Patton was the American version of a blitzkrieg commander and quickly completed his assigned run, ready to join Montgomery in an effort to catch and squeeze the German forces. But the cautious Montgomery moved his forces at a slower pace than that of Patton, which had the effect of allowing a great many enemy armour and infantry units to escape the trap through a corridor at Falaise. While Eisenhower and U.S. General Omar Bradley were dismayed at General Montgomery's apparently leisurely approach, Patton reportedly said to Bradley: "Let me go on to Falaise and we'll drive the British back into the sea for another Dunkirk." Montgomery, however, was probably the shrewdest of all the players, having learned much about his opponent's armoured tactics from studying their performances in North Africa and the Russian Front.

Believing that Allied air superiority over the

Normandy region denied his tanks the mobility they desperately needed to fight their kind of war there, Rommel was uncharacteristically slow to mount a counter-offensive. When he finally did so, the German armour was overwhelmed by that of the British at Caen, which fell to the Allies on 9 July. With American forces proceeding effectively from the west near St Lo, and the substantial German losses near Caen, Rommel's armour was now forced to make a fight in the *bocage* in support of his under-strength infantry. Still, in Montgomery's opinion, the Allied effort to crush the enemy in the region was not progressing as it should and he planned a major attack south from Caen, using three armoured divisions supported by infantry divisions and preceded by a huge air bombardment. In the assault, *Operation Goodwood*, his Cromwells, Churchills and Shermans, with their 75mm guns, would have to face the better-armed Tigers and Panthers and the excellent anti-tank guns of the Germans.

Of the nine Panzer divisions in Normandy, seven were gathered to face approximately 1,350 British tanks by 21 July near Caen. On the 19th just 400 German tanks had appeared, but the fighting was disastrous for the Allies who lost 300 tanks in the first three days of the battle. The American M4 Shermans struggled to break out of the thick *bocage* against the vastly superior German Tigers, but by 25 July momentum had shifted in favour of the Yanks, who were moving south towards Avranches at a steady rate. As Montgomery's *Goodwood* armoured units and infantry were frequently bogged down in traffic delays, Patton's seven fresh armoured divisions (100,000 men and 15,000 vehicles) were making enormous gains beyond Avranches by 30 July. By 4 August, Patton's Army reached Rennes, the Brittany capital.

On 7 August Lieutenant-General G.G. Simonds launched *Totalize*, the first key Canadian attack, an effort to drive his tanks from Caen to Falaise through the German lines. Waiting to greet his force *en route* were many Tiger tanks and a large number of 88mm guns that could be deadly in the anti-tank role. Simonds intended to attack by night and minimize his tanks' exposure on the broad plain south of Caen. He would run two tank columns, one along each side of the Caen-Falaise road. Many of his lead infantry were to be transported in armoured carriers. The Canadians were to move in four parallel columns to the right of the road while the British elements would go as three columns to the left of the road. In the darkness the force would have searchlight beams and continuous tracers from anti-aircraft guns, as well as their compasses, to guide their movement. The way would be paved for them by Allied heavy bombers hitting German concentrations and by a massive artillery barrage. Simonds planned to push about four miles through the German lines before stopping his initial drive.

The Simonds force moved out on the 7th and, as they entered enemy territory, the German troops were thrown into chaos and confusion. Their commander, Major-General Kurt Meyer, rallied them, however, and they began an effective defence. The Allied advance did not resume until the afternoon of 8 August. For the next few days the Canadians were badly beaten up by the Germans who destroyed 150 Allied tanks and halted the Canadian and British armoured columns, creating some spectacular traffic jams as well as filling many of the fields on the plain south of Caen with wrecked, smouldering tanks. The Polish armoured division accompanying the Canadians lost 26 of its tanks and an entire Canadian armoured regiment was wiped out by the Germans. When the faltering *Totalize* was called off on 10 August, the Allies had gained roughly nine miles of German territory.

Again, from *The Battle of Normandy*: "To those fighting there [on the Caen-Falaise plain] this area seemed to have been dedicated to battle by the Germans, who had evacuated all the inhabitants of the field. They first try to knock out the machine guns at each corner. They do this with hand grenades, rifle grenades and machineguns.

Usually, when the pressure gets on, the German defenders of the hedgerow start pulling back. They'll take their heavier guns and most of the men back a couple of fields and start digging in for a new line. They leave about two machineguns and a few riflemen scattered through the hedge, to do a lot of shooting and hold up the Americans as long as they can.

Our men now sneak along the front side of the hedgerow, throwing grenades over onto the other side and spraying the hedges with their guns. The fighting is very close—only a few yards apart—but it is seldom actual hand-to-hand stuff. Sometimes the remaining Germans come out of their holes with their hands up. Sometimes they try to run for it and are mowed down. Sometimes they won't come out at all, and a hand grenade, thrown into their hole, finishes them off.

And so we've taken another hedgerow and are ready to start on the one beyond.

continued on page 124

above left: M4 Sherman tanks advancing on Falaise. below left: Field Marshal Erwin Rommel and Generalfeldmarshall Gerd von Rundstedt.

above: A neon sign at Auberge John Steele. Steel was the American paratrooper whose 'chute became entangled on a church steeple at Saint Mère Eglise during the airborne assault of D-Day, 6 June 1944.
right: *Staffordshire Yeomanry in a French Orchard*, a painting by T.B. Hennell.

and most of their livestock. From the end of July until after the middle of August, the sun was so hot here that, by early afternoon, any man touching exposed metal burnt his bare skin. Vast numbers of vehicles pounded the dry ground and the dust was so dense that desert veterans recalled their North African days with nostalgia. Driving at anything except a snail's pace raised a huge cloud of this dust and, in the forward areas, shelling and mortaring inevitably resulted. Well provided with long-range Moaning Minnies, the Germans knew the range to most targets; the huge notices saying DUST CAUSES DEATH emphasized the dangers of speed to all who neared the forward troops. One effect of this chalky dust was to turn everyone's hair grey, youth seemed to have departed, leaving only an army of prematurely aged and grimy men.

"Dry weather had ripened the tall uncut corn, which could not only hide snipers, but also caught fire easily; many a wounded soldier was literally roasted to death when he lay helplessly on the ground, the corn all round set ablaze by a mortar bomb or a smoke shell. A drought added to the discomfort, little water could be found locally and it had to be brought up in the water trucks, whose arrival came to be the most important event in the day, even more eagerly awaited than the mail from home.

"Finally, the insect life flourished. In the daytime persistent hordes of flies swarmed round the soldiers and their food; great fat flies bloated from their feasting off tens of thousands of human and animal corpses which lay rotting on the battlefield itself, or its environs; others fed off the large quantities of human excrement which lay on the hard, dry ground. Stomach upsets became common. By night, the mosquitoes took over to plague the troops. They were larger and more ferocious creatures than any that even the most hardened veterans had encountered elsewhere and seemed to find little inconvenience in making

their nightly journey from the Ore or Dives Valleys to the Caen Plain. If a mosquito decided it would dine off your knees, then dine it did, battledress or no battledress; and as it sucked, its friends would be wriggling happily inside your gaiters to nibble your ankles while others clamped down in hordes upon your wrists and face. They appeared to relish the anti-mosquito paste."

By 7 August Hitler had decided to mount a major panzer counter-offensive to breach the American line at Mortain in order to cross the 25-mile stretch to the coast and re-take Avranches. In so doing, he hoped to cut off Patton's army from its supplies and bring the American general's tank units to a standstill. He expected his panzers to cause such a stir in the rear of the American units as to panic and demoralize them, creating entirely new opportunites for German forces in the Normandy region. The German commander of this operation was Field Marshal Hans von Kluge, who managed to form a panzer group of 185 tanks.

The panzers were now between the proverbial rock and hard place, compelled to take up mobile warfare and in so doing, exposed to unrelenting tank-busting attacks from the skies. The effect of these rocket-firing attacks on the Germans was actually more psychological than material. The RAF Typhoons were scoring few hits (and very few actual kills) on the German tanks. The accuracy of the Allied fighter-bomber rocket attacks was minimal against the panzers, though the attacks certainly took a heavy toll of German supply and transport vehicles. Most of the German armour destroyed, disabled or silenced there were victims of ground-based anti-tank fire, mechanical breakdown or had simply run out of fuel.

After these losses, Hitler sacked von Kluge. He then appointed Field Marshal Walther Model to command all German forces in Normandy, most of which had been in some form of retreat for much of the previous week. Most senior German commanders there expected the worst in an Allied

This hedgerow business is a series of little skirmishes like that clear across the front, thousands and thousands of little skirmishes. No single one of them is very big. But add them all up over the days and weeks and you've got a man-sized war, with thousands on both sides being killed.
— Ernie Pyle, with the 4th Division in Normandy, August 1944

By day I studied the whole process of the landing of supplies and troops, both at the piers, in which I had so long been interested, and on the beaches. On one occasion six tank landing-craft came to the beach in line. When their prows grounded, their drawbridges fell forward and out came the tanks, three or four from each, and splashed ashore. In less than eight minutes by my stop-watch the tanks stood in column of route on the highroad ready to move into action. This was an impressive performance, and typical of the rate of discharge which had now been achieved.
— Winston Churchill, Normandy, July 1944

right: American soldiers on an armoured scout car in France, 1944.

trap at what had become known as the Falaise Pocket, where sixteen entire German divisions were, in fact, cut off. The Canadian units had entered Falaise on 16 August and by the 22nd the pocket had been almost completely sealed off by the Allies. In the fighting that followed, an estimated 10,000 Germans died and 50,000 were captured, while 40,000 managed to escape, crossing the Seine near Rouen. The German soldiers thereafter referred to Falaise as "the killing ground". General Eisenhower later said of it: "It was literally possible to walk for hundreds of yards at a time stepping on nothing but dead and decaying flesh."

With the successful Allied breakout from the Normandy *bocage*, and the progress of the British and Canadians around Caen to the east, Allied armoured units would now have to pursue their enemy to Germany on a wide front. Once the pursuit was in full swing, Montgomery's armoured forces moved amazingly quickly to seize Antwerp and the vital port facilities there, while his 7th Armoured Division took Ghent. By 5 September the British divisions had accomplished these tasks, having covered 230 miles in just seven days. The U.S. 1st Army had made its way through the Ardennes to the Siegfried Line and the German frontier, while the U.S. 3rd Army, to the right of the 1st, had to overcome fierce resistance by German forces to establish a bridgehead over the Moselle between Metz and Nancy. The Allied armies had now stretched their supply lines to the breaking point. On reaching the Siegfried Line defences, the Allied pursuit ground to a halt, as did that of the Russians approaching from the east, giving the Germans a breather in which to regroup and reassemble a substantial armoured fighting force.

In the Battle of Normandy, the Germans had suffered more than 300,000 casualties; Allied casualties amounted to nearly 210,000.

THE PUSH ON GERMANY

BY THE END of summer 1944 the Allies had liberated Paris, which was saved from the last-minute devastation ordered by Hitler when his commander there, General Dietrich von Choltitz, negotiated the surrender of the city, agreeing not to destroy it in exchange for the safe withdrawal of his occupying garrison. The logistics of liberating the city cost the Allies dearly in personnel commitments, fuel, other resources and, more importantly, time—delaying their advance on the Rhine and Germany. Elsewhere, the Germans were feeling the pressure of the Russian advance from the east, Yugoslav partisans in the Balkans and the American forces pushing into Belgium and making inroads towards the Rhine.

It was at that point that a major dispute arose between Eisenhower and Field Marshal Sir Bernard Montgomery (later referred to by Ike as "a thorn in my side"). Montgomery strongly favoured an assault on Germany along a narrow front, followed by a concentrated attack on Berlin, while Eisenhower planned an approach to Germany on an extended front. Ike saw the need to allow his supply system to catch up with his armies which had outrun it, and to consolidate their position along the Rhine, before commencing the final push on Germany, as the highest priority.

In September an extensive Allied airborne operation against the Dutch towns of Arnhem, Nijmegen and Eindhoven resulted in a shambles and the British First Airborne Division incurred 75 per cent casualties in the fighting. This was followed in October by the American capture of the German city, Aachen, which had once been the capital of Charlemagne's empire. From Aachen, the Yanks entered the Hürtgen Forest where they suffered heavy losses in the snow-covered German minefields.

Despite the many successes of the Allied tank operations in Normandy, it was the inability of the Allies to adequately support their three-pronged attacking forces in the campaign that

The Sergeant is the Army.
– Dwight D. Eisenhower

My men can eat their belts, but my tanks gotta have gas.
– Lieutenant-General George S. Patton

left: *British Scorpion Mine-Destroying Tanks in France*, by C.A. Russell.

below: Lieutenant-General George S. Patton, was nicknamed "Blood and Guts." An armoured brigade tank veteran of World War I, Patton led the Allied Invasion force in North Africa, was a leading figure in the invasion of Sicily and later lost his command after a famous slapping incident in a U.S. Army medical facility. He was restored to command in summer 1944 and led the U.S. Third Army across Europe into Germany. He died of injuries received in a freak auto accident near Mannheim, Germany on 9 December 1945 and is buried in Luxembourg.

followed which prevented them from ending the European war in 1944. By September, when the Allies reached the vaunted Siegfried Line, their forces had been considerably weakened by the effort and could no longer be supplied with the fuel, ammunition, food, spares and maintenance essential to continue their advance. The Russians, having similar supply problems in their approach to Germany from the east, were also stalled. This was the break the Germans desperately needed. They took full advantage of it to put together a substantial armoured fighting force with which they intended, once again, to shove the Allies into the sea and regain the upper hand. It would be their last real opportunity of the war.

To assemble this impressive armoured force, the Germans had to redouble the mobilization of their country, contain the Russian advance in Poland, take thousands of workers from their declining industrial base to replace the heavy manpower losses they were incurring in the fighting, and somehow find the wherewithal to mount, equip, at least partially train, and field nine complete new Panzer divisions and twenty infantry divisions.

While managing the near-miraculous resurrection of their armoured capability, Hitler's forces could do little to stem the flow of precious oil from their war reserves. Germany's entire infrastructure was in ruins near the end of 1944. Her strategic oil reserves had been reduced to slightly more than 300,000 tons, from more than a million tons in the spring. Allied bombing had crippled her synthetic oil production facilities and, in August, Russian forces approaching the vital Ploesti oilfields of Romania had cut off that source. The shortage compelled the Germans to move their tanks by rail, using the remains of their coal supply, rather than further strain their oil reserves. However, with Allied air superiority growing daily, bombers (and fighters in the ground-attack role) were busy with the destruction of the German railways, making life ever more miserable for those trying to

move panzers to where they would be required. They were forced to confine such rail movements to the night.

Shortly after the D-Day landings, Hitler had sought to recapture the initiative and alter the likely outcome of the war through the introduction of an entirely new terror weapon, the V-1 flying bomb. Referred to by Britons and Americans as "Doodlebugs" or "Buzzbombs", the small, pulse-jet-powered weapons were an early type of cruise missile, but not capable of reaching and striking a specific target with any degree of reliability or accuracy. Still, by the end of the summer of 1944, the V-1s, fired from launch sites on the Channel coast of France, had killed more than 6,000 people in the south of England and destroyed 75,000 buildings. The Nazis followed the V-1 campaign with something much more terrible in September— attacks on Britain by supersonic V-2 rockets which arrived silently and without warning, devastating much greater areas than the V-1s had done. But these terror weapons came too late to change the course of the war for the Germans.

It was probably Hitler's need of V-weapon launch sites in Northern France for further attacks on Britain, together with his desire to recapture the Antwerp port facilities, that most influenced the decision to make his final strike at the Western Allies, rather than the advancing Russians.

He elected to attack through the Ardennes forest of Belgium, owing to the relatively sparse American forces there, and the vagaries of the weather in that region which would virtually guarantee minimal enemy aerial reconaissance and opposition. Efficient initial assembly and early mobility for the panzers was practically assured.

He hoped to cut the enemy supply lines, split the Allies and crush their morale sufficiently to re-direct the course of the war and force a negotiated peace. He had little respect for the American soldier, believing that this blitzkrieg surprise attack would terrorize and crack the enemy troops. The final planning conference for the operation was held on 11 and 12 December .

" 'Gentlemen, before opening the conference I must ask you to read this document carefully and then sign it with your full names.' The date was 3 November 1944, and I had assumed that the conference would be merely a routine meeting of the three army commanders who held the northern sector of the Western Front under Field-Marshal Model's Army Group B. Each officer present had to pledge himself to preserve complete silence concerning the information which Jodl intended to divulge to us: should any officer break this pledge, he must realize that his offence would be punishable by death. I had frequently attended top secret conferences presided over by Hitler at Berchtesgaden or at the 'Wolf's Lair' both before and after 20 July 1944, but this was the first time that I had seen a document such as the one which I now signed. It was clear that something most unusual was afoot.

"The German commanders knew the terrain in the Ardennes well. We had advanced across it in 1940 and retreated through it only a few months before. We knew its narrow, twisting roads and the difficulties, not to say dangers, they could cause an attacking force, particularly in winter and in the bad weather conditions which were an essential prerequisite to the opening of our operation. The main roads contained many hairpin bends, and were frequently built into steep hillsides. To get the guns of the artillery and flak units as well as the pontoons and beams of the bridging engineers around these sharp corners was a lengthy and difficult business. The guns and trailers had to be disconnected and then dragged around the corner by a capstan mechanism, naturally one at a time. Vehicles could not pass one another on these roads."
– General Hasso von Manteuffel, General Officer Commanding, 5 Panzer Army
"All I had to do was to cross the river, capture Brussels and then go on and take the port of Antwerp. And all this in December, January and February, the worst months of the year; through the Ardennes where snow was waist deep and there wasn't room to deploy four tanks abreast, let alone six armoured divisions; when it didn't get light until eight in the morning and was dark again at four in the afternoon and my tanks can't fight at night; with divisions that had just been reformed and were composed chiefly of raw untrained recruits; and at Christmas time."
– General Sepp Dietrich, General Officer Commanding, 6 Panzer Army

On the morning of the 16 December, taking advantage of the cover of heavy fog, eight panzer divisions slashed through the frail Allied defences along the 85-mile forest front.

At first, the German advance through the Ardennes piled up significant gains against the totally surprised Americans. The campaign became known as the Battle of the Bulge because of the dent the Germans made in the Allied line. But when the panzers approached the American-held town of Bastogne, they encountered a robust defence by members of the 101st Airborne Division under the command of Brigadier-General Anthony McAuliffe. Losing his initial momentum and determined to press the offensive, the area German commander, General von Lüttwitz, issued a surrender ultimatum to McAuliffe on 22 December. It had been typed on a captured American typewriter and read: "To the U.S.A. commander of the encircled town of Bastogne. The fortune of war is changing. This time the U.S.A. forces in and near Bastogne have been encircled by strong German armoured units. More German armoured units have crossed the River Our near Ortheuville, have taken Marche and reached St. Hubert by passing through Homores-Sibret-Tillet. Librimont is in German hands.

"There is only one possibility of saving the encircled U.S.A. troops from total annihilation: that

The Third (British) Division had been tasked to take Caen by the evening of D-Day. It didn't happen. It took a full month of intense military activity to achieve that goal. D-Day found Lieutenant-Colonel Sir Delaval Cotter, Bt, DSO, who died in April 2001, aged 89, in command of a squadron of 40 duplex-drive "swimming" tanks. The tanks were to provide fire support for the attacking Third Division infantry, but a delay in their turn to beach their tanks caused Cotter's squadron to become bogged down in intense fighting at the exit points from the beach. From Cotter's obituary in *The Times* (London) 26 April 2001: "Exactly two months after D-Day, Cotter won an immediate DSO for his tenacity and leadership in command of his squadron during the battle for Mont Pinçon, south of Aunay-sur-Odon, which barred exploitation of the breakout from the bridgehead west of Caen. His squadron was assigned to hold the village of La Variniére on the centre line of the assault, west of Mont Pinçon, with an infantry battalion already seriously depleted by casualties.

The area had not been cleared and Cotter found the surrounding woods and orchards full of the enemy. Despite intense shelling and accurate continued on page 132

above left: Charles Shenloogian, far right: Steve Joseph. Both were U.S. Army tankers in the European Theatre of Operations, World War II. above right: An American Sherman tank stands in a snow-covered field near Manhay, Belgium after defeating the partially-concealed overturned German Panther (upper left) in the Battle of the Bulge, December 1944

is the honourable surrender of the encircled town. In order to think it over, a period of two hours will be granted, beginning with the presentation of this note.

"If this proposal should be rejected; one German artillery corps and six heavy anti-aircraft battalions are ready to annihilate the U.S.A. troops in and near Bastogne. The order for firing will be given immediately after this two-hour period.

"All the serious civilian losses caused by this artillery fire would not correspond with the well-known American humanity."
– General Heinrich von Lüttwitz, General Officer Commanding, XLVII Panzer Corps

General McAuliffe's reply: "Nuts."

Eisenhower ordered General George Patton to come to the aid of the American forces at Bastogne and his 37th Tank Battalion commander, Creighton Abrams, Jr., spearheaded the armoured column that broke the German encirclement of Bastogne. Abrams would go on to become a prominent four-star general, commanding all U.S. forces in the Vietnam war. The current American main battle tank is named in his honour.

In his book *Soldier*, General Matthew B. Ridgeway stated: "I remember once standing beside a road leading through a pine wood, down a slope to the road junction of Manhay, where a hot fight was going on. That whole Ardennes fight was a battle for road junctions, because in that wooded country, in the deep snows, armies could not move off the roads. This particular crossroads was one of many that the Germans had to take if they were to keep up the momentum of their offensive, and we were fighting desperately to hold it. I had gone up to this point, which lay not far forward of my command post, to be of what help I could in this critical spot. As I was standing there, a lieutenant, with perhaps a dozen men, came out of the woods from the fighting, headed towards the rear. I stopped him and asked him where he was going and what his mission was. He told me that he and his men had been sent out to develop the strength of the German units that had reached Manhay, and that they had run into some machinegun fire that was too hot for them, so they had come back.

"I relieved him of his command there on the spot. I told him that he was a disgrace to his country and his uniform and that I was ashamed of him, and I knew the members of his patrol were equally ashamed. Then I asked if any other member of the patrol was willing to lead it back into the fight. A sergeant stepped up and said he would lead it back and see to it that it carried out its mission."

Again, General Ridgeway: ". . . another incident occurred which I remember with regret. In the fierce fighting, the town [Manhay] changed hands several times. The Germans had brought up some flat trajectory guns, and they started shelling our little group. Fragments whizzed everywhere. One struck an artillery observer, who was standing by me, in the leg, and another punctured the [fuel] tank of his jeep. As this shell exploded an infantry sergeant standing nearby became hysterical. He threw himself into the ditch by the side of the road, crying and raving. I walked over and tried to talk to him, trying to help him get hold of himself. But it had no effect. He was just crouched there in the ditch, cringing in utter terror. So I called my jeep driver, Sergeant Farmer, and told him to take his carbine and march this man back to the nearest M.P., and if he started to escape to shoot him without hesitation. He was an object of abject cowardice, and the sight of him would have a terrible effect on any American soldier who might see him.

" . . . That's the sort of thing you see sometimes. It is an appalling thing to witness—to see a man break completely like that—in battle. It is worse than watching a death—for you are seeing something more important than the body die. You are witnessing the death of a man's spirit, of his pride, of all that gives meaning and purpose to life."

The following passage recounts the participation of one American armoured unit in the Battle of the Bulge.

When Generalfeldmarschall Gerd von Rundstedt launched the German counter-offensive in the Ardennes on 16 December 1944, the principal elements of the U.S. 11th Armored Division were crossing the English Channel to France. The 11th arrived at Cherbourg on the 17th and was ordered south to Lorient and St Nazaire to contain the enemy forces in those vital seaports.

While en route south, the surprise German assault through the Ardennes caused the American command to redirect the units of the 11th northward on 20 December towards Reims. Heading to the River Meuse, they were assigned to defend a 30-mile sector between Sedan and Givet and to hold themselves in readiness as a mobile reserve force.

Covering more than 500 miles in just three days, the Division entered the combat area, was made part of the VIII Corps of Patton's Third Army and moved on to Belgium's southern frontier. They met heavy opposition on 30 December from the 15th Panzer Grenadier Division (which had distinguished itself in the Afrika Korps) when they attacked the Germans northeast of Neufchateau. German forces of the 3rd Panzer Grenadier Division engaged elements of the 11th in fierce fighting at the towns of Acul and Chenogne on 31 December, at Rechrival on 1 January and at Senonchamps on 2 January 1945. Through their victories in these intense engagements, the men of the 11th succeeded in defending the essential Neufchateau Highway supply link to Bastogne, keeping the enemy from cutting off the crucial flow of supplies to the Americans there.

For the next ten days the men of the 11th Armored Division had the jobs of patrolling and protecting key road junctions and roadblocks, reconnoitering for tank and infantry positions in German territory and lending support to the U.S.

It had many defects and teething troubles, and when these became apparent the tank was appropriately rechristened the 'Churchill'.
– from a speech by Prime Minister Winston Churchill to the House of Commons in July 1942.

mortar fire, Cotter cleared the village and held it against repeated attacks for the vital 24 hours it took the other two squadrons of the regiment and the supporting infantry of 129 Infantry Brigade to secure the decisive lodgement on the western sector of Mont Pinçon.

A few days later, after the advance had resumed, Cotter's tank received a direct hit from a German 88mm gun. Two of his crew members were killed but he climbed out without injury. He survived in command of his squadron to the end of the campaign in North-West Europe and left his regiment in 1945 to attend a course at the wartime staff college in Palestine."

17th, 87th and 101st Airborne Divisions in the area. Then, on 13 January, the 11th Armored launched a powerful offensive against the 9th Panzer Division, the 130th (Lehr) Panzer Division and the 26th Volksgrenadier Division at Bertogne. By 16 January, after a fire fight with the 27th Volksgrenadier Division at Velleroux, the 11th occupied the town and linked up with the U.S. First Army at Houffalize, stopping the German advance and containing the famous "bulge" the enemy had made in the Allied line on 16 December at the start of its counter-offensive.

Now the 11th was advancing steadily across Belgium as German forces were withdrawing ahead of it. The Americans reached the border with Luxembourg on 22 January, having liberated two dozen Belgian towns along the way. For their rapid march across France to reach the scene of the fighting in the Ardennes, and their slashing pursuit and engagement of the enemy in the great Battle of the Bulge, the members of the 11th Armored Division, United States Army, were given the nickname "Patton's Thunderbolts".

Although significant combat engagements were still to come, initiative and momentum shifted to the American side on 26 December. By Christmas Eve the prolonged bad weather and thick fog had lifted, permitting Allied fighter bombers, including the tank-busting Typhoons of the Royal Air Force, to mount a powerful attack on the enemy armour, much of which they quickly destroyed. The Germans had again tried an assault on Bastogne, engaging in a large scale armoured action, but this too was unsuccessful and 5th Panzer Army commander General Hasso von Manteuffel now knew that the German counter-offensive had failed and a retreat was in order. The full-scale pursuit of Hitler's forces towards Germany was under way.

In the Battle of the Bulge, American losses were 10,276 killed, 47,493 wounded and 23,218 missing.

The British forces suffered 1,400 casualties with 200 killed. It is believed that German casualties were approximately 100,000 killed, wounded or captured.

The fighting in the Ardennes in late 1944 and early 1945 was among the most savage and intense of the entire war. The aggression of the German forces had been whipped up to great intensity at the beginning of the campaign by a rumour circulating among them that the American and British armies were about to turn over their German prisoners to the Russians. Therefore German troops engaged the Allies in Belgium with unprecendented ferocity and a number of their commanders were subsequently tried for war crimes committed during the campaign. But in the majority of the armoured battles, the American forces in their initially defensive role, and later when they were able to take the fight to the enemy, were more prudent than the Germans in the use of their tanks, preserving them and their mobility to a far greater extent than did the panzers.

As American armoured and infantry forces were advancing on the retreating German units from the south, the British were chasing them from the north. Much of the remaining panzer strength had been rushed to Poland in a vain attempt to hold off advancing Russian armour there. This left only small armoured reserves to cope with the on-rushing Allies in the west. By 22 March 1945 there were no more German soldiers fighting west of the Rhine.

The final push is ably described in this account of the U.S. 745th Tank Battalion as it rolled into and across Germany in the last weeks of the war. It is taken from a speech by Captain S. Scott Sullivan to the final reunion of the 745th at Fort Knox, Kentucky in September 1999. "Mid-February 1945 found the battalion halted, performing much-needed maintenance, and getting ready for a massive attack against the defenses in the Roer River area. The 745th launched the drive to the Rhine River with

Able Company being the first to cross the Roer. The battalion moved across the Cologne plain and encountered stiff resistance. The Germans had laid thousands of mines and hid numerous anti-tank guns to ambush the Americans. As a result, the 745th began to conduct more and more night attacks. The fighting was so severe that, by the end of February, Able and Dog companies were down to two tanks total—due to the enemy's guns and the deep, muddy sugar beet fields.

"The battalion fought its way from one small village to another—always moving toward their objective, the city of Bonn and its bridge across the Rhine River. In early March, the battalion conducted a night attack to capture this critical bridge. Able Company moved in with the elements of the 16th Infantry Regiment and sneaked quietly into the city. They found the bridge and began to secure the area but not before the Germans unfortunately blew it up right in front of them. The battalion continued to clear the city, even destroying a tank and anti-tank gun on the university campus. The ancient city of Bonn was now in the hands of the American Army.

"While the 745th secured the city and conducted resupply and rearming, twenty miles down the river, the 9th Armored Division was luckily able to capture a railroad bridge in the city of Remagen. This allowed the Allies to continue the attack into the very heart of Germany. The 745th moved down to support the expansion of the bridgehead and crossing. They crossed the Rhine and continued the fight. The Germans were putting up a heavy fight, attempting to push us back over the Rhine. Artillery and mortar fire was continuous. As the 745th pushed deeper into Germany, the Wehrmacht threw everything they had at them. The 745th took town after town and repulsed multiple counter-attacks. All of these actions directly contributed to the American Army keeping the bridgehead and building enough combat power to break out into the Ruhr Valley and link up with the American 9th Army. As the 745th moved through following the breakout, their job was to eliminate tough pockets of resistance which were bypassed earlier.

"The battalion then pushed on to assist the Big Red One in seizing and clearing the Harz Mountain area. Here the Germans were well organized and the mountainous terrain kept tanks mostly on the roads. The 745th met the challenge, and from April 12th through 21st fought bravely and scored record numbers of kills and prisoners. Incidents like 1st Platoon, Able Company's performance on 18 April were an example of how formidable and experienced the 745th had become. The platoon alone captured 50 enemy vehicles near Rubeland and went on to ambush an enemy column the same day to destroy 30 more vehicles and capture a thousand prisoners. The combined effects of actions like these broke the German will and mass surrenders began. The German Army was crumbling and the war in Europe nearly over.

"The 745th went on to relieve elements of the 97th Infantry Division on the Czech border. It was now the beginning of May and all indications were that the Germans were about to quit. The 745th didn't quit—although given the mission to defend—they kept attacking and edging deeper in Czechoslovakia. They pushed so far that the division had to give them orders to stop on May 6th, but not before Dog Company had made the historic linkup with Russian forces at Karlsbad. The German High Command surrendered two days later—the Allies had taken Fortress Europe."

Fritz-Rudolf Averdieck was a Radio Operator Sergeant with Armoured Grenadier Regiment 90 of the German Army in World War II. He rode an armoured personnel carrier (Schützenpanzerwagen or SPW) which was used by his commander as a command centre during operations. The SPW was a light armoured vehicle with half-tracks. It was also used as a troop carrier, was open at the top and

Once in combat, it was virtually impossible to get replacement tank maintenance mechanics, and equally difficult, if not more so, to get trained replacement tank crews. As a result, it was necessary for the ordnance maintenance battalion to develop a two-fold function. We not only did the maintenance, repair, and replacement of the shot up tanks, but we actually became involved in the training of new tank crews. After severe tank losses and comparable losses in the crews, the armored regiments ran out of good tank crews. It was necessary for the ordnance to take raw infantry recruits who had just come off the boat from the United States and train them to be tank crews. In some cases the training time amounted to only several hours or maybe a day at the most. These inexperienced crews in turn suffered more severe losses due to their lack of training.
– from *Death Traps* by Belton Y. Cooper

By 22 March 1945, no German soldier was fighting west of the Rhine.

right: British soldiers and a Sherman Crab flail tank in a mine-clearing operation near the Dutch border. bottom: A war-time painting by Adolf Hoffmeister.

mounted a machinegun. The wireless operator sat beside the driver, with the commander behind him on the carrier. The SPW was thus a command-communications and fighting vehicle. "In early 1945, the last barrier before Berlin was the Seelow Heights near the Oder River. After incurring heavy casualties in our numerous attacks which failed to throw the Soviet bridgehead back over the Oder, the great Soviet offensive began on 16 April. The superior strength of the enemy overwhelmed our battle-weary troops, and reached the Seelow Heights. Our weakened regiment counter-attacked, but was unable to regain the old front lines. Nevertheless, we strengthened and held a position on the Heights the night of 19 April. But the continuous Soviet heavy artillery and mortar fire took a heavy toll, tearing large rents in our lines. One thing was clear from the sounds of the ongoing battles. The enemy had already passed us to the north and south on its march to Berlin.

"The remnants of the Regiment were retreating in stages towards Berlin. Attempts were being made to delay the advance of the enemy with repeated counter-attacks, but the front had been broken at various points and the Soviets were attacking us with tanks from the rear and on the flanks. A tank attack on our flank the morning of 18 April caused our SPW and remaining vehicles to be sent back a few kilometres to Worin, a small abandoned village. We took up a position behind a house near a crossroads. A rain of mortar shells and artillery salvoes fell on us, wounding some soldiers. The Regimental Commander was seriously wounded and the adjutant took over for him.

"In the late morning, the rest of the Regiment came into Worin. Regimental command was now directly at the front. We were at the divisional command post a few hundred metres further into the village and our signal operations were constantly breaking down during this period.

"It was our misfortune to have a mixture of petrol and diesel fuel in the tank and the SPW could only be driven slowly and it had frequent breakdowns. A young lieutenant who had joined us a few days earlier, daringly planned to route the SPW over open ground along a downhill path. We reached the protection of a hollow without incident. We then had to go uphill, however, and the lame carrier came into full view of the enemy, attracting mortar fire and salvoes from Stalinorgels. The SPW crawled and bucked through it and we were expecting a direct hit in our open carrier at any time, which would have been the end of us. After long moments we came to a protected depression and drove behind a barn where a number of other vehicles of various types had gathered.

"As Russian tanks penetrated into Worin, I decided to leave the village with my lame SPW and, luckily, after crawling up a hill, I reached the edge of a wood. Explosions overhead forced us to move deeper into the forest. We were supposed to be in Müncheberg by that afternoon and columns of vehicles were rolling through the forest towards Jahnsfelde on their way to the main track to Müncheberg. Some of them returned later with the news that we were surrounded and the Russians were only two kilometres to our rear. Jahnsfelde had fallen. We could hear the machinegun fire of fights on our left and right flanks and there was no way out. The divisional communications unit elected to break out on its own and three of our five men fell into Russian hands. The Russians were now directly behind us and we prepared for the worst, protecting ourselves with our machinegun. We also got ready to blow up the SPW.

"By the late afternoon, all our infantry, tanks and other vehicles were gathered in the forest. The only hope for us was to take an unknown track to break through to our lines. Our commander, a lieutenant, organized the infantry. The SPW was towed by a Tiger tank. We took up positions at the edge of the wood at dusk and heard the enemy firing behind us. As darkness fell, we moved out of the wood and through the burning ruins of Jahnsfelde. We met no

27/28 April 1944
FRIEDRICHSHAFEN
322 Lancasters and 1 Mosquito of 1, 3, 6 and 8 Groups. This was a raid with some interesting aspects. The Air Ministry had urged Bomber Command to attack this relatively small town in moonlight because it contained important factories making engines and gearboxes for German tanks. But the flight to this target, deep in southern Germany on a moonlit night, was potentially very dangerous; the disastrous attack on Nuremberg had taken place only 4 weeks previously in similar conditions. However, Friedrichshafen was further south and on the fringe of the German night-fighter defences; because of this and the various diversions which confused the German controllers, the bombers reached the target without being intercepted. However, the German fighters arrived at the target while the raid

resistance.

"We set up new positions near Müncheberg. Our SPW was brought to a workshop in the rear and repaired during the night. The next day, 19 April, Soviet tanks broke through again and, together with our auxiliaries, we retreated back to Rüdersdorf. Huge columns of wretched, miserable civilian refugees hindered our movement until about 3 a.m. We stayed in Rüdersdorf until noon of the 20th.

"Only 90 soldiers were left of our entire regiment,

so a further 90-man company was assembled from the auxiliary troops, who were normally non-combatants. Men from the intelligence units were also assimilated into the infantry. This 'support' company moved out and came under continuous Russian air harassment. Shortly afterwards we followed, with two lieutenants, in the SPW. A bomber let loose a hail of bombs on us. We joined the divisional command in the woods near Hennickendorf-Herzfeld as fighters flew low over the trees, but they did not see us.

"In the evening, we were ordered to block the neck of land between two small lakes with our 180-man contingent, but only the 90-man 'support' company was at hand. At sundown the troops marched out under a hail of explosives and phosphorus bombs. We on the SPW had to use the road frequently, which was lit up by numerous burning flares that we called 'Christmas trees'. We had to wait a long time in the vehicle for the company to catch up with us. It was now just a 60-man contingent. 30 soldiers had nipped off and there was no trace of our 90-man original Regiment.

"We took up positions previously held by an SPW company, with two Tiger tanks. Against us were enemy tanks. Earlier, a Stalin tank had broken through the lines after putting a Tiger out of action. It now rattled along the road a hundred metres from us and was stopped by anti-tank obstacles. A bazooka shell ricocheted off it with a spray of sparks. The enemy tank tried to retreat but was put out of action by the second Tiger. A nearby petrol and ammunition dump went up in flames and the air crackled with detonations as in a fight. Then the air strikes stopped. We drove the SPW from the road to the edge of a wood and camouflaged it. We were a few kilometres from Rüdersdorf, along a road that passed through fields and pine groves. I tried to sleep with the snapping sounds of the fire from the dump in my ears.

"When I awoke it was dark and I could still hear the rattling sounds, followed shortly by shouts from our left and right along the road. The Russians had broken through again and the 'heroes' of our support company had taken to their heels. The helplessness of our lieutenants had nearly cost us our SPW. Now dawn was breaking.

"Trusting to luck we drove along the edge of the wood. Under machinegun fire we drove through a ditch. We could hear the enemy tanks as we approached the outskirts of Herzfelde under the protection of a light early morning fog. Some Tigers and 88mm artillery batteries from our division had been positioned here and began a duel with some Russian tanks that came out of the woods. We watched as tracer grenades ricocheted off the Russian tanks. A short time later one of our tanks was hit on the side and went up in flames. At least the hazy, rainy weather spared us the fighters. As our regiment no longer existed, the two lieutenants decided to drive to Berlin to search for the Divisional Command or the rest of the 'support company.'

"While underway we observed some peculiarities in the defences of Berlin. They consisted only of fighting units that had organized themselves independently. Hitler Youth were in position at some places. Strangely, we came under continuous fire along the way over Schönebeck to Schönblick. We now felt that defeat was inevitable. BERLIN REMAINS GERMAN was written on a signboard at the edge of the city. We heard a rumour that the city was preparing for its defence and was full of SS. We found our missing 'support' company in Schönblick in very comfortable quarters, and all of us were put off. In the afternoon we were on the road again as part of a long column. With frequent stops, we passed beautiful residences and well-kept gardens with spring flowers, baths and parks. The Russians were already at Köpenick and threatened to cut us off. We met troops moving outwards. Then we passed through Köpenick, over the River Spree and through Adlershof and Altglienicke into the housing estate of Rudow where we took up quarters. The small fighting

was taking place and 18 Lancasters were lost, 5.6 per cent of the force.

1,234 tons of bombs were dropped in an outstandingly successful attack based on good Pathfinder marking; Bomber Command later estimated that 99 acres of Friedrichshafen, 67 per cent of the town's built-up area, were devastated. Several factories were badly damaged and the tank gearbox factory was destroyed. When the American bombing survey team investigated this raid after the war, German officials said that this was the most damaging raid on tank production of the war. A civil report states that 136 people were killed and 375 injured in Friedrichshafen, and that 656 houses were destroyed and 421 severely damaged.
– from *The Bomber Command War Diaries* by Martin Middlebrook and Chris Everitt

above left: Tea break for the crew of a British AVRE, an armoured special-purpose tank utilized in demolition and other duties. left: Under the protection of an M4 Sherman tank, Soldiers of the U.S. Army 60th Infantry Regiment advance into the Belgian town of Spangle on 9 September 1944.

We arrived in Paris on Christmas Day. I was given another tank and we were on our way again, to take the city of Trier. We approached the city in the middle of the night and at dawn we were hit by a barrage. As we started towards the city, the point tank and a half-track were knocked out. Shells were flying all around us. I spotted an 88 and got my gunner on it and knocked it out. Then we were hit with three rounds. One went through the front, killing my driver and starting a fire. He never knew what hit him. Another broke my tracks and the third exploded under the tank near the escape hatch. I got my badly-wounded assistant driver out and helped him to some medics. I then put out the fire in my tank.
– Charles Shenloogian, World War II U.S. tanker

above: Lieutnant Ludwig Bauer of 33 Regiment 'Prinz Eugen,' 9th Panzer Division in World War II.

units of our division set up their positions at Adlershof. We began our own Battle of Berlin."

Ludwig Bauer was a lieutenant with 33 Regiment, 9th Panzer Division of the German Army. He fought in Russia, on the Western Front in the Ardennes in 1944, and in the Ruhr Basin near the end of the war. His tanks were knocked out nine times and he was wounded seven times. While a commander of the 1st Panzer Regiment, 33, "Prinz Eugen", he was awarded the Knight's Cross. "At the beginning of April 1945 I was leading what remained of the Panther Company (5th Tank Regiment, No. 33), five Panther tanks. We were in the Seigen area. I was put under the command of a neighbouring division and ordered to report to a Captain Adrario in Erndtebrück. After engaging in various operations we took up positions there as it was reported that the Americans were marching towards us with superior strength.

"We had not been out of our tanks for weeks and were dead tired after all of the action. I reported to Captain Agrario and received a special bonus of tobacco for the troops. I intended to take my tanks to a previously reconnoitred position, but the captain was of the opinion that we had had enough for the day. He ordered me to go to a house which was situated diagonally opposite the command post of an infantry unit in the middle of the town. There I introduced myself to the company commander. I informed the troop captain of the position of my tank and asked him to wake me and raise the alarm should there be the slightest cause for concern. Then I lay down with my crew in the ground-level room of a shoe-maker. Our tank stood in front of the house. We were only separated from it by the wall of the house.

"I thought I was dreaming. Suddenly, I heard shooting and American voices. It must have been five or six o'clock in the morning. My driver, Gustl Medack, woke me up: 'The Americans have

arrived!' At that moment they shot through a window and called out in typically American accents, 'Hello comrades, come on out. The war is over.'

"As quickly as I could, I snapped on my belt, put on my cap and, as I couldn't get out of the front door, ran up the narrow staircase. In the tumult that followed, I couldn't tell whether any of my men had followed me. I paused momentarily at the first floor and, with the Americans pursuing me, dashed further up the stairs. Then, standing there, I realized that I hadn't got any shoes on. In my rush to get away I had forgotten them. The Americans then began to search the house. I ended up in the loft. It was a hay store and as they entered it, I crawled into the hay. They shot into the hay a few times and then went downstairs again. Now it was essential that I find out if any of my men had also come upstairs (I later learned that they had all been picked up), so I crawled out of the hay and evaluated the situation. The Americans were talking out on the street. I was able to watch them through a small window in a door which served as a lift for the hay. I could see my tank and what was going on in the street.

"The arrival of the Americans had come as a surprise. As relatively few shots had been fired, either by the German infantry or the tanks which were positioned around Erndtebrück, I suspected that the enemy had been directed in by someone via an unsecured route. In any event, the Americans were there and I estimated their strength to be three companies.

"I stood there, upstairs in that house, without my shoes, my Panther down below. Our infantry had either been picked up or had escaped. What was I to do now? First, I had to find out if any of my crew were still hidden in the house. I crept downstairs and searched through the rooms but found no one. Between two and three hours dragged by. I continued to watch the goings-on through the window. By this time the Americans had completely cleared out the tank. It seemed they only valued things to eat or drink. They emptied a bottle of cognac amidst a lot of noise. They ate the salami sausages that we had received as special rations. They tossed out bags of underwear, papers and photos. Then an officer joined them. I thought that they were going to blow up the tank. Instead, after considerable to-ing and fro-ing, a tank-disabling chemical (an acid) was thrown into the Panther. It caused thick, billowing smoke and, apparently, as far as the Americans were concerned, that was that. My tank was still standing in front of the house, undamaged. I decided to make my getaway with it. I considered the situation and crept down the stairs. I had left our cigarette supply under a bench in the kitchen and, above all, I wanted to save that, come what may.

"In front of the house my tank was surrounded by Americans. Two of their soldiers were observing it from between the hall and the kitchen. After their long march they had made themselves comfortable by removing their shoes. At an opportune moment I grabbed a pair of their shoes, along with my cigarettes, and raced up the stairs. While putting on the shoes and stuffing my pockets with cigarettes, I heard some cursing from downstairs. Obviously, something had been missed.

"In time I could hear the sound of our own artillery shells. I certainly did not want to die there in the loft as a result of this bombardment. The other Panthers of the company had realized what was happening and vacated their positions, some of them firing as they moved off and rolled through the town at about nine o'clock.

"Slowly, peace and quiet returned. It was after twelve o'clock. My heart was pounding as I made my move. I went downstairs and slipped into a neighbouring barn, hoping that one of my crew might be hiding there. Unfortunately, I didn't find anyone. I crawled up to my Panther and hauled myself up at the rear. I wriggled my way

to the open driver's hatch, diving in head first. Once inside I could barely manage to get into the normal sitting position. I was just about to release the steering mechanism when three Americans suddenly arrived and began looking over the tank. Then they climbed up on top and into the turret. Their inspection seemed to take forever, though it was only minutes. One of them actually clambered through the wireless operator's hatch to the inside of the tank where he stayed for a few minutes. He must have been a stickler for detail. He even stuck his head in through the driver's hatch. I had pressed myself as far forward as I possibly could. Still, he could not have been more than 15cm away from me. My heart was hammering so fast I felt sure he must have heard it.

"At last, the Americans jumped down from the tank. It was now or never. I pressed the starter. 550 horsepower roared into action and I ambled off in first gear. The Americans who had been standing in front of the tank, jumped to one side, horrified, while I rolled the 20 metres to the main road, turned left and continued away from the locality. I then began having problems with the gears and the clutch, and soon the tank came to a standstill. I finally managed to put it in third gear and roared off. On the way I received three bazooka hits. The suspension of the gun was damaged and it fell down with its muzzle tilting to the front and came to rest on the top of the tank. The camouflage netting which had been resting on the barrel of the gun slipped forward, leaving me with a slit of about 2cm of glass through which I could see.

"I got away from Erndtebrück safely and later stopped on the crossroads to Schameda to get my bearings. I was under way again when, after a bit, I misjudged a bend, turned too sharply to the left and drove down an embankment into a field. I rolled to a stop, intending to remove the camouflage netting which was draped over the

When you're wandering around our very far-flung front lines that in our present rapid war are known as "fluid" you can always tell how recently the battle has swept on ahead of you. You can sense it from the little things even more than the big things. From the scattered green leaves and the fresh branches of trees still lying in the middle of the road. From the wisps and coils of telephone wire, hanging brokenly from high poles and entwining across the roads. From the gray, burned-powder rims of the shell craters in the gravel roads, their edges not yet smoothed by the pounding of military traffic. From the little pools of blood on the roadside, blook that has only begun to congeal and turn black, and the punctured steel helmets lying nearby. From the square blocks of building stone still scattered in the village street, and from the sharp-edged rocks in the

roads, still uncrushed by traffic. From the burned-out tanks and broken carts still unremoved from the road. From the cows in the fields, lying grotesquely wiht their feet to the sky, so newly dead they have not begun to bloat or smell. From the scattered heaps of personal debris around a gun. (I don't know why it is, but the Germans always seem to take off their coats before they flee or die). From all these things you can tell that the battle has been recent—from these and from the men dead so recently that they seem to be merely asleep. And also from the inhuman quiet. Usually battles are noisy for miles around. But in this recent fast warfare a battle sometimes leaves a complete vacuum behind it.

The Germans will stand and fight it out until they see there is no hope. Then some give up, and the rest pull and run for miles. Shooting stops. Our fighters move on after the enemy, and those who do not fight, but move in the wake of the battles, will not catch up for hours.

There is nothing left behind but the remains—the lifeless debris, the sunshine and the flowers, and utter silence.

An amateur who wanders

above: A U.S. Army M4A4 Sherman crossing the Dortmund-Ems Canal in 1945.

driver's hatch and at that moment the tank took a direct hit. It immediately burst into flames and I tried, as quickly as I could, to get out. In doing so, my cap fell off and my hair immediately 'melted.' I felt the air disappear from my lungs. Everything around me was ablaze. After my failed attempts to remove the netting my strength seemed to ebb away and I thought: 'Now it's all over.' I fell back onto the seat, exhausted. Then I noticed how the fire engulfing me was beating its way through the mesh netting, and my will to live returned. I tore wildly at the burning netting. At the last possible second I made it out of the tank and landed on the grass. I looked up to see three German soldiers a few hundred metres away. I ran to them and they led me away. Thus I got back to my own company's tanks."

Former German Army tank driver Ernst Kröfel: "Suddenly our missing tank, that which my comrade Gustl Medack had driven, came roaring

towards us. I was pleased and thought at first that Gustl had somehow got away from the Americans. When the tank was about 1,000 metres from us we could see thick smoke escaping from the engine compartment. The tank had clearly received an American bazooka hit. The tank was moving at high speed. Alongside us on the six-metre-wide road by the forest was a Hetzer [tank destroyer] with its 75mm cannon. We weren't watching it and the commander, a bearded warrant officer, had not spoken to us. Then, as our missing Panther drew closer to us, the Hetzer fired a shot; the Panther received a direct hit and burst into flames. We saw the driver throw himself out of the tank and, because his uniform was on fire, roll himself in the grass. He then came over to us. His face was terribly deformed by the burns and I only recognised him when he was right in front of us. It was Lieutenant Bauer."

Ludwig Bauer: "The Hetzer commander

maintained that he had mistaken my tank for one that had been captured by the Americans and that was why he had fired on it. On 10 April 1945 I had survived my ninth hit. After receiving emergency treatment and reporting the incident to the sectional commander in charge, I was admitted to Olpe Hospital. The burnt skin was removed, along with sooty shreds of uniform that were stuck to the skin of my back. I left the hospital a day later so as not to become a prisoner. With my head and hands swathed in bandages, I found my way back to my section where I remained until the fighting ceased."

As they rolled across Germany in late April 1945, elements of the U.S. Army's 12th Armored Division arrived at Landsberg, an area that contained eleven concentration camps. Starting in 1933 with their "model camp" at Dachau, the Nazis systematically constructed such camps throughout Germany and German-occupied Europe, initially to hold political prisoners and, later, Jews, Gypsies and others they considered enemies of or threats to the state. The camps were a source of slave labour for the Nazis and although only a handful of camps in Poland were designed as extermination centres, vast numbers of inmates in the other camps perished from ill-treatment, illness and malnutrition. Members of the 12th Armored Division recount their experiences on arriving at one such Landsberg camp, Kaufering IV, also known as Hurlach.

"The GIs went into Landsberg and collected about 200 citizens and marched them out to the camp. No one there had money unless he was a Nazi. These were fat Nazis, well-dressed. Out at the camps, they were divided into two groups. One group dug mass graves. Each grave was 30 feet long and 15 feet wide, rows of them. The GIs were in charge. Rifle butts and bayonets were used freely. The released Russian had the run of the place. He was one of the busiest people I have ever seen. His working tool was a club

similar to a baseball bat. He just wandered back and forth among the civilians, picking out the slackers. He used that working tool. Sometime before we got there, the soldiers brought a captured SS man to work. This particular trooper had been a guard at the camp and had beaten the Russian many times. The trooper, it seemed, couldn't stand the pace. His body was added to the ever-growing pile of dead awaiting burial. This big, husky 'superman' was quite noticeable among the emaciated corpses.

"Other civilians were paired off and marched to an area more than a mile away, to bring back the dead. One fellow claimed inability to carry such a heavy load. He was allowed to bring back separate heads, legs and arms found strewn around. We walked the railroad track to find the scene where bodies had been dismembered. Here some 60 inmates had been made to dig their own graves with spoons and dishes. Everyone of these prisoners was then violently murdered, chopped to pieces. The axe was still there.

"As we drove away from the camp, we saw some prisoners who had escaped. Either the injections hadn't taken effect or they had been skipped. Some were lying dead, two or three miles away, and some were walking, the walking dead. They could barely move their legs and were stooped almost double. One fellow I will never forget. He heard our jeep coming before we got to him. With the most painful effort he turned toward us, brought himself to attention and saluted. The amount of effort it cost him to do that was, I'm sure, far more than he could spare."
— Robert T. Hartwig, 12th Armored Division, U.S. Army, World War II

"We gave all the food we had (mostly K-rations) to the survivors, radioed battalion headquarters of what we had witnessed, and moved out."
— A. G. Bramble, 12th Armored Division, U.S. Army, World War II

in this vacuum at the rear of a battle has a terrible sense of loneliness. Everything is dead— the men, the machines, the animals—and you alone are left alive.
— Ernie Pyle, August 1944

They carry no shadow in sunlight, the past like a slate Rubbed out on a future that arrived too late. / Their faces are maps of a landscape, whose ghosts hover / Around them, an arena of ruins that are all like each other.
— from *Stateless Persons* by Alan Ross

There are no words to be said: Let the future recommend / The living to the luckless dead. Tomorrow night a war will end.
— from *Midnight: May 7th, 1945* by Patric Dickinson

TRAINING

Today we have naming of parts. Yesterday, / We had daily cleaning. / And to-morrow morning, / We shall have what to do after firing. But today, / Today we have naming of parts. Japonica Glistens like coral in all of the neighbouring gardens / And today we have naming of parts.

This is the lower sling swivel. And this / Is the upper sling swivel, whose use you will see / When you are given your slings. And this is the piling swivel, / Which in your case you have not got. The branches / Hold in the gardens their silent, eloquent gestures, / Which in our case we have not got.

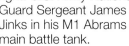

This is the safety-catch, which is always released With an easy flick of the thumb. / And please do not let me / See anyone using his finger. / You can do it quite easy / If you have any strength in your thumb. The blossoms / Are fragile and motionless, never letting anyone see Any of them using their finger.
– from *I-Naming of Parts* by Henry Reed

right: U.S. Army National Guard Sergeant James Jinks in his M1 Abrams main battle tank.

"We were at Fort Knox, Kentucky and we had to know our machineguns. The cadre took us out into the woods to teach us about the .30 calibre machinegun. We sat around on empty ammunition boxes and went through all the nomenclature of the weapon. Then the sergeant who was teaching us said, 'Everybody, shut up,' and we all shut up. I'm from New York state and I'd never seen a rattlesnake in my life, but the sergeant was from Texas and he took off his jacket, tipped over the ammunition box that I was sitting on and put his jacket over the rattlesnake. Then he cut the rattlers off."
– John R. Schaeffer, World War Two U.S. Army tanker

TO THE SOUTH of Death Valley, in the Mojave desert of California is the National Training Center of the United States Army. It is part of the Army's Fort Irwin, an old post where General George S. Patton saw to the training of armoured units in the 1940s. Fort Irwin occupies an immense area and, situated as it is in virtually the middle of nowhere, provides a near-perfect environment for armoured training and battle simulation. It is a giant sandbox, ideal for the war games and manoeuvring of the Army's tanks and other armoured fighting vehicles.

It was due to the widespread inefficiencies and inadequacies of U.S. Army performance in the Vietnam War that the Army determined to establish a specially tailored training facility that would enable its soldiers to "fight battles" in a monitored, controlled environment. At Irwin they can engage in force-on-force battle training, taking on opposing force (Opfor) units in realistic, highly demanding combat scenarios which are recorded and played back to help the trainees learn from their mistakes and take pride in their achievements.

In the high summer at Irwin the temperature can exceed 110°F, making tank training even more of a challenge than it normally is. The heat, however, is just one aspect of what tankers may endure during

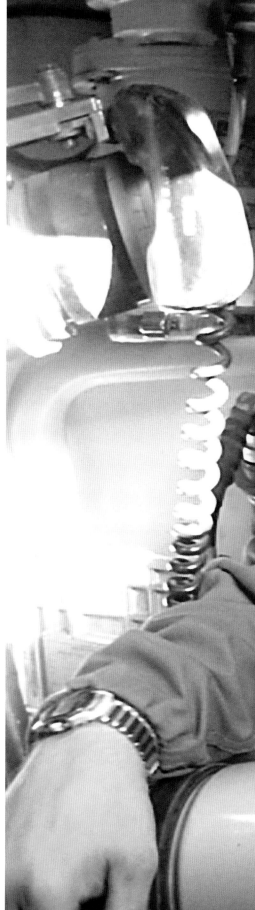

142

right: Chrysler-built M3
Grant tanks and crews
on training manoeuvres
in the California desert
early in World War II.

their three-to-five-week training stints at the NTC. While there the soldiers' skills are examined in the field, checking proficiency in a whole range of capabilities including maintenance, logistics, weapons operation and vehicle manoeuvring. It is a punishing, round-the-clock regime that is grounded in the kind of discipline and standards needed to guarantee that the lessons essential to success and survival in real combat are mastered in these controlled circumstances. At Irwin, the tankers of the U.S. Army hone their skills in the amazing M1 Abrams main battle tank.

The M1 Abrams is operated by a crew of four: a tank commander, a driver, a gunner and a loader. The job of the commander is to be the eyes, ears and mouth of the crew. Of the four, he is the one who communicates with the other tanks, and with his driver and the other crew members, to maintain the tank on course and in its proper position among the other tanks of his platoon. The rest of the crew is dependent on his eyes and his judgement to keep them out of trouble as he constantly scans the area around the tank and directs the driver. He is the only member of the crew whose position offers the sort of visibility required by his broad responsibilities. As tank commander he is also responsible for the daily servicing and maintenance of the vehicle.

"On my first tank crew qualification, the battalion had a great gunner and a great loader; he was a weightlifter and that guy could really slam rounds in there. We had a fantastic driver too. When we came off the course at about 2:30 in the morning, we came back for our debrief and the tank crew evaluator recounted each engagement for us. As he was giving us the points for each engagement and showing us what we did, I had a little calculator with me and I was adding up the points. As he got to the very last engagement, which happened to be a fifty calibre one, I could see on the video that the last tracer out of my fifty hit that target and gave me the points for it, I knew we had

qualified and possibly qualified high in the battalion. The crew knew it too. They just erupted. I was very proud of all of them. At this point I had been up for about 24 hours. We finished the debrief, pulled off the range and went back to our cots. The next morning at about 06:30, I was in my sleeping bag on my cot and I felt somebody shoving my shoulder: 'Hey sir, wake up, wake up.' I could barely see; I was pretty tired. And here were my platoon sergeant and all the tank commanders from my platoon, with a big bucket of ice and water. I still have a picture in my mind of the three tank commanders high-tailing it out of that barracks, and me freezing cold in my underwear chasing 'em out the door.

"Years ago I was in Germany and we were training at night. When it starts snowing, it doesn't really bother us tankers. The snow can get pretty deep when we are rolling cross-country and that really doesn't affect us. But if you happen to cross a road or a trail and you get three or four tanks there, by the time that fourth tank gets through, the snow is usually pretty well packed down. It's ice at that point. So here was this tank company lined up on a tank trail, a dirt road, in the middle of the night and they are getting ready to move. They had been in position for about five minutes, waiting to move. No one is going anywhere at this point. The tanks are stopped, the vehicles are idling, and then the most unlucky tank company commander appeared out of nowhere. Mysteriously, his tank just flipped over. His was one of the tanks in that column and it was as if God said: 'Your tank is flipping over.' He was parked there on that ice and while the vehicle was idling, just imperceptibly, the tank was sliding sideways on the ice towards the shoulder, and then suddenly the shoulder gave way and the tank was upside down. Thank God nobody in that tank was killed, but that tank commander took no end of ribbing for that. The only thing that broke was the barrel of the fifty calibre machinegun; that got bent down in a U.

"When I was notified that I had been selected for this command, I couldn't believe it. I was going to command First Battalion, 33rd Armor. My first assignment out of West Point was to this very battalion when it was in Germany. My platoon sergeant was Staff Sergeant Neil Ciotola, who is now our Command Sergeant Major Ciotola. Even then, we all knew he was the *standard*. And over the years, whether he knew it or not, he has been the standard by which I have measured NCOs ever since. There are just none better in the army. I've not met one better. He knows tanks, he knows tankers, he cares for them like they are his kids. He's a wonderful man and a great American.

"At the time in Germany, all the tanks were up-loaded with all their go-to-war ammunition and tank commanders would wear their personal weapons with live ammunition because the terrorist posture was pretty high at the time over there. Wherever we rolled we brought our live ammunition. We were alerted every month, we rolled every month. I remember the phone calls coming in in the middle of the night. With no notice, we rolled. The scouts would leave; they were out the gate in about an hour. The tanks would follow at about two hours. We'd go out to the local dispersal area; we'd move in to the assigned wood line and we'd stay there and wait for orders. That was exciting stuff. We'd spend 24 or 48 hours there, then we'd go back to battalion. But one time we arrived and the orders came down and I didn't know what to think. I was actually the scout platoon leader at the time. We rolled all the way up to the border, about a 60-kilometre road march and we spent the next two weeks up there. That was right at Fulda Gap. It was *the* piece of Germany that was of most interest to us. This was before the wall came down. It was where we expected to fight if we had to fight on a big scale.

– Ernest Audino, U.S. Army tanker

In the Abrams, the driver's seat is in a separate compartment in the forward part of the tank. He

left: Lt Col Ernest Audino. below: Breakfast at the tanks. far left: American-built M3 Lee tanks of a Canadian Armoured unit in World War II England.

147

I enlisted as a private in 1985 in the California Army National Guard, as a tank crewman. Basic training was fourteen months long for Armor crewmen. I finished 2nd in my class and served as Platoon Leader for my unit. After a "Team Spirit" deployment to South Korea, I was asked to attend the California Military Academy to become an officer. I finished 3rd in my class and was fortunate to be branched in Armor. I would have gone crazy otherwise. I was trained in M48A5s, M60A3s, M1s, M113s and M2 Bradleys. I commanded M60A3s. I always wanted a career in heavy metal. Fourteen 52-ton tanks was perfect. I did one National Training Center rotation. The most important lesson of all my training experiences was how important it is to paint a picture of the battlefield so that commanders can act. Planning is essential to prepare for contingencies, but after the shooting starts and the radio goes berserk, it's imperative that reporting procedures are quick and concise. Of course, the radios hardly

is able to steer the vehicle from either of two positions, depending on conditions and the circumstances. With his hatch open and his seat raised to the fully elevated position, his visibility is nearly as good as that of the commander. He is, however, subject to the worst of the sand, dust, and churned-up mud as well as being exposed to enemy lead and steel in the air. When cranked down in the "buttoned up" position, with his seat fully lowered and his hatch closed, he is protected from those hazards, but then becomes dependent on the eyes of his tank commander and the periscopes and night vision device at his position.

"Every time we come out to do an exercise we go through an operation we call Railhead. Companies prepare by tieing down the gun tubes so they won't move on a train. We drive them up on the train, which can be particularly hazardous because the [tank] tracks hang about six inches on either side. We carefully guide them up and then cable them down with shackles and cables, eight in the front, eight in the rear; a really aggravating exercise. Then when we get up to the Yakima area we unbuckle them and carefully drive them off, drive them up here, shoot them and then repeat the process to go back home again."
– James Jinks, U.S. Army tanker

"These tanks hold 544 gallons of diesel fuel and they'll go through that in about seven or eight hours of operation. It's a huge cost, but it's a big payoff in operations that require intimidation and firepower. Your average tanker, especially in the American Army, is about 60 per cent mechanic. He is constantly working on these things to keep them up. A lot of guys talk bad about their tanks, but they also have a lot of pride in them."
– Charles L. Ross, U.S. Army tanker

"My wife has driven a tank. We used to sponsor spouse driver training classes. It's nice to let the wives see what the husbands do and let the kids see what dad does. And when I arrived in this battalion, I was determined to try to do this. We

have all these great things and I couldn't live with myself if I let these opportunities to share them with the families go by. So we put together a spouse driver's training programme where we would bring spouses with driver's licenses out with us in the field on a specific day. We would give them a one-hour class to orient them to the controls of the vehicle, put them in the driver's hatch, with some tankers, and take them out on the course. We would allow them to do one or two brake tests so they could understand that they had the power to stop that 70 tons. Then we would let them go out on the course for about a kilometre, not really that long, very simple, relatively flat, no challenging terrain. But when the wives came back after driving that 1500 horsepower, the smiles were from ear to ear. We'd have a photographer right there and the ladies, of course, had their helmets on, beaming. We took pictures of them so that some day, when they are grandmothers, they can point to their picture and say: 'That's when grandma used to drive tanks.' "
– Ernest Audino, U.S. Army tanker

The gunner must search for his targets by peering through an optical sight. He is isolated in the tank, with no hatch of his own and sits in front of and slightly lower than the tank commander. He controls the great main gun of the vehicle through control handles that the tankers call "Cadillacs" because they are manufactured by Cadillac-Gage. Using them, he can adjust the elevation of the gun, traverse the turret through the entire field of fire, control the laser range-finger and fire the weapon. His is a highly skilled role demanding superb co-ordination.

"Each individual crewman carries a 9mm pistol. We have two M4 carbines. If we go to war we'll have eight fragmentation grenades, eight thermite grenades, 24 smoke grenades and a total of 40 main gun rounds, and that may not seem like a lot, but is when it's designed to take out enemy vehicles of this calibre of tank. We also have 11,400

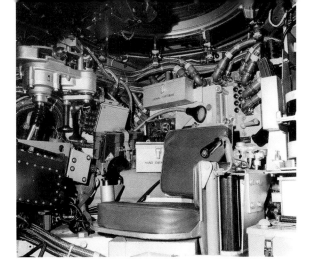

rounds of co-ax ammunition and a thousand rounds of calibre fifty. [In the tank it smells of] diesel fuel and cordite, the main gun residue. The system is designed so that the gases from firing don't come back in here, 'cause they are toxic. The cordite has a sulfurous smell; it stinks. There are guys who, when they start smelling it, get excited 'cause they know it's big-bullet time.

"Hydraulic blast doors . . . if we get hit in the back, all the combustibles, if all that went off at once . . . that protects us. There are big plates on there that blow off, called blow-up panels. When an explosion goes off in there, they'll go about 200-300 feet in the air. The crew will be safe inside here. On our Nomex suits . . . the rear end has a couple of sewn-in panels. The Nomex guys you'll see have flaps hanging down on the back of their rear ends. We call those blow-up panels also."
—James Jinks, U.S. Army tanker

The job of the loader is to serve the gun, with either the "sabot" or "HEAT" (High-Explosive Anti-Tank) rounds depending on the target. The sabot round is essentially a thin bolt of depleted uranium or tungsten carbide encapsulated in an aluminium "shoe" or "sabot" that enlarges the bulk of the round to a diameter of the bore of the Abrams' main gun. Without its sabot the anti-tank round looks a bit like a big dart. It carries no explosive material. It derives its power from the kinetic energy imparted at the firing

and is capable of driving and burning through the armour of another modern tank, causing a deadly shower of "spall" in which fragmentation from the enemy tank's armour is blasted into its interior space, exposing the enemy crew to a terrible flak. This spall phenomenon can result regardless of whether or not the tank's armour has been fully penetrated. In the Persian Gulf War of 1990-91, many hapless Iraqi tank crews fell victim to Abrams-fired bolts as they struggled to put up opposition in their outclassed Russian T-72s. The HEAT round is basically a cone-shaped liner surrounded by a high-explosive shaped charge, together forming the warhead. When the round strikes a target, the shaped charge drives a jet of molten metal foward at velocities up to Mach 25.

In addition to the loading chore, the loader, when not engaged in his primary role, stands and mans an externally-mounted machinegun near his hatch.

One of the key people in the United States Army, one of those who keeps it ticking over smoothly is 25-year tanker Command Sergeant Major Neil Ciotola: "When I was growing up I lived in New Jersey. McGuire Air Force Base was right down the highway from us and there would be 'deuce-and-a-halfs', the old Army trucks, loaded with soldiers in the back and I sat up there in the front seat of the Buick Le Sabre that my dad bought in 1967. I was nine years old and I looked up and waved and a soldier waved back.

ever work like you want them to, so now you know why you spent all night planning for the next day.

Artillery was available and we trained on the application of artillery all the time. We never spent enough time to get artillery properly implemented at the tank commander level. Having to command a tank or two, read the map, check for artillery, change radio frequencies and make a proper call for fire was very intensive work, especially when guys were supposed to be shooting back, and, oh yes, watch out for that tree. In a battle, everyone is yelling and screaming, especially the gunner and the tank commander. Then you have the loader, who is *really* stressing because he can't see out of the tank and is getting all his information from the two guys that are screaming stuff like, "Where is he?" "He's right there, pointing his gun at us." "I don't see him." "Fire!"
"I can't. I don't see

anything."

"Just pull the f . . . . . . trigger!"

I used to laugh at car salesmen who said, "It's built like a tank." I would respond, "So, it requires eight hours of labour for every hour of operation and it breaks down all the time?" There is nothing fun or glorious about breaking down. With proper driving habits you can avoid a lot of problems. I have never been in a tank that threw a track. Concertina wire wrapped around the idler wheel, yes, but we didn't throw a track. I don't want to count the times I broke track due to maintenance.
– Jeff Babineau, U.S. Army tanker

right: A column of Russian T-55 tanks in a training exercise along a trail in the Leningrad Military District. below: A Tank Crossing warning road sign near Tidworth, England.

What made me join the Army? It was that guy in that deuce-and-a-half who waved back.

"I wanted to be a pilot. My father was in the air force. He used to tell me that I would never amount to anything and that I would have to join the Army. I went ahead and took a flight physical. My eyes weren't good enough. My second choice was armored cavalry. I was eighteen years old and I wanted to be a tanker. It's been 25 years now and I've never looked back. If I have any regrets about my job, it's what I've put my family through doing it. Every time I went to school, I took my wife with me and she studied with me every night. My successes are as much my wife's successes. When I made Staff Sergeant she revelled in it as much as I did. When I made First Sergeant . . . and it wasn't just the money, it was the prestige, it was the sense of responsibility, it was the people that, not only I would be able to touch but my wife would be able to touch as well. My wife has multiple sclerosis and it has really taken a toll on her in the last five years, but she is still, by any measure, a very vivacious woman. And her goal [for me], as well as my goal, has always been to become a Command Sergeant Major in the United States Army. I've been one now for the last five years and she's ready to stop. She's moved with me nine times. That's nine different households she's had to set up. We have a wonderful little boy. He's twelve years old, and my missing his baseball games and stuff like that . . . but he's pretty tolerant. Now, my wife wants a home and I owe her that.

"There are a lot of misconceptions about people in the Army . . . that we're a lot of blood-thirsty killers and all that. I've been to combat. I don't want to see it again. I'm tired of getting shot at.

" In my service in the army, I've met some of the most wonderful people in the world, and I just don't ever want to know what it's like to not be a part of that. But I know that I'm coming to the end of my career and that I'll do as I've always

150

right: The superb British Challenger I main battle tank has a Royal Ordnance 120mm L30 rifled gun and Chobham/steel armour protection.

done in the past. I try to give back everything I possibly can. The wonderful thing about the Army is, our product is people, and in order for us to be successful, if we want to be here for another 226 years, we have to perpetuate ourselves every day and the only way for us to do that is to give back everything that we know.

"Another wonderful thing about the Army is, they forced me to exist with my fellow man, my fellow Americans. Nobody else, other than the armed services, demand that you get to know one another. People tell me the United States Army can't adapt. My men have been out there in minus twelve with the wind-chill factor minus 35. They've been out there changing engines and transmissions, taking their work in ten-minute shifts because their hands start to freeze . . . and people tell me the United States Army can't adapt and the United States Army is soft. They can kiss my ass. They have no idea what the Army is made of. We live in a nation that provides its citizens with many more freedoms and much more latitude than any other nation on this planet.

"People talk about the new army and the old army. I was in the old friggin army. I came in right after Vietnam. My first tank unit was nothing but Vietnam veterans. The problem with the old army was they confused abuse with discipline. But they didn't serve alongside *these* soldiers, who are every bit as honorable, deserving and capable as those who went before them. Are they selfless? Yes, they are. Are they cut from the same cloth as those who served in World War II? No, they're not. Are we motivated in the same way as this country was motivated then? No, we're not, but we've got to stop living in the past. We need to learn from it, we need to revel in it, we need to respect it and respect those who did what they did, but, if there's a difference between the soldiers of today and the soldiers of yesterday, sociologically speaking, the kids today want to know *why* . . . and we tell 'em why. When you convince a young

below: The M-48 Patton mounted a 90mm gun, had a range of 289 miles, a top speed of 30 mph and was notorious for using fuel at the rate of nearly four U.S. gallons per mile.

[this time] fatally, in the act of dressing his wounded driver.

During the whole of this period he was in full view and short range of enemy machineguns and rifle pits, and throughout by his prompt and heroic action showed an utter disregard for his own personal safety.

man or a young woman that you'll tell them why they have to do something when it's required, when you tell them to execute and execute now, they know because you've treated them that way, and they'll execute. There's nothing wrong with the Army. Our toys are more expensive, it's harder to keep everybody in all of that nice stuff. It's always gonna be hard to buy that stuff. But, fundamentally, philosophically, ethically, morally, there is nothing wrong with the Army. I know that the same things went on in the Army before; it's just that you can't hide anything any more. What happens to one person in one unit is everybody's business now.

"When I was a young NCO, I used to think, 'I'm a tanker. I'm the cock o'the walk. I'm the King of Battle. I ride in a 70-ton iron monster. I don't need anybody else.' Well, an M1A1 consumes 500 gallons of diesel or JP-8 in a day, and after that's gone, if you don't have the support facility, you're screwed. You can only eat MREs [Meals Ready to Eat] for so long, you can only exist on one five-gallon water

can for so long. If everybody isn't doing their jobs, you're screwed. So, the Army isn't about any one particular facet; the Army is about people acknowledging that what they do is important, and my job is to make sure that they understand how important each of their jobs are, because if I took out any one facet of my battalion, it would cease to function. Take my medical team away, somebody would die. My job is not only to kick people in the ass; it's also to pat 'em on the back and give 'em a hug. Just like when the winds are kicking up to 50 and 60 miles an hour, my job is to make sure my First Sergeant gets those tanks around those tents, to keep them from going down, but then after that, it's just to stand there and let my soldiers see me. Wherever my soldiers are, I am.

"When I was a young private in 1977 and my tank had just manoeuvred up to an infantry command post and we were talking big shit, and this infantry Sergeant First Class who'd had two tours in Vietnam, reached up and literally hauled me out of the turret and dragged me across an open field.

He pushed my face into an anti-tank mine and said, 'You see that, you son of a bitch. That's called an M-15 anti-tank mine.' He dragged me a little closer to the tank and said, 'You see that? That's another fuckin' mine. And he dragged me a little further and said, 'That's another Goddamned mine. Next time you think you're the King of Battle, you'd better go ahead and pull your head out of your ass and realize that it takes everybody to do this shit.' After I got done wetting myself I got back in my tank and I was a very quiet, submissive, stupid young Private First Class again and I just sat there.

"I *am* the United States Army. I establish the standards in this unit and the soldiers will abide by those standards. If you cross the line you will answer to the Command Sergeant Major. If you don't accept my perception of what a soldier should be, you will go home. The Marines talk about the few, the proud, and see if you're good enough. You have to be good enough to be a soldier too, whether you are a man or a woman. You have to be deserving to wear the uniform of your nation. We're affable and we're fallible. We make mistakes every day and we do hundreds of things right every day. We're made out to look like the bad guys sometimes. But we're the first one they call when the wife says that her husband is not taking care of her. We take that husband out of there to protect that woman. Somebody said a long time ago that the Army takes care of its own. It takes care of its soldiers, its wives, its children. The system that has been established is a wonderful one that is vested in this sense of integrity that everybody has. My soldiers deserve consistency. That's another thing that I'm supposed to bring. When they wake up, I'm there. Taking PT [physical training], I'm there. It's all about doing the best they can, and the best I can. And they'll get the recognition they deserve. It doesn't necessarily have to be an award or a medal. It just has to be a pat on the

back. I hate the fact that the phone rings at least 25 times a day . . . somebody is hurt, somebody got arrested, somebody did this, somebody did that. I hate it. But there's another part of me that . . . I don't know what I would do if I wasn't doing it. They call me because they rely on me. I have to understand the goals and objectives of my Battalion Commander and I have to help him fulfill the destiny that he has charted for this battalion and I do that by, number one, being his sounding board, number two, being his confidant, number three, being a sanity check, and number four, talking to my non-commissioned officers and articulating the significance of the agenda he has established. Colonel Audino is my fourth Battalion Commander and the only agenda that he has set for himself and this battalion is for them to be a well-trained, combat-ready unit. He loves being around his soldiers and he believes, just like I do, that we have a great privilege and honour; him to be commander of a tank battalion of 557 Americans; me, with the power and authority that I wield and the responsibility that I have as a Command Sergeant Major.

"I walk out in my uniform in the morning and I have spit-shined jump boots on and starched fatigues and my wife is there and she looks at me and says, 'God, you look good.' I get in front of my battalion and call them to attention and that's how we start off every Monday. I say, 'Listen up, you sons of bitches. This is what we're gonna do. It isn't what *you're* gonna do; it's what *we're* gonna do. Get your head out of your ass. Go ahead and shake off the cobwebs. You got any alcohol left in your system, you should have run it off this morning at 6.30. It's time to take a Darvon and drive on. We've got 44 iron monsters and 150 other vehicles down at the motor pool that need our tender, loving care. We've got people to take care of, we've got equipment to repair and we've got a nation to defend.' "

To lead uninstructed people to war is to throw them away.
– Confucius, 480 B.C.

TANKS PLAYED a pivotal role in the hell that was the Pacific Theatre of Operations in World War II. They were a key factor in the great Allied island-hopping campaign at Balikpapan and Brunei on Borneo, Bougainville in the Solomons, Guam in the Marianas, Tarawa in the Gilberts, Peleliu in the Palaus, and at Cape Endaiadere near Buna on New Guinea. But in the Pacific war, as well as the later conflicts in Korea and Vietnam, there was little actual tank-versus-tank engagement. The Japanese, North Koreans and Viet Cong were not well-equipped with tanks or other armoured fighting vehicles. They utilized their armour largely in an infantry support capacity, and in the Korean action, tanks were frequently used to supplement artillery. In this pictorial section, selected colour and black-and-white images depict some of the armoured operations in these conflicts.

PACIFIC WARS

left: Australian Matilda tanks landing on Brunei. below: More Aussie Matildas, these operating on Wewak.

right: The Matilda turret with its 37mm cannon. below: The M5 Stuart and its .30 calibre machinegun. far right: Australian Matildas in support of Aussie infantrymen clearing the oil refinery facility at Balikpapan, 3 July 1945.

above: Closed down for
immediate action, an
Australian Matilda rolls
towards Slater's Knoll on
Bougainville in April 1945.
right: U.S. Sherman tanks
assembled for a mopping-
up patrol near Hollandia.
far right: U.S. Marine
tanks on patrol near
Chunchon, Korea in 1951.

In the Vietnam War of the 1960s and '70s, the initial American emphasis was on infantry supported by substantial air power and helicopters as gunships, transport and evacuation aircraft. In time though, and with tremendous effort, medium tanks and armoured personnel carriers were employed. The Viet Cong, however, proved an elusive and demoralizing foe for the U.S. and South Vietnamese tank crews hunting them in the grasslands and jungles. The VC were proficient at hit-and-run tactics, short-range ambushes and anti-tank warfare using simple mines. They were adept at silently slipping away and evading their enemy in most situations. Significantly, most of the American armoured fighting vehicles used in Vietnam had been designed for operations in an entirely different arena, the nuclear battlefield of Europe and were not well suited to the narrow-fronted encounters of Vietnam.

above: A U.S. 25th Infantry Division tank churns up dust in Vietnam during January 1969. right: *Tank and Crew*, Vietnam, 1969, a painting by James R. Drake.

The conduct of the fighting during the French and U.S. wars in South Vietnam was heavily influenced by the weather and the topography. Monsoon rains hit the mountainous northern regions in the winters, while the Mekong Delta area of the south experienced them in the summers. The enormous rainfall, the mud, swamps, rice paddies, dikes and ditches of the Delta, and the poor visibility, made tank operations virtually impossible in much of the country. Only the central Piedmont region, with its broad plains and rolling hills, was suited to armoured warfare.

162

In New Guinea the great mountain ranges with their high peaks and deep gorges, the dense jungles which cover almost all of the huge island, the reeking *nipa* and mangrove swamps— "a stinking jumble of twisted, slime-covered roots and muddy 'soup' ' —the hazardous jungle trails, the vast patches of *kunai* grass, with its sharp-edged blades growing to a height of six or seven feet, the swollen streams, the ever- present mud, the dangerous off-shore reefs, most of them uncharted, the poor harbours— these terrain characteristics exerted a constant and adverse influence on troops and military tactics.

The problem of climate and health were no less severe. The penetrating, energy-sapping heat was accompanied by intense humidity and frequent torrential rains that defy description. Health conditions were amongst the worst in the world. The incidence of malaria could only be reduced by the most rigid and irksome discipline and even then *continued on page 168*

left: In the great Pacific island-hopping campaign, U.S. Army and Marine Corps M4 Sherman tanks were involved in clearing the Japanese from Peleliu and the other islands of the Palau group. They were ably assisted by the big guns of U.S. Navy warships just offshore.

Were you ever inside a tank when it got hit? The spot inside the tank where the shell hits turns a bright yellow, like a sunrise.
– from *Tarawa: The Second Day*
by Robert Sherrod

far left: A derelict Sherman tank that was destroyed by the Japanese on Guam in World War II. left: U.S. Marine tankers study the snow-covered slope of a Korean hill in search of enemy positions. below: A free ride for U.S. Marines during the Korean War.

right: American infantrymen with fixed bayonets crouch behind a Sherman tank during their advance against Japanese forces on the island of Bougainville in the northern Solomons. This action followed shortly after the March 1944 establishment of a beachhead at Empress Augusta Bay in which 5,000 Japanese soldiers were killed. Cut off from all further supplies, the remaining Japanese forces on the island faced certain annihilation or capture.

the dreaded disease took a heavy toll. Dengue fever was common, while the deadly blackwater fever, though not so prevalent, was no less an adversary. Bacillary and amoebic dysentery were both forbidding possibilities, and tropical ulcers, easily formed from the slightest scratch, were difficult to cure. Scrub typhus, ringworm, hookworm and yaws all awaited the careless soldier. Millions of insects abounded everywhere.
– from the Douglas MacArthur historical records

We must trade time for space, hold the high ground as long as possible. Defend in depth. Keep a reserve. Watch your flanks. Protect your artillery. Maintain communications at all costs. Don't get decisively engaged.
– General Walton Walker, Korea

We win here or lose everywhere; if we win here, we improve the chances of winning everywhere.
– General Douglas MacArthur, Korea

left: An American tank of the Army of the Republic of Vietnam participating in the final battle for Saigon, in April 1975. On 30 April North Vietnamese troops and armoured elements entered the South Vietnamese capital. By then, most remaining Americans and many South Vietnamese were being evacuated. Soviet-built North Vietnamese T-54s quickly surrounded the Presidential palace and the capital fell as South Vietnamese forces offered little resistance.

below: In August 1950, a U.S. Army half-track driver shaves in the field with the assistance of several Korean children. right: Jeeps escorting an M8 armoured car of the Canadian Army's Lord Strathcona's Horse Regiment, Korea, 1951.

AMONG THE MOST RESPECTED armoured corps in the world is that of the Israeli Defence Force and Israel is often perceived as one of the leaders in modern tank technology. It was not always so. In its initial combat engagement on 16 October 1948, the then battalion-strength Israeli tank organization was ordered into battle against an Egyptian force that had gained control of Lod airport. In the brief action, Israel's ten French 1930s-era two-man Hotchkiss H39 light tanks all failed embarrassingly, breaking down or ending up in anti-tank ditches, without getting within range of their enemy. These tanks were World War II leftovers, obtained in the Middle East after the conflict. Their two British Cromwell infantry tanks were also quickly out of action.

In those days, the Israelis didn't know much about tanks or armoured warfare. They did know that they faced a prolonged fight for their very survival against the Arab enemy. They knew that they would have to hold their tiny territory with an unrivalled tenacity and play for time in which to gather strength and improve their fighting capability. They knew, too, that in the coming years they could not possibly prevail in a war of attrition. They were the few; the Arabs the many. The Israelis were extremely limited in equipment, weaponry, ammunition, technology, geography, money and manpower. Their enemy had all the advantages in numbers. Knowing this about their opponents, the Arabs determined to force the Israelis into fighting that defensive war of attrition. The Israelis realized that their only hope was always to control the situation and strike swiftly and powerfully in short campaigns that would be decisive. They had to take and keep the offensive in the struggle to come.

To control the situation, and survive, the Israelis needed to ensure that their land battles would take place in wasteland regions whenever possible, far from the hard-won cultivated areas where most of their population resided. Somehow, they had to develop a highly effective, technologically sound, well trained and disciplined armoured fighting force, a tall order for a small country with severely limited resources.

Since 1948, the state of Israel has fought six wars with Arab nations of the region. In the course and aftermaths of these conflicts, the Israelis have learned many lessons about tanks and tank warfare. It was in the Sinai Campaign of 1956 that the Israel Armoured Corps began to transform itself from a rather ragtag outfit to something resembling an efficient and effective war machine.

Late in 1955 the Egyptian government under Gamal Abdel Nasser, the former army officer who had served as prime minister and president of Egypt, and later as president of the United Arab Republic, negotiated a large arms agreement with Czechoslovakia, which led Israel to fear it would have to embark upon a Middle East arms race. Because the Egyptians were also providing support to the anti-French elements in Algeria, France was disposed to provide armaments to the Israelis in the form of 250 tanks, most of them Shermans. Noting how effective some Shermans had become against German Tigers and Panthers during the 1944 Normandy campaign when the British had retrofitted them with a 17-pounder gun, the Israel Armoured Corps followed suit and had their Shermans mounted with French CN75-50 guns.

The Israelis attacked the numerically stronger Egyptians in the Sinai desert in late October 1956, following a pattern of horrific attacks and reprisals, and the nationalization of the Suez Canal by Nasser in July—an action which infuriated Britain and France. While there was substantial disagreement among the various Israeli army commanders about how, and even whether, their tanks should be used in the conflict, their 7th Armoured Brigade moved out to the southern front of its own volition and quickly spearheaded the initial assault on the Egyptian forces. Impressively, the 7th advanced more than 250 kilometres to the Suez Canal in

MIDDLE EAST AND PERSIAN GULF

The 1973 Yom Kippur Arab-Israeli War featured one of the classic defensive armoured battles of all time. It was the battle for the Golan Heights, which Israel had captured in 1967 and which Syria wanted to regain. The Syrian army had fielded five divisions for an attack it planned to launch on 6 October. They brought 1400 tanks to the scene, including 400 T-62s 1000 T-54/55s. They also utilized a number of obsolete T-34s which they had dug into concrete bunker positions on the front lines. Together with the Egyptians, who would attack across the Suez Canal, they intended to launch a co-ordinated surprise offensive on two fronts and hoped to destroy a maximum amount of Israeli armour, stagger the Israeli command structure, and, if possible, retake the Golan and perhaps make further territorial gains in Galilee.

The Israelis were well positioned defensively. They

left: Heavy losses among Israeli tank crews in the October 1973 war motivated Israel's tank planners to develop the Merkava (chariot in Hebrew), probably the best tank ever built in terms of crew protection.

under 100 hours. On the way, they engaged and destroyed a larger Egyptian armoured brigade. The surprising, extraordinarily effective Israeli blitzkrieg contributed mightily to the defeat of the enemy forces by early November, but the victory was also due to the intervention of the French and British whose forces destoryed Egypt's air force on the ground within three days and went on to land at Port Suez in an attempt to seize the Canal. The intervention of the United States led to a U.N.-brokered ceasefire on 5 November. But the Sinai Campaign was the turning point for the Israel Armoured Corps. The tank had been accepted as a key player in the future defence of the young state.

In the 1967 Six-Day War, the Syrian Army had 70,000 men in six infantry and two armoured brigades, as well as one mechanized brigade. They were well deployed along the Golan Heights and were backed up by a sizable mobile reserve. Their armour at the front consisted of 40 Russian T34 and T54 tanks from a total force of 750 tanks. Most of the early action took place in the Sinai peninsula while the Syrians confined their activity to shelling Israeli settlements from the Golan positions.

The escarpment of the Golan rises 1,000 metres above the Sea of Galilee and the Jordan Valley. In 1967 three roads climbed the Golan, all of them heavily defended. The slopes had been turned into a virtually impregnable fortress by the Syrians, with defensive positions and fortifications, roadblocks and minefields.

The head of the Israeli Defence Force Northern Command, Major-General David Elazar, had only three brigades available to him when he was called upon to seize the Golan. They were supported by Sherman tanks of the 8th and 37th Armoured Brigades on 9 June when General Elazar set out to climb the Golan and clear the Syrian positions.

Syrian resistance was intense as the Israeli infantry and tanks pressed along the mountain track. It was a slow advance with the Israelis

did have to construct an anti-tank barrier across the so-called Purple Line, which ran from Rafid to Kuneitra and was established after the cease-fire in the 1967 Six-Day War. The barrier was simply meant to delay the Syrians advance and buy time for substantial Israel reserve forces to be brought to the front. The Syrians wanted to get to the Jordan River bridges in time to hold off those Israeli reserves. For the coming battle the Israelis were only able to field a single two-battalion armoured brigade which was equipped with modified Centurion tanks. They did maintain emergency back-up armoured formations deployed below the Golan Heights.

The combined Syrian-Egyptian offensive was launched at 2 p.m. on 6 October, chosed with the aim of achieving maximum surprise on the sacred Jewish holiday of Yom Kippur.

Syrian intelligence on the strength and disposition of the Israelis was accurate.

left: Israeli tanks advancing into Egyptian territory after crossing the Suez Canal during the October 1973 Yom Kippur War. Following the crossing, the tanks of General Ariel Sharon proceeded to cut off the Egyptian Third Army in one of boldest armoured warfare moves ever undertaken.

right: The Israeli Merkava main battle tank is special and unconventional. Its ultra-low design enables it to hide behind most relatively low obstacles, minimizing its exposure to enemy fire and presenting a very small target. The slender turret enhances the compact, efficient shape. below: The body of an Egyptian soldier killed during the 1967 Six-Day War lies near his wrecked tank. overleaf: Israeli Armoured Corps MBTs on the roll.

suffering many casualties along the way, but the Syrian fortifications were gradually overcome. Several of the Shermans received hits from deadly accurate enemy fire, but they pressed on.

The leading tank battalion was supposed to outflank the heavily defended fortification at Qala, but was hampered by substantial artillery fire as it approached. Instead of being able to outflank the Qala site, the Israelis were held up and engaged with it, and were taking many more casualties.

At this point the second Israeli tank battalion, realising the predicament of the first, came forward and assaulted the rear echelon stronghold of Zaoura. After securing it, they turned west and attacked the Qala position from the rear. Now the Israeli tanks of the pinned-down battalion were rallied by a young officer and redirected in a renewed attack on Qala. They not only came under intense defensive fire, but encountered a mined anti-tank barrier. The young officer continued the advance, however, and soon three of the Shermans, including his own, were hit. He scrambled down from the tank, ran to another and continued to command from it. The fight went on into the night when, at last, the two tank battalions managed to join up and defeat the Qala fortification, leading to the end of Syrian resistance along the Golan front. The Syrians were in full retreat and the war on the Syrian front was at an end.

The war had begun when, following lengthy skirmishes along the Sinai frontier and the withdrawal of U.N. observers, the Israelis found it necessary to launch a pre-emptive assault on Egyptian positions in the Sinai. The Israelis were taking their own version of blitzkrieg to the Egyptians, who were set in a Soviet-style defence, having been schooled and equipped by the Russians. By 1965 the Israel Armoured Corps had accumulated about 1,000 tanks, a combination of

American Shermans and Pattons, British Centurions and French AMX-13s, while the Egyptians had 1,300 tanks, mostly Josef Stalin 3 heavies and T34s, but their total also included 450 more modern Russian T54s and T55s.

Until 1964, the quality of Israeli tank gunnery, and tank maintenance, was at best uneven. With the arrival of the Pattons and Centurions, such a casual approach was no longer tolerable. These vehicles were far more sophisticated and demanding than the IAC's old Shermans and suddenly a great deal more was required of the crews and personnel. This was the moment when Major-General Israel Tal took command of the IAC and forced through a programme of reforms that completely revitalized it. He showed his men how to operate and fight their new tanks with confidence and inspiration. He instilled a high level of discipline, standardized and tightened training procedures and introduced an expertise that had been unknown in the Corps before his arrival. By 1967 the crews of the IAC no longer feared their tanks; they had mastered them and developed a great respect for their capabilites.

In the early action the Israeli Air Force attacked the Egyptian airfields with the aim of eliminating the enemy air force on the ground, while three IAC tank columns rolled in a surprise attack on Egyptian positions. The Israeli plan called for frightening the Egyptian defenders into retreat. The IAC armour would then maintain the pressure until the fleeing enemy was exhausted. The Israelis smashed through Egyptian defences, incurring some losses to enemy tanks, mines and anti-tank guns. But these were essentially token actions on the part of the Egyptians who appeared to lack the will for the fight and tended to crumble after offering only marginal resistance.

The mobility and excellent gunnery of the Israeli tank crews, the surprise factor in their attack, and the immobile defensive stance of the Egyptians in their JS3s and T34s both contributed to the Israeli triumph in little more than 24 hours. By the time

They knew that the Israelis had deployed fewer than 200 against their own armoured force of 1400.

Early in the afternoon of the 6th, MiG jet fighters appeared and strafed the Israeli 7th Armoured Brigade headquarters at Nafakh, which immediately sent the tanks of the 7th racing to reach their assigned positions at the front ahead of the Syrian armour. In the first hours of the offensive, Syrian artillery and air support were hammering the Israeli front. The tanks of three Syrian infantry brigades were rushing towards the Jordan River bridges along a 40-kilometre front, hoping to be there before Israeli reserve forces could reach the bridges. Overhead, Israeli Air Force Mirage fighters had engaged Syrian Sukhoi fighter-bombers in furious air battles.

Within two hours of the start of the offensive, the Israeli tanks were being overwhelmed by the huge numerical superiority of the Syrian tank force. The Israeli tank crews were having to fight a virtually hopeless delaying action against the advancing Syrians while waiting for the reserves to support them. Israeli tanks were being destroyed at a furious rate.

When the masses of Syrian tanks and mine-clearing armoured vehicles approached the tank barriers and minefield, an immense traffic jam developed, halting the Syrian advance.

Trailblazing Syrian tanks soon began rolling through the minefield, followed by bridging tanks whose job was to make it possible for the balance of the Syrian tanks to cross the anti-tank ditch at the far end of the minefield. The vastly outnumbered Israeli Centurions fought valiantly but were unable to contain the flood of Syrian T-55s rolling through towards their objective.

Soon two brigades of T-54s were firing on the Centurions of the Barak Brigade positioned on the near ridge as more Syrian tanks swarmed onto the field below. Firing at a range of 2,000 metres, the armour-piercing rounds of the Centurions gradually began to score hits on the tanks of their opponents. Many Syrian tanks blew up in the battle, but the Israelis desperately needed the help of the reserve tanks which were on the way to the front.

With nightfall, the advantage appeared to swing back to the Syrian tank forces whose T-55s were equipped with a superb night vision capability, while the Israeli Centurions were ill-equipped for night-fighting. Aircraft of the IAF tried to illuminate the battlefield with flares but they didn't help much. The Syrians took full advantage of the situation, advancing towards their enemy in the darkness.

In the moonlight the crews of the Israeli tank units watched the blinking coloured lights of the

previous spread: Israeli
Tank Corps crewmen
awaiting orders at their
vehicles. right: Flares
illuminating a battlefield
and Israeli tanks in the
Northern Sinai during the
1973 Yom Kippur War.

approaching Syrian tanks, and held their fire as the enemy vehicles climbed towards them. When at last the Syrians crawled into short range of the Israelis, the Israeli armoured commander gave the order to his crews to fire on sight. More than a dozen Syrian tanks were burning in the first few minutes of firing, temporarily slowing their assault. But the superior night-fighting capability of the T-55s soon brought their 100mm guns into play at a range of only 300 metres. Gradually the backdrop of the raging tank fires across the battlefield made targets for both sides highly visible.

Shocked and wounded tank crews of both sides scrambled for cover in the rocks of the ridge. The leading Syrian tanks had nearly reached the top of the ridge and tanks were firing at each other from as close as fifty metres.

The Israeli armoured commander managed to rally his tank crews in an effective counter-attack along the ridge line, which surprised the Syrians, causing them to withdraw. Now the Israeli tanks went after their opposite number with a vengeance, flaming many more of the T-55s.

Egyptian T54s and T55s appeared on the battlefield, it was too late. Although the situation had the makings of a major tank-versus-tank engagement the Egyptian tank crews were all but hypnotized by Israeli tanks that were outflanking them, rolling through terrain that the Egyptians had thought impassable for tanks. Under massive attack on their exposed flanks, they lost 70 tanks to the Israeli action in less than three hours.

In less than four days of fighting, IAC tanks had defeated and captured 850 Egyptian tanks as well as knocking out 35 Jordanian Patton tanks during the invasion of the West Bank and East Jerusalem.

Lieutenant-Colonel David Eshel was a founding member of the Israeli Armoured Corps and its Chief of Signals. On retirement, he became proprietor and Editor-in-Chief of the magazine, *Defence Update International*. In his book, *Chariots of the Desert*, he comments on the 1967 conflict: "The Egyptian handling of their armoured

forces was totally ineffective and unimaginative. With almost three times as many tanks as the Israelis, their armour was kept static, far behind the battle-front. Such armour as was used, was engaged piecemeal and reluctantly without precise orders about their objectives. The state of supreme confusion under which the Egyptian command operated was signified by the handling of their crack 4th Armoured Division, a force which, had it been employed decisively, could have caused the Israeli armoured commanders considerable headaches. Still, some credit must be handed to the Egyptian formations operating under complete Israeli air supremacy, which deprived them of any operational movements in daylight.

"At the tactical level, the Israeli tank gunners showed that they were more than a match for their Egyptian counterparts, even when heavily outgunned. For example, the 90mm Patton gunners were so effective against the monster

122mm JS 3s that they knocked them out without losing a single tank themselves. Similarly, the AMX-13 crews showed that they could out-shoot the 100mm T-55 at night by out-manoeuvring them and penetrating their superior sloped armour from a flank with their 75mm high velocity guns.

"On the other hand, the Israeli armoured infantry proved insufficiently trained, as had also been the case in the 1956 war. With the exception of the 9th regular battalion, the rest of the armoured infantry performed poorly, a fact, which was to have far reaching consequences in the future shaping of the Israeli armoured forces. The Israelis also found out very quickly how badly they suffered from the lack of modern night fighting equipment, in contrast to the well-equipped Egyptian T-55s. Xenon searchlights proved extremely dangerous to the crews.

"There was marked disparity in the standards of tactical leadership between the two sides. Whereas the Israeli commanders led from the front, sometimes even too much so, with brigadiers moving immediately behind their vanguards, ready to intervene at once when necessary, and battalion commanders leading each assault, exercising their battle leadership by personal example, the Egyptian commanders normally remained in their headquarters—confused by conflicting reports from the front and unable to influence the battle by exercising their authority to support actions or to move their reserves to endangered sectors.

"Lack of initiative or motivation caused their armoured attacks, those that were executed at all, to peter out at the first enemy response. Egyptian tank crews usually fought buttoned down and so with limited visibility. Hence, at Jebel Libni, a complete brigade of T-55 tanks was outflanked and destroyed. While the Israeli crews sometimes fought for more than sixty hours without rest, the Egyptians were employed on short sorties only. Nevertheless, in spite of their fatigue, the better trained and motivated Israeli crews outfought the relatively fresh Egyptian crew in all battles."

In the years after the Sinai Campaign, the pioneers of the Israeli armour force, and especially Major-General Tal, began the lengthy process of planning and developing a tank weapon of their own, an indigenous vehicle that would be tailored to their particular needs, the Merkava (Hebrew for chariot).

Tal and the Israeli tank planners well understood the predicament that has faced all tank designers since the development of the first British vehicle in World War I; the inevitable compromise between the three great tank requirements: mobility, firepower and crew protection. It was the substantial losses of tank crews that Israel suffered in their October 1973 War which caused them to give crew protection the highest prority in early planning for the Merkava. Their challenge was to find a way to design in the desired degrees of firepower and mobility, but not at the expense of crew survivability. It may have been the only occasion in the history of the tank when a nation has chosen to approach the problem in this way.

Their extensive experience of armoured warfare has taught the Israelis much about what happens to tanks and their crews in battle. That experience enabled them to conduct what may be the most thorough and exhaustive studies of ballistics as related to the tank, ever attempted. Their conclusion was that it is just as important for the tank itself to be protected, as its crew—something even more difficult to achieve. Greater protection, they reasoned, would enable the tank to get in closer to the enemy.

To provide maximum crew protection, the designers of Merkava positioned the entire crew at the centre of the tank so that they would be surrounded not just by the armour of the vehicle, but also by all the other elements and materials, for additional layers of shielding from incoming fire. Most modern main battle tanks have the engine located at the rear of the hull. For Merkava it was

Dawn revealed the spectacle of hundreds of burning and smoking Syrian tanks below the Israeli positions. But with the daylight came a renewed attack by more than 500 Syrian tanks on the relatively few remaining Israeli tanks. The Israeli armoured commander called for help from the IAF who responded quickly with jet fighters in an effort to halt or at least slow the progress of the Syrian tanks, but to little avail. All that remained for the Israeli tank commander was to gather his surviving tanks and take up a position in defence of the Nafakh camp brigade headquarters. The command group leader and most of his officers died in their tanks in the last ditch effort.

When Israeli reserve tanks wound their way up the ridge and surmounted it, they encountered a mass of Syrian T-54s, which they quickly destroyed. But in the previous actions the Israelis had lost most of their tanks and crews and were facing the real prospect of defeat. It was then that veteran armoured commander Jossi Ben Hannan, who had been abroad on leave, arrived and rallied the remaining Israeli tank forces in a new assault on the Syrians, who were also exhausted. The action broke the will of the Syrian force which began to withdraw from the battle arena which would be remembered by the combatants as the 'Valley of Tears.' The first phase of the Yom Kippur war was over.

"The great tank battles in the Sinai on 8 and 14 October [1973] involved close on 2,000 tanks on both sides. This number exceeded the great tank battles in North Africa during World War II as well as those in Normandy. Only the battle of Kursk in the summer of 1943 surpassed it. It is interesting to note, that while the British deployed some 1,100 tanks at El Alamein, the Germans had barely 200 tanks to counter them, with an additional Italian force which counted for little. However, while the Eighth Army lost almost half their number, nearly three times those lost by the Germans, their losses could easily be replaced, while those of the Germans became an almost total loss. The same situation applied to the Egyptian losses on 14 October. Another interesting aspect is the comparison between human losses. Although firepower and lethality had increased substantially when compared with World War II, with much more powerful tank guns available, the loss in human life actually decreased markedly.

"While losses of over 15,000 dead were suffered by the German and Italian forces at El Alamein, with the Eighth Army losing some 5,000, only a few hundred men were

right: Tank repair in field conditions is always challenging. Even the superb Merkava can be subject to breakdown.

decided to place the engine and transmission towards the front of the tank, adding another barrier between the crewmen and their enemy. The designers' guiding precept was that every operating part of the vehicle had to function optimally *and* be positioned in such a way as to add to protection. Even the diesel fuel tanks are designed into the walls of the Merkava hull which consist of an outer layer of cast armour and a welded inside layer, with the fuel contained between the two layers. In a brilliantly innovative concept, the fuel tanks have been developed to generate a hydrostatic pressure on impact from an incoming projectile. This pressure turns the fuel itself into a more resistant medium which actually pushes back at the projectile, turning the projectile's own energy against it.

To further expand the protective characteristics of Merkava, Israeli designers developed a system of panels of high explosive sandwiched between metal plates, which explode outward when hit by an incoming projectile. This Explosive Reactive Armour was in place on the early Merkavas but has been superseded on the most recent generation of the tank by a newer passive system of modular panels that can be quickly and easily replaced.

The Merkava driver is positioned forward and to the left, with the engine to his right. The engine, a Teledyne Continental AVDS-1790-6A is an uprated version of that used in the American M60 tank, which is also part of the Israeli arsenal. The later generation of Merkava is equipped with an Israeli-designed Ashot transmission system, so efficient that the tank's range has been increased by the changeover from the early mark's Allison to the Ashot. The tops of the tracks are shielded by steel covers which are backed with plates of a "special" armour to protect the tracks and the suspension from damage by HEAT (High Explosive Anti-Tank) weapons.

The turret of the Merkava is well-sloped at the front and has a small cross-section, offering a minimal target to enemy gunners, and it is also

reported killed by the Egyptians in the great tank battles. Even more amazing are the figures of tank losses in the British three-division tank attack during Operation 'Goodwood' in 1944. From a total of 650 medium tanks engaged, about half were stopped by enemy fire, of which 150 became a total loss. In some units, losses surpassed 80 per cent—the Germans lost 109 tanks, all of them totally. Such percentages were suffered by Israeli tactical units during the first stage of the Egyptian offensive only, the rate sharply reducing later on, as the front stabilised and tactics returned to normal. The Egyptians suffered severely during their later attacks, some units being virtually annihilated, mostly by accurate Israeli long-range tank gunnery.

"While the Egyptian 100mm gun, mounted in their T-54s and T-55s contrasted sharply in performance with the Israeli 105mm mounted in Centurion and Patton, the Soviet 115mm smoothbore gun was greatly respected. But superior Israeli tank gunnery achieved kills of Egyptian T-62s, even by the 75mm gun-mounted Sherman tanks in the Kantara sector, when fired from good hull-down positions. One more point which proved decisive in tank versus tank battles was the elevation and depression of tank guns. The marked difference of this factor between the Soviet

protected with a layer of the special armour. Inside the turret, to the right, sit the commander and the gunner, with the loader to the left. While many Merkavas feature an Israeli-produced, licensed version of the British L7 105mm gun as their principal armament, the current version of the tank has been fitted with a new 120mm high-pressure smoothbore gun that is said to be capable of amazing accuracy. The gun is equipped with a tracking device which can lock it onto a target and keep it aimed accurately even when the tank is moving at speed.

There are other aspects of this impressive vehicle that contribute to it being truly special. It can accommodate additional personnel and has a low-level entrance at the rear making escape, or the ability to evacuate infantrymen under fire, easier. It is also one of the most fire-proof tanks. It is believed that few, if any, Merkava crewmen have suffered burns in the tank resulting from combat. This is partly due to the crew being positioned in a dry, electrically-operated fighting compartment, and to the employment of fire-proofed munitions containers. The latest Merkava, the Mark III, is probably the safest tank in the world, affording its crews protection and confidence never before known by tankers of any army.

Coming out of a costly eight-year war with Iran, Saddam Hussein presided over a nearly bankrupt Iraq in 1988. He eyed neighbouring Kuwait, and her $22 billion a year oil income with more than casual interest. Kuwait's oil wealth in his pocket would provide just what he needed politically and economically to put Iraq back on her feet and reinforce his power base.

Sensing that the Western nations would raise little more than token complaints, he mustered a force of one million men, 6000 tanks and 600 aircraft and began massing troops along his border with Kuwait in the summer of 1990. While bridling at his move, Western leaders continued to

cling to the hope that Saddam was just blowing smoke, but on 2 August that hope was dashed as Iraqi forces moved into Kuwait and took control of 20 per cent of the world's oil resources.

The West was shocked, not only by Saddam's audacious move on his neighbour, but by the chilling implications of the ease with which he had accomplished it. Would he now try to extend his gains by continuing on into Saudi Arabia? Would he be emboldened to attack Israel?

In the evening of 2 August, American senate and congressional leaders, and the U.S. administration, began work on a reaction to the Iraqi move. After much debate they finally agreed on the necessity of developing a "coalition" of allied nations, united in its response to the Iraqi aggression. It would be essential to enlist the participation of Arab countries in this coalition and, while far from being unanimous in their support, the Arab League did vote to condemn Iraq. The United Nations resolved to condemn Iraq's actions and her assets in the West were frozen. After some difficult negotiation with the Russians, for whom Iraq had been a good customer over the years, and considerable discussion with Arab states about the matter of deploying American and other Western troops on Muslim territory, the coalition was formed and committed to use all necessary means to force an Iraqi withdrawal from Kuwait by no later than 15 January 1991.

With America taking the lead role in the coalition, U.S. General Norman Schwarzkopf was put in charge of the military operations, Desert Shield and Desert Storm. The chain of command was headed by President George Bush and included Secretary of Defense Dick Cheney and Chairman of the Joint Chiefs of Staff General Colin Powell. The coalition military build-up began immediately. As the planners saw it, it was essential to complete the build-up rapidly, and achieve their goal before March, the beginning of high summer in the Gulf region.

The nightmarish logistics involved in organizing

and transporting everything that would be needed to supply and equip the allies proved far more complex and difficult than anyone had imagined. In addition to weaponry, materiel, ammunition, supplies, vehicles and other equipment, there was the matter of coordinating vast numbers of troops and personnel from several coalition nations.

The first phase of the allied effort involved keeping Saddam's forces in a figurative box; denying them any possibility of escalating or widening their adventure, while the allies gathered strength and the wherewithall to begin the second phase. This would involve driving the Iraqis from Kuwait, a job seen by allied planners as potentially very tough. It was believed then that Saddam would welcome the coalition forces with everything he could muster—massed artillery, minefields, flaming oil-filled trenches and barbed wire as well as half a million troops and the armoured formations of the elite Republican Guard. The use of chemical weapons by the Iraqis was anticipated and extremely high allied casualties were predicted by some.

The coalition "air war" laid the foundation for the ultimate ground war, which Saddam would call "The Mother of All Battles." Using a standard of technology that the Iraqis could only dream of having, the allies began the operation on the evening of 16 January with strikes by cruise missiles and F-117A stealth fighter-bombers, destroying the Iraqi radar installations. The action virtually guaranteed that allied planes and missiles could operate in Iraqi skies with impunity. Within a month most of the objectives of the allied air campaign had been accomplished. The Iraqi supply and transport system, and most of their bridges, were destroyed, as were 1,300 of the 4,000 tanks Saddam then had in Kuwait.

By 22 February the coalition's preparations and build-up for their ground offensive against the Iraqi forces were complete. George Bush gave Saddam one last opportunity to withdraw his troops from Kuwait. The Iraqi leader responded with a boast that "the coalition troops would tumble into the great crater of death." The ground war was on.

On 23 February allied ground troops and armoured units rolled across the Saudi-Kuwaiti frontier. It was immediately apparent that allied estimates of the resistance they would meet were greatly overblown. Allied tank crews rolling to the border came to the dreaded "flaming trenches" and found them to be rather narrower than had been rumoured. American bulldozers quickly filled in crossing points and the tanks rolled on towards Kuwait City, followed by the arrival, some 70 miles inside Iraq, of the U.S. 101st Airborne Division. There they set up a base which was immediately occupied by American infantry and armoured cavalry elements.

Resistance by Iraqi tank crews proved futile against the vastly superior armour, training and technique of the allied tankers. The highly capable M1 Abrams American main battle tank was the primary weapon of the coalition armoured force. It performed brilliantly against the Soviet-built armour of the other side and easily gave the lie to pre-Gulf War critics who had claimed that the Abrams was excessively complex, difficult to maintain and out of action for servicing much of the time. In fact, the serviceability rate for the M1 in the Gulf conflict was 90 per cent. Only four of the 2000 M1A1 Abrams tanks in the Gulf War were put out of action in combat. None were destroyed. M1A1s destroyed more enemy tanks than any other weapons system of the war. Every one of the 57 Russian T72s operated by an Iraqi brigade in their flight from the conflict on 26 February was destroyed by the advancing allied tanks. By that date some 25,000 Iraqi troops had surrendered. Along what came to be known as the "Highway of Hell", hundreds more Iraqi soldiers were killed in their tanks and trucks when coalition aircraft attacked the road, destroying more than

ballistically well-designed, round-shaped turret, allowing limited depression and the higher turret of the Western design, especially the Patton, gave a substantial advantage for long-range tank gunnery during critical stages in the battle. Firing from well chosen hull-down positions against advancing enemy tanks within tactical ranges, the Israeli tankers were in their element.

"There is no doubt that by the end of the great tank battles on 14 October, the Israeli tanks had regained their marked superiority, placing the Egyptian ATGW [anti-tank missile] to its rightful place as a secondary support weapon in the regular combat mix."
— from *Chariots of the Desert*
by David Eshel

Israeli tank crews first encountered the formidable and numerically massive Egyptian Sagger ATGW and RPG-armed tank-killer infantry teams in the 1973 Yom Kippur War. Initially, the Israelis were shocked by the devastating effect of these weapons.

The Merkava was the inspiration of General Israel Tal, an important figure in the 1967 war. Tal believed instensely in the importance of designing a homegrown tank which would be tailored to Israel's specific requirements and ease her dependence on the United States and Britain for weaponry.

1,000 of the vehicles.

The entire ground action lasted about 100 hours. Iraq lost approximately 25,000 men. Coalition losses amounted to 150 dead. So much for the "Mother of All Battles".

"I was a Staff Sergeant at the time. I was platoon sergeant and a tank commander in 3rd Platoon, Bravo Company, 4th Tank Battalion. My crew was Corporal James Brackett (gunner), Lance Corporals Sean Edler and Rick Freier, loader and driver respectively. There were four tanks in each of the three platoons and two in the headquarters section; one for the commanding officer and another for his executive officer. A total of fourteen tanks in the company. My tank [an M1 Abrams main battle tank] was call sign "Titan Four," the fourth tank in 3rd (Titan) Platoon. Our crew nicknamed her the Rockin' Reaper after a tattoo on Brackett's arm that showed the grim reaper playing a guitar.

"Bravo Company, 4th Tanks, is a reserve unit from Yakima, Washington. They meet once a month for a weekend and two weeks each summer. They were trained on M60A1 tanks when they were called up for Desert Storm. We spent about two weeks, from 26 December 1990 to 15 January 1991, on new equipment training to learn the M1A1. We deployed to Saudi Arabia on 16 January and went into the desert the next day. We did not come out of the desert until late March.

"The day the war started, we had thirteen tanks. One had fuel problems, but we found the parts in the Army's Tiger Brigade and our fourteenth tank joined us as we sat waiting to go across the border. We crossed the border just before 5 a.m. and led the battalion as we approached the first minefield. The engineers attempted to breach the minefield, but lost three tanks and an amtrak in doing so. Our tanks started through, but the first one hit a mine. The crew was unhurt but the tank was a mobility kill [immobilized, but still able to fight].

In the Persian Gulf War of 1990-91, American M1 Abrams tanks destroyed more than 2,000 Iraqi tanks without the loss of a single Abrams in combat.

above: An oilfield fire near the end of the Persian Gulf War of 1990-91. Hundreds of oil wells were fired by the Iraqis in a final gesture of defiance. left: The M1 Abrams crew of tank commander Jeff Dacus in the Gulf. In addition to the excellent Chobham layered armour protecting the crew of the Abrams, the tank is equipped with an advanced thermal sight and laser range-finder system affording the gunner or the tank commander the ability to spot, identify, target and destroy their enemy even through smoke, dust storms, the extremes of weather and the dark of night. As for reliability, the M1s had a 90 per cent readiness for combat rate in the ground action phase of the Gulf War.

below: Chinese-built Iraqi T-69 and T-62 tanks of the Gulf War, on display at the Tank Museum, Bovington, England.

We went around the vehicle and continued on through the second minefield.

"We engaged in our first combat after reaching an east-west road that was heavily defended by dug-in troops and tanks. Infantry officers requested our assistance and my vehicle engaged the Iraqi trenches with coaxial machinegun fire. Iraqis poured out of their positions after that. Recalcitrant enemy forces were pounded by our tank guns. Dozens of enemy soldiers walked towards and through our company to prisoner of war cages. All the while, our guns engaged the enemy from 2,000 to 3,800 metres. My wingman, Corporal Glen Carter, destroyed two enemy tanks at ranges in excess of 3,700 metres. Enemy troops attempting to escape from the Marines to the east of us, used small vehicles; Ford Broncos or Toyota Land Cruiser types, to drive past us. Only the first one got by. They were travelling at upwards of 60 miles per hour, but our guns easily destroyed them. We

fought until the evening forced us to pull back. Mortar fire and the possibility of artillery had threatened our infantry support and they withdrew, leaving us in the lurch. This was called the Candy Cane Engagement because of the red and white striped towers that lined the east-west road.

"We coiled up for the night. Just before six the next morning, Captain Hart recognized the sound of Russian vehicles and two Marines, using thermal sights, spotted a brigade of Iraqi mechanized troops aiming for the logistical trains of our battalion and using a road that served as the boundary between our division, and the First Marine Division to our right. Despite the fact that most of the Marines were asleep, the effect was electric. Our company moved from a coil to a line formation and began firing. Due to morning haze, dust and darkness, they never saw us. The guns of their T72s were slightly elevated, indicating that they were attempting to load. They were

"The Egyptians, at first hard-hit, rallied fast. Infantry teams carrying Sagger anti-tank missile cases crept into position along ramparts on the east bank, dodging the bullets pinging around them as they went. The Egyptian artillery resumed its deadly barrage. The Israeli tanks were hit—and so were a number of enemy infantrymen, cut down by the artillery assigned to support them. Ranges were down to zero.

"Yaron's tank was hit below the turret by an Egyptian RPG rocket. Flames immediately blazed from the rear deck. Calmly, the tank commander stopped the driver and ordered fire extinguishing drill to be executed, as in training. But, despite the precision drill, the fire quickly got out of control, forcing the crew to bail out. A nearby tank stopped to pick them up. As they crowded into the already cramped interior, Yaron's crew did their best to stay out of the way, as their host tank went about its fighting business.

"Suddenly a flash of blood-red light enveloped the tank next to the one which had picked up Yaron's crew. The whole front of the turret seemed to melt into a reddish mass of molten steel. As the eight men huddled inside the rescuing tank watched horrified, a blazing shape thrust itself out of the commander's hatch and jumping to the ground,

rolled itself over and over in the sand, trying to extinguish the flaming overalls it wore. A crewman—the driver—jumped free of the tank; the other two were nowhere to be seen. Then with a fearsome roar, the tank exploded, flying fragments struck the commander and driver, killing them instantly."
— from *Chariots of the Desert*
by David Eshel

What's the greatest threat I might face in a tank? Anyone who can kill me without me seeing him. I have had good experiences in defense against choppers, but when the enemy comes in with a Hellfire missile, it's just too scary. Mavericks look like they are hard to defend against, but the few times I've been attacked by aircraft, we were in woods and my very strict policy was, don't flinch. Let the jet pass you by. The last thing you want to do is let a jet know where you are. Tracers work both ways. I really felt sorry for those Iraqi tankers who just died without being able to see who to shoot at.
— Jeff Babineau, U.S. Army tanker

obliterated. Our guns hit them from 1,200 to 1,800 metres from the side. The T72s blew up one after another, their turrets flying into the air. One flew up twenty or thirty feet before crashing back down. Several older tanks were also destroyed. A T55 took five hits and one round went completely through the turret. We looked at it after the battle and could see sunlight showing through from the other side. It was all over in about 90 seconds. We destroyed 34 enemy tanks, most of them T72s. We thought they were Republican Guard, but it turned out they were part of the Iraqi 3rd Mechanized Division. Several armoured personnel carriers were also flamed. There were few survivors, although Iraqi infantry surrendered when their armour was wiped out. This battle was called the Reveille Engagement because it happened as the Marines were being awakened for a 6:30 jump-off of the day's attack.

"We moved out at about 1300, north towards Kuwait City in poor visibility. We encounted enemy forces retreating and there were many short, sharp engagements. My favourite shot was a 2,000-metre hit on a T62 while we were moving at 30 kph. My thermal sights went out during the day, which was unfortunate as it was pitch black at 1600 due to oil smoke and dust. We reached our second night's position at an intersection of a fence and the north-south road. We spent the evening destroying enemy vehicles and killing infantry as the Iraqis attempted a counter-attack through their retreating troops. We received only desultory mortar fire in return.

"The next morning we moved on to Kuwait City. There was little opposition. Occasionally, a tank would spot a target and quickly destroy it, but the Iraqis were plainly heading out of town as fast as possible. We reached the edge of the main freeway that afternoon. We would be there for several days, through the ceasefire."
— Jeff Dacus, U.S. Marine tanker, Gulf War

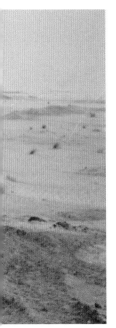

above left: An Iraqi T-72 abandoned south of Kuwait City after Operation Desert Storm. above: An Iraqi T-55 after the 100-hour Gulf War ground campaign. left: A U.S. Marine Corps Abrams tank during Desert Storm.

We make war that we may live in peace.
– Aristotle, 325 B.C.

In war there is no second prize for the runner-up.
– General Omar Bradley

Friends may come and go, but enemies accumulate.
– unknown

HOW TO STOP A TANK IN ITS TRACKS

WHEN THE TANK first entered military service with the British Army in World War I, its primary mission was to break through the enemy defences and enable British infantry elements to penetrate the German line and engage the opposition in open battle. The early successes caused the Germans to think about ways to defeat the new mechanical threat. Since then the world's armies have concentrated great resources on the design, development, production and utilitzation of both tank and anti-tank weaponry. Each new, seemingly invincible, tank design has ultimately been countered, or seriously threatened, by anti-tank weaponry, whether gun, rocket, grenade, mine or other device.

It was initially thought that a heavily armoured tank was more easily put out of action through wounding or killing the crew than through damaging the vehicle itself. The early tank was armoured with a form of boiler plate, protecting the crew from rifle and machinegun bullets and small shrapnel fragments. The driver operated the vehicle while peering through a narrow vision slit at the front of the tank, leaving him somewhat vulnerable to fire from German infantry ahead. Even though the likelihood of the enemy actually hitting the driver through that slit was slim, he and the eight other crew members were extremely vulnerable to metal fragment splash from rounds hitting near the slit. They soon adapted chain-mail visors or steel masks to protect against the splash effect.

Next to killing or seriously wounding the crew of a tank, the objective of the opposing force was to stop the vehicle by any means available, making it a stationary target and thus easier to destroy or eliminate as a threat. When a slow-moving tank of 1916 managed to breech the enemy line and advance into the open, it often became relatively easy game for opposing artillery which was likely to stop it.

The First World War brought other anti-tank concepts. Enemy infantry tried lobbing grenades onto the hulls of tanks as they approached, in an effort to injure the crew and cause damage within the vehicle by blowing a hole through its roof. Tank designers were quick to protect against this threat by putting a sloped, triangular "roof" of wood and wire netting over the tank. When a grenade landed on the roof it either exploded away from the hull itself, or fell off and exploded on the ground, doing little or no damage to the tank. Infantry personnel also tried, with varying success, to explode set charges beneath tanks as the vehicles crossed them. Attempts to stop enemy tanks with ditches or trenches often failed as the tanks were designed to cross such gaps.

In its infancy the tank was probably its own worst enemy, being slow, underpowered and unreliable. More often than not, it bogged down in mud, succumbed to some insurmountable obstacle or simply broke down mechanically, becoming an easy mark for enemy gunners.

As tanks became faster, more manoeuvrable, more reliable, better armed and better armoured during the 1920s, the efforts to find an effective counter intensified. The designers of anti-tank weaponry now focused on the most vulnerable aspects of their target. Apparent weaknesses in the tank structure such as the tracks, suspension and hatches were quickly exploited. The tank crew was re-targeted with new emphasis put on burning them out of action by attacking the inflammable fuel and ammunition carried in the vehicle. The use of rifle and machinegun fire to kill the driver either in his open hatch, or through his vision block was also emphasized. Greater attention was paid to finding weak points in a tank's armour as it became clear that the tank planners of the day were utilizing the heaviest armour on the turret and front of the hull, with thinner plating on the sides, rear and top surfaces.

In 1936 the Spanish Civil War provided a unique opportunity for the testing and evaluation of a wide variety of weaponry, from bomber and attack

196

aircraft through tanks (both light and heavy) and anti-tank systems. Italian and German light tanks there proved highly vulnerable to the relatively small-calibre anti-tank guns of the time, and to an early form of Molotov Cocktail, used by the Soviet-supported Republican forces. The most interesting tank-related lesson of the conflict, in terms of the approaching Second World War, was a German experiment in which their gunners employed a small number of 88mm anti-aircraft guns against a few hapless Soviet BT-4 tanks. So devastating was their effect on the tanks that the future development of German tank armament was dramatically influenced by the experiment.

By the end of the 1930s a new sophistication had invaded the field of tank design. The previous flat-slab look began to give way to a somewhat contoured shape as the advantages of a sloping surface came to light. It was realized that the probability of an enemy round deflecting off such a sloped surface was far greater than was the case with a slab-sided structure. Soon a combination of this "ballistic shaping" and a new welded-and-cast type of armour was defining the tank weapon for the 1940s. The use of welded seams in place of rivets increased the protection factor for tank crews substantially by eliminating the possibility of rivets being turned into potentially lethal missiles when the tank hull was struck by incoming rounds.

Tanks were now more powerful and faster, making them more difficult targets for enemy gunners to hit, but new anti-tank guns were able to fire larger, higher-velocity rounds with improved penetration which increased their lethality when a tank was hit. The new rounds soon reached a point of diminishing return however, when it was discovered that beyond a certain velocity, they actually shattered on impact with the new tank armour, leaving the vehicle relatively undamaged.

As the armour grew in thickness, strength and resistance to penetration, industrialists working on ways to defeat the tank turned their attention to the problems with their ammunition. Part of the trouble with existing anti-tank rounds was the steel of which they were made. The search for a harder, denser, more shatter-resistant material was on in earnest. The solution seemed to be tungsten carbide, but this, although affordable, was considerably heavier than steel and projectiles made of it therefore achieved much lower velocities than comparable steel rounds. At this point a German idea from the 1920s resurfaced when the Rheinmetall company succeeded in building a light anti-tank gun with a tapered bore. The new gun fired a shell with a tungsten core and a soft steel body mounted with "skirts" which were compressed around the body of the projectile as it travelled through the barrel of the gun. The effect gave both the high velocity and increased penetration power that the makers wanted. The new weapon proved quite effective in the North African desert engagements of 1942.

By 1943 work was under way in Britain on one of the most important anti-tank weapon concepts ever; the Armour-Piercing Discarding Sabot (APDS). A sabot is a lightweight carrier in which a projectile of a smaller calibre is centred so as to permit the projectile to be fired from within a larger calibre weapon. The carrier fills the bore of the weapon from which the projectile is fired and is normally discarded a short distance from the muzzle. The result of this effort, a 3 1/4 pound (at loading) round capable of achieving a muzzle velocity of 1,234 metres per second and penetrating 146mm of armour at a range of 915 metres, made its combat debut in Normandy during June 1944. This was progress and an impressive achievement. But the Germans, whose own supplies of tungsten were so limited that they were unable to allocate any of the precious material for further use in ammunition, had managed to develop and field vehicles in the form of the Tiger II and Jagdtiger (the latter a tank destroyer) with armour capable

overleaf: In his painting *Typhoon Target*, Robert Bailey depicts a German King Tiger tank, low on gas and nakedly exposed to air attack, running for the cover of trees, pursued by two Typhoon fighter-bombers of 440 Squadron, 143 Wing (RCAF), 2nd Tactical Air Force.

Robert Bailey ©2002

In the Soviet T-34, the Germans faced a masterpiece of tank design. Even with its 28-ton weight, the ground-bearing pressure on its 19-inch tracks was only ten pounds per square inch, giving it an amazing ability to cross soft ground. It also sported the revolutionary shaped, sloped armour which easily deflected many German gun rounds.

Among the most formidable tanks of World War II was the infamous German King Tiger, a 63-ton monster mounting an extremely accurate and deadly 88mm gun adapted from the highly-effective 88mm anti-aircraft gun. With room aboard for 64 88mm rounds, ample speed and heavily armoured, the King Tiger posed a major threat to Allied forces wherever it operated. But it was far from trouble-free. In combat conditions, it required an excessive amount of maintenance and was a difficult, demanding weapon to drive and fight.

right: Soviet BMP-1 armoured personnel carrier vehicles rolling in a Red Square parade in Moscow, 1967.

of standing up to the APDS. Additionally, the 88mm gun of the Tiger II was an overmatch for any tank at a range of 1,500 metres or more, while the 128mm gun of the Jagdtiger could deliver a round able to smash through armour of 200mm thickness at a 1,000 metre range. Their ammunition was developed without the use of tungsten.

In World War II several techniques were devised to attack and defeat tanks—methods which often relied on daring, skill and rather unsophisticated weaponry and which frequently placed the tank-killers at considerable personal risk. A lone soldier might, for example, attempt to sneak up on a tank to toss a grenade at it, or drop one into it through an open turret or hatch. The turret itself would sometimes be targetted in an effort by an enemy gunner to hit the turret ring, jamming or disabling the turret, and possibly the tank through injury to the crew. With the turret disabled, the tank was often a sitting duck, unable to offer much fight or defend itself. Another choice target was the engine compartment. It was sometimes attacked with explosive charges placed or attached appropriately, but this generally involved an heroic action on the part of the attacker at extremely high risk to himself.

The use of fire as a means of halting a tank by destroying or severely injuring the crew was thoroughly explored in that war. Many approaches to firing tanks were tried, with particular emphasis upon those which would ignite the ammunition and fuel supplies in the vehicle. The fear of being burnt to death while trapped inside must have caused many a tank crew to operate their vehicle in a completely buttoned-up condition in combat, to minimize the threat from such attacks. Opposing soldiers facing such closed-down tanks had to lob their Molotov Cocktails above the vehicle's vents in an attempt to fire the interior and either kill the crew or force it to evacuate the tank.

Among the most difficult of targets for the tank attacker were the tracks. These could theoretically be broken or damaged through the use of explosive charges or mines. If the charge failed to immobilize the tank by causing it to throw a track, suffcient damage to the suspension might still halt the vehicle.

It was the Soviets who, in the 1960s, determined to get the very most out of a tank gun by mounting a smooth-bore weapon on a tank. The idea involved reducing friction and thus gaining greater velocity by eliminating the barrel rifling. Of course, it was the rifling that stabilized the round in flight and added considerably to its accuracy on target. In time the Soviets solved the problem of how to have both velocity and accuracy by what became known as fin-stabilization. It enabled them to use the highly effective Armour-Piercing Discarding Sabot in the form of a long dart with a tungsten core surrounded by a sabot designed for the smooth gun bore. The result was greatly improved penetration and accuracy. In the '60s and '70s all nations operating tank forces became devotees of the Armour-Piercing Fin-Stabilized Discarding Sabot (APFSDS). The weapon itself was soon enhanced by the replacement of the tungsten core with one of depleted uranium. This nuclear by-product offered significant advantages over tungsten, not least being its greater density and punching power.

The next important achievement in the tank v. anti-tank competition came with the early '70s British development called "Chobham Armour", a still-secret compound believed to contain steel, plastic and ceramics, with tungsten blocks and rods embedded in it. It is considered most efficient in defeating both the APFSDS and the shaped-charge or HEAT (High Explosive Anti-Tank) weapon. A shaped-charge is one in which explosives are "shaped" around the outside of a copper cone. With the explosion of the warhead, the resultant energy is directed inwards and forwards, which creates a stream of gas and molten metal, forcing a metal slug to the front, which then melts through the tank armour. At the same time, Israel was creating Explosive Reactive Armour, a system which has become standard with most major tank users since the 1980s.

There is no more remarkable example of tank versus tank action than that of Hauptsturmführer Michael Wittmann against the tanks of the British 7th Armoured Division near Villers Bocage, Normandy on 13 June 1944. Born in Vogelthal, Upper Pfalz on 22 April 1914, Wittmann had entered the German Army in 1934 as a regular soldier before transferring to the Waffen SS in 1936. In September 1939 he participated in the Polish campaign as the commander of an armoured car and was promoted to Untersturmführer. After his participation in the invasions of France and Yugoslavia, he became a member of an SS Panzer Division and in November 1942 began training on the Tiger E heavy tank. On the Eastern Front he served with 13 Company of SS Panzer Regiment 1 Leibstandarte Adolf Hitler fighting in the Battle of Kursk, followed by service in Italy and another stint in Russia. Promoted to Obersturmführer in January 1944, he was transferred to Belgium, and then to France in time for the Allied invasion of Normandy.

As commander 2 Company SS Heavy Tank Battalion 101, he led a unit credited with destroying 119 Russian tanks and was heavily decorated for his achievements to June 1944.

At dawn on 13 June only four of the six Tiger tanks led by Michael Wittmann were serviceable. They lay in thick cover on a hill above the village of Villers Bocage, perfectly positioned to observe the tanks, personnel carriers and half-tracks of the 7th Armoured Division's A Squadron 4th County of London Yeomanry and A Company 1st Rifle Brigade as they rolled through the village and halted in a column.

Wittmann acted immediately. His lead Tiger

far left: A depleted uranium bolt in its sabot surround. The dart-like projectile of this Armour-Piercing Discarding Sabot round can penetrate the thickest tank armour. above: The interior of an FV 433 Abbot self-propelled gun's turret. An armoured fighting vehicle served by a crew of four, the compact, Rolls-Royce-powered Abbot was able to fire a wide range of ammunition including high-explosive squash-head rounds for use against everything except heavy armour. left: The 105mm projectiles for the Abbot gun.

In July 2000 it was reported that German landowners along the 650-kilometre Siegfried Line, a system of tank traps, concrete bunkers and gun emplacements from World War II, were furious about government plans to remove the last traces of the Line. The German government had announced that it would be spending millions to erase the fortifications of Nazi Germany's western defence line and that it expected some landowners to pay for the clearance of such facilities from their land, as it would benefit these farmers who would then have more land to farm. Strongly supported by environmentalists who want the Siegfried structures to stay because they are perfect havens for foxes, badgers and bats, the farmers steadfastly refused to cooperate with the German government in the plan. Enter hundreds of local politicians and war veterans who have joined the argument, taking the view that the Siegfried structures should be preserved as a massive memorial to the thousands of soldiers of both sides who died in the fighting there. They claim that the government is simply out to remove one more reminder of the the nation's Nazi past. The enormous stretch of concrete bunkers and anti-

emerged from its cover and took up a firing position adjacent to the village main road. His first shot destroyed a British half-track and the wreck lay blocking the road. With his Tiger rolling slowly along a lane parallel to the road, he fired round after round, methodically picking off the enemy tanks and other vehicles. The British tanks returned fire but the majority of their rounds made no impression on the heavily armoured Tiger. Now Wittmann's tank moved onto the village road itself and travelled into the village where he encountered and destroyed a number of artillery observation Sherman tanks along with a Cromwell attempting to position itself for a shot at the German. Satisfied with the morning's work, he withdrew from Villers Bocage, returning to the cover of the nearby hill.

In renewed tank fighting at the village that afternoon, the panzers faired less well, losing three Tigers and having three immobilized (including Wittman's). But the Germans had clearly won the day, having destroyed 25 7th Armoured Division tanks, 14 personnel carriers and 14 half-tracks. The British were forced to withdraw to the west of the village. As a result of this engagement, Michael Wittmann was promoted to his ultimate rank of Hauptsturmführer and received the Swords to his Knight's Cross. He was also offered an appointment to a German Officer's tactical school, which he declined, preferring to remain with his unit. It is generally believed that he was killed on 8 August near Caen while engaged in combat with British Sherman Firefly tanks, but this has been disputed in recent years. It has been claimed that his tank and crew were actually the victims of a rocket attack by an RAF Typhoon fighter-bomber. Other reports indicate that his demise resulted from an attack by heavy artillery.

In the summer of 1983, members of the German War Graves Commission, assisted by French and

British volunteers, found the remains of Michael Wittmann and his crew. These remains were later buried in a communal grave at the German war cemetery near La Cambe in Normandy.

Stopping tanks isn't always about weaponry. The weapons are the tools required and when one side has superior weaponry, the odds are that it will triumph. But frequently, what tips the odds is human judgement, intelligence and opportunism. Wittman's Tiger was indeed superior in many ways to the tanks of the 7th Armoured Division that June day in 1944, but the factors which led to such a one-sided victory for the Germans were more human than mechanical. The decision on the part of the British armoured commander to bring his tank column to a halt at Villers Bocage in a tight nose-to-tail column that morning effectively trapped all of his vehicles where they sat. They were left with no possibilty of escape and little ability to defend themselves, much less take up an offensive role against an enemy tank force that was known to be in the area. Wittman, on the other hand, observed, intelligently assessed and seized his opportunity, taking the fullest advantage of its possibilities. It is conceivable that he might have achieved a similar result had he been in command of a tank less formidable than the Tiger.

The idea for the tank destroyer stemmed from the assault gun, a weapon originally intended by the Germans to accompany advancing infantry and support them by knocking out anything likely to impede their further progress. Conventional wisdom suggested that mounting such a gun on what essentially was a tank chassis, provided increased mobility and protection for the crew, as well as a more economical alternative to the tank. This less costly, highly capable vehicle was simple in concept and construction. Lacking a rotating turret, it was easier to build and, with proper armament, proved extremely effective on the offensive as an anti-tank weapon, particularly when employed in an ambush position.

Little good can be said about the results of American and British efforts to build effective self-propelled tank destroyers in the early 1940s. It was not until late 1944 that the U.S. Army became fully operational with its evolved M-36, which mounted a 90mm gun firing a 24-pound armour-piercing shell able to penetrate 122mm of armour at a range of 915 metres. It was also capable of using a tungsten core round which had nearly twice the armour-penetration capability of the standard round. The U.S. 2nd Armoured Division was quite successful with the M-36 against various panzers in the final assault on Germany in early 1945. U.S. Army enthusiasm for offensive, highly-mobile tank destroyer vehicles able to aggressively hunt and kill enemy tanks culminated in the best tank dragon's teeth became widely known via the wartime song "We're Going to Hang Out the Washing on the Siegfried Line". The German government insists that the remaining structures of the Line must be removed because they are dangerous and the government is liable for any injuries that people suffer there. Farmers who live and work along the Line have been notified by the government that the work of filling in the old bunkers and dragging away the anti-tank defences was to begin within weeks.

left: Soviet troops exiting from their BMP armoured personnel carrier. The vehicle is armed with a 100mm gun.

above: The Skoda-built
German Jagdpanzer
Hetzer tank-destroyer of
World War II. right: The
interior of the Hetzer.

206

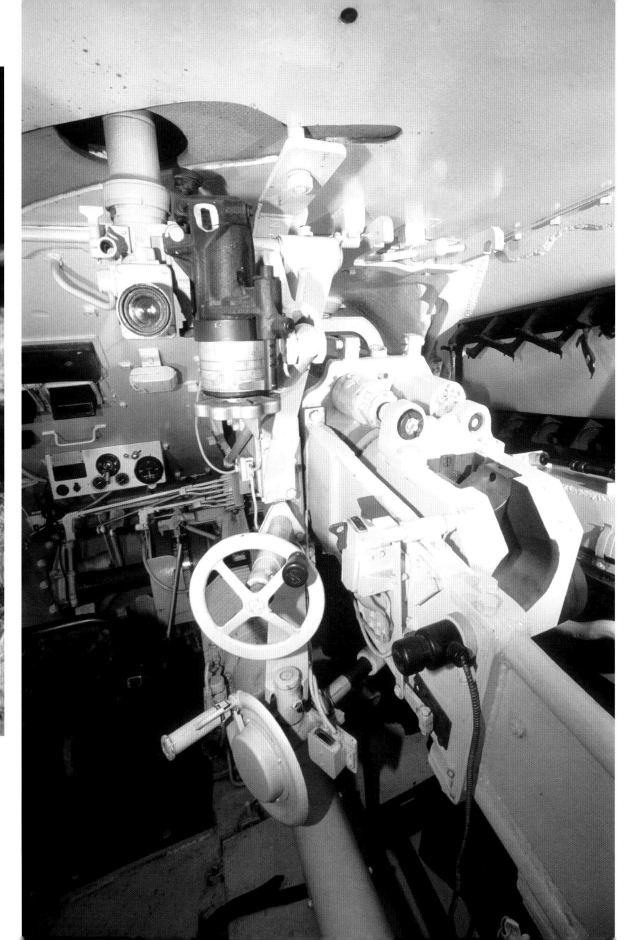

The only novel weapon of offence introduced was the anti-tank rifle. This was a huge affair, 5 1/2 feet long, and provided with biped legs and an ordinary wooden stock. It fired armour-piercing bullets of .530 [inch] calibre and had no magazine. It was obviously too conspicuous and too slow a weapon to be really effective against tanks, though the steel core could penetrate the armour of British tanks at several hundred yards' range. The chief disadvantage of the anti-tank rifle, however, was that the German soldier would not use it. He was untrained in its use, afraid of its kick, and still more afraid of the tanks themselves. It is doubtful if more than one per cent of the anti-tank rifles captured in our tank attacks had ever been fired.
– from *The Tank in Action* by Captain D. G. Browne, MC

below: U.S. 1st Marine Division M4s which have lost their footing on the icy roads of Korea in November 1950. right: The skipper and gunner of an American Whippet tank northwest of Verdun, France in 1918.

American example of the war, the M-18. Considerably smaller than the M-36, it weighed far less, had a better gun and was the fastest tracked vehicle of the war. With relatively light armour protection, M-18 crews counted on their manoeuvrability, speed and firepower to get them out of trouble in combat situations. It served with the U.S. and other armies into the 1960s.

Russian efforts to develop an effective counter to the newly-introduced German PzKpfw V Panther tank produced an important result in 1943, the SU-85, a clever modification of the very successful T-34 tank. In the SU-85, the T-34 turret was replaced by an armoured compartment mounting an 85mm anti-aircraft gun. It was a competent, useful weapon which eventually was redeveloped to accept a Soviet 100mm gun, making it more than a match for any German tank.

The impressive German Panther led directly to development of the Jagdpanther, a tank destroyer of great size (103,000 pounds) and capability. The Jagdpanther, with its 88mm gun, was able to kill any other tank at a safe range of 2500 metres.

Of the various types of anti-tank vehicles devised since the 1950s, the best is probably the Austrian SK 105 Jagdpanzer, a light-tank design with a 105mm gun. It is equipped with an automatic loader, eliminating one crew member, and fires a shaped-charge round capable of penetrating armour of 360mm thickness at a range of 1,000 metres. Another notable anti-tank vehicle is the Swedish Stridsvagn 103 (S-tank) developed after World War II. An indigenous heavy tank without a turret, its 105mm gun was fixed to the chassis and was aimed by turning the vehicle and adjusting the suspension height.

Following their involvement in the Spanish Civil War, when they provided Polikarpov aircraft to the Republicans and saw the planes used effectively against Italian-supplied tanks, the Soviets directed their Ilyushin design bureau to go to work on a

The German *panzerfaust* could penetrate our tanks with impunity, even through the extra armor we'd put in front of the driver and on the ammunition boxes on the side. These *panzerfausts* were obviously more powerful than our American bazookas.
– from *Death Traps* by Belton Y. Cooper

left: Crewmen of an American M1 Abrams main battle tank replenish their supply of High-Explosive Anti-Tank (HEAT) ammunition.

new anti-tank aircraft in 1937. The product of this effort was the Shturmovik ground-attack aircraft. More than 36,000 Shturmoviks were produced in World War II, and it was perhaps the best anti-tank aircraft of the war. The initial version carried only a pilot, but his vulnerability to attack from the rear led to a two-seat version in 1942 which accommodated a rear gunner for the protection of pilot and plane. Still, the attrition rate of Shturmoviks and their crews was terribly high. But their effectiveness against German tanks and other armoured vehicles was such that, coupled with Soviet industry's ability to produce the plane in numbers far surpassing the losses incurred, the Shturmoviks ultimately overwhelmed their adversaries. They pioneered successful aerial rocket attacks on German tanks while braving intense anti-aircraft fire.

Certainly, the British Hawker Typhoon ground-support fighter-bomber, which suffered a number of early developmental problems, came into its own as a very good and high-achieving machine by the time of the Normandy landings in mid-1944. Armed with four 20mm **Hispano cannon** in the wings and eight rocket rails under them, the 400 mph Typhoon became a near-perfect firing platform, excelling in ground attack and pounding German tanks in a performance second to none.

The main American aerial tank-killer in the final year of World War II was the Republic P-47 Thunderbolt, a big, heavy, escort fighter that could dive much better than it could climb. The Thunderbolt carried eight .50 calibre machine-guns and two three-tube rocket clusters and was on a par with the Typhoon in its ability to seek out and destroy enemy tanks, trains and other vehicles. But the greatest achievement by the Americans in the field of aerial anti-tank warfare is undoubtedly the Republic Fairchild A-10 Thunderbolt II, also known in the U.S. Air Force as the Warthog. Like its Second World War P-47 ancestor, the 1970's A-10 is a rugged aircraft, able to absorb and survive substantial battle damage. It brings a unique, amazingly powerful armament to the combat zone, a 30mm General Electric GAU-8/A Avenger seven-barrel Gatling-style cannon able to shoot at a rate of up to 4,000 rounds a minute. It carries up to 1,350 rounds of either high-explosive/incendiary or armour-piercing shot, the latter having a depleted uranium core with exceptional armour penetration capability. The A-10 delivers 65 of these rounds in a two-second burst, a barrage that has devastating effect on most modern tanks. The A-10 is the universally acknowledged king of the aerial tank killers.

With the coming of age of the combat helicopter in the 1960s and 70s Vietnam War, it became possible to mount a sighting unit on the rotor mast of such an aircraft, together with a small video camera, giving the crew the ability to hide low behind trees or hills while stalking a tank, sight, aim and rise briefly to launch a fire-and-forget missile before departing without ever having been a target themselves. What would become the state-of-the-art attack helicopter of the 21st century, the Boeing McDonnell Douglas AH-64 Apache, an awesome anti-tank weapon, entered development in 1976 armed with the American AGM-114 Hellfire (Helicopter-borne Fire-and-forget) missile. With a semi-active laser guidance system, the Hellfire can be launched either directly at its target, or indirectly, when the weapon will seek and find the target. It can follow the Apache laser designator to the target over a range of up to 3 1/2 miles. For the modern tank crew the Hellfire is the most fearsome of threats.

In 1916 German soldiers began using anti-tank rifles and machineguns, both of which fired armour-piercing (AP) bullets in an effort to cause bullet splash fragments to enter the British tanks and injure their crews. Such weaponry was only marginally successful and, in the early 1930s, a British Royal Artillery Lieutenant-Colonel named

Blacker began work on a design for a small high-explosive anti-tank bomb which could be placed over a rod or spigot and launched to a range of about 90 metres. In trials his "Baby Bombard" failed to impress, but later, in the hands of Major Mills Jefferis, Blacker's notion was revised and reinvented as the Projector, Infantry, Anti-Tank (PIAT) weapon, an awkward, cranky, extremely demanding device with the reputation of being almost as intimidating to the shooter as it was threatening to the target. Despite its quirks, the PIAT was used used effectively by the British Army through much of World War II.

Another significant method of attacking tanks in that war was the 60mm anti-tank rocket launcher known as the "Bazooka". Created by a U.S. Army colonel named Skinner, the bazooka was intended to provide the individual American infantryman with an appropriate way of defending against or attacking an enemy tank. It was simply a shoulder-supported steel tube for launching a rocket. It had two grips for aiming and the rear grip housed the trigger. Its rocket was capable of penetrating three inches of steel. It became the Bazooka when U.S. Army Major Zeb Hastings decided to name it after the musical instrument used by Bob Burns, the "Arkansas Traveller", a radio comedian of the time. The improved M-9 version could be broken down into two sections, making it easier to carry. A larger, 88.9mm version followed which was an excellent anti-tank weapon in the Korean conflict from 1951. It was known as the Super Bazooka. Nearly half a million bazookas were used by the U.S. and Allied armies in World War II.

The Germans also developed a bazooka-type weapon, an 88mm adaptation called Panzerschreck (Panzer terror) and it was even more effective than the bazooka. But they had an acute shortage of the required nitrocellulose rocket propellant and began development of a shaped-charge alternative. The result was the Panzerfaust (Armoured Fist), a disposable anti-tank launcher capable of firing a round that could penetrate 140mm of tank armour and ruined the day of many an Allied tank commander. The Panzerfaust contained a hollow-charge bomb at one end, which was propelled by a small charge of gunpowder and the firing was nearly recoil-less. The early version was difficult to aim and was soon replaced by the Panzerfaust 30, whose warhead had a substantially larger diameter than that of the launch tube. The new bomb had four flexible fins which were wrapped around the boom. The fin section fitted into the tube and the shooter held the launch tube under his arm, aimed and fired. The range of the weapon was about 30 metres. It entered full production in late 1943 and was followed in mid-1944 by two advanced versions offering increased ranges of 60 and 100 metres.

After the war, the Allies learned that the Germans had been making important progress in their development of an anti-tank missile known as the X-7. It was to be the forerunner of all such future weapons. The X-7 could be directed onto its target and deliver a far more destructive payload than that of any anti-tank gun. A French derivative of the X-7 was first used in combat by the Israelis in 1956. They later found themselves on the receiving end of a Soviet version called the Snapper in their 1967 conflict with the Egyptians.

Little was achieved in the area of individual anti-tank weaponry after World War II until the 1960s when the Russians came out with the RPG-2 (a weapon similar in style to the Panzerfaust), having a tube which launched an oversized grenade with fins and did so without recoil. While the range of the RPG-2 was just 150 metres, the shot could penetrate up to 180mm of armour. The weapon was later cloned by the Chinese who reworked it to fire a High-Explosive Anti-Tank (HEAT) warhead which could go through 250mm of armour. Then the Russians went one better with the RPG-7, in which the grenade was now powered by a small rocket motor. The warhead was still fired initially

He woke the other two men in his foxhole. They had been curled in their ponchos, and they got to their feet uncertainly. At the same moment an orange signal flare shot up from the Japanese lines. A singsong voice shouted into the night, and an avalanche of screaming forms bounded suddenly into view. With their bayonets gleaming in the light of sudden flares, they charged toward the Marine foxholes, throwing grenades and howling: *"Ban-zai-ai!"* like a pack of animals.

The Marines awoke with a start. Along the ridge, wet, groggy men bolted to their feet and grabbed their weapons. Grenades exploded like a crashing curtain against the onrushing Japs. A man on a telephone yelled for uninterrupted flares, and flickering lights began to hang in the air like gian overhead fires.

All along the line the enemy attack was on. Red tracer bullets flashed through the blackness. Japanese orange signal flares and American white illumination shells lit up the night like the Fourth of July, silhouetting the running forms of the enemy. On the right and the left the attack was stopped cold. As fast as the Japs came, they were mowed down by automatic rifles and machine guns. The enemy assault gradually focused on a

by the old recoil-less charge, but once it left the tube its little motor ignited and dramatically accelerated it to the target up to 500 metres away. On arriving it could penetrate 320mm of armour and do appalling damage to the interior of a tank. The secret of its success lay in a new recipe for the explosive and a new way of "packaging" it. The Americans first experienced the effects of the RPG-7 when hit with it by the Viet Cong in 1966. The RPG-7, and an American one-man anti-tank weapon developed at about the same time, the M-72 LAW(Light Anti-Tank Weapon), were also significant in that they caused many nations to re-focus on the need for a really effective advanced one-man anti-tank weapon system. During this period the RPG-7 became the standard type for all Soviet-bloc countries, while the M-72 was adopted by the NATO alliance and some other Western nations. The M-72 was most effective at 300 metres and was able to penetrate 300mm of armour at that range. It was a 66mm rocket launcher made up of two concentric tubes which fired a shaped-charge warhead with a small rocket motor. It was shoulder-fired and was used to great effect in Vietnam and in the 1982 Falklands War.

Among the most interesting weapons of that era is the Swedish Carl Gustav, an 84mm recoil-less anti-tank gun that is fired from the shoulder and can utilize a range of ammunition types to tackle a variety of combat tasks. Another superb weapon is the BILL, (Bofors, Infantry, Light and Lethal) which is also a Swedish design. The BILL is a truly revolutionary missile system. It contains a thermal imaging (TI) sight to detect heat from such sources as tank and armoured fighting vehicle engines. Wire-guided, the BILL is specifically intended to target the vulnerable upper surfaces of tanks, which it attacks by overflying the target at low-level. When its guidance computer senses that the missile is in proper position, it detonates a downward-firing shaped-charge which then penetrates the thinner upper-surface armour of

draw where some American tanks were parked. The tanks fired their 75s at the charging masses. At first the Japs attacked the steel monsters like swarms of ants, firing their rifles at the metal sides and clambering up and over the tanks in a vain attempt to get at the crews inside. They screamed and pounded drunkenly on the turrets and locked hatches, but in their excitement they failed to damage a single tank. Finally, as if engaged in a wild game of follow-the-leader, many of them streamed past the tanks, down the draw toward the beach.

The rest, cringing before the tank fire, moved to the left, hoping to break through our lines and get to the draw farther down the slope of the ridge, behind the tanks. The front they now charged was that of B Company. Here, against the 75 men, the full force of the Japanese attack broke.
– from *Banzai on Guam* by Alvin M. Josephy, Jr.

left: The German World War II military cemetery at La Cambe, Normandy, France, where the tank ace Michael Wittman is buried.

215

the tank with deadly effect.

As impressive as the various shoulder-launched shell and rocket projectiles were, they made relatively little difference to the heavy tanks of the day with their massive front armour. Furthermore, in some conditions they could be hazardous to their users. These limitations and drawbacks, together with significant advances in shaped-charge technology, led directly to the development of one of the best such weapons yet devised, the British LAW 80 94mm rocket. Incredibly, the LAW 80 warhead can penetrate more than 700mm of armour at an effective range of 500 metres. This amazing weapon is part rocket launcher and part 9mm aiming rifle. The operator simply fires a tracer/ explosive bullet from the aiming rifle at the target tank. If his shot is accurate, he selects "rocket" and fires again, this time sending a 3.7 inch missile to the same aiming point hit by his tracer round. If his aiming round missed the target, he fires another tracer, and another, until he hits the tank. He then shoots it with a rocket.

Of the so-called "smart" weapons, two are quite special: the TOW and the MILAN. The TOW(tube-launched, optically tracked and wire guided) is a 1960s product of the American Hughes company and has been steadily upgraded and improved since the initial model whose range was 2750 metres. It is the best anti-tank guided missile there is. The current version is able to penetrate armour plate of 800mm or 31 inches. The missile, in a sealed tube, is clipped to the back of a launcher tube which is equipped with the sight and guidance system. Refinements have included a shaped-charge warhead version designed to defeat explosive reactive armour, and one which is dedicated to attacking the thinner and more vulnerable upper surfaces of tanks, utilizing special sensors and charges that can fire downwards while the warhead overflies the tank. Since establishing

From a May 1943 U.S. Army Orientation Course:
You can crack that tank!
1. BUTTON HIM UP—Tank crews have limited vision even with the ports open. Accurate rifle fire will force them to close up.
2. THEN BLIND HIM—Continued fire directed at the periscope and slits prevents the crew from shooting back at you accurately.
3. DUCK! DON'T RUN—Above the ground where you are visible you make an easy target. Hide in your foxhole until the tank passes. THEN—let him have it with a well-placed Molotov cocktail splashing burning gasoline over his ventilator or any other vulnerable spot.

left: June, 1918. A French "37" in firing position on a parapet in a second-line trench, ready and waiting for an enemy tank.

217

To me, one of the greatest tragedies of World War II was that our armored troops had to fight the Germans with a grossly inferior tank compared to the heavy German panzer units. Before we went into Normandy, we had been led to believe that the M4 Sherman main battle tank was a good tank, thoroughly capable of dealing with German armor on an equal basis. We soon learned that the opposite was true. The 3rd Armored Division entered combat in Normandy with 232 M4 Sherman tanks. During the European Campaign, the Division had some 648 Sherman tanks completely destroyed in combat and we had another 700 knocked out, repaired and put back into operation. This was a loss rate of 580 percent.
– from *Death Traps* by Belton Y. Cooper

right: A line of "dragon's teeth" anti-tank obstacles at Cripp's Corner, Sussex, England.

itself as the king of sophisticated anti-tank missiles when operated by Israel in the 1973 Arab-Israeli War, it has become the anti-tank weapon of choice in the inventories of many armies the world over. MILAN (Missile, Infanterie, Légère, Anti-char, or infantry light anti-tank missile) is the product of a French/German consortium, Nord Aviation and Bölkow (later joined in the effort by British Aerospace.) It is a wire-guided infantry missile fielded by two men. It can be set up and ready to fire in seconds and, once fired, a hit is assured as long as the shooter keeps his sight aligned on the target. The advanced MILAN 3 carries a warhead with two shaped charges. One charge is on an extended probe ahead of the main warhead charge. This "precursor" charge hits and destroys any reactive armour that is protecting the main armour of the target tank. This action is followed instantly by the detonation of the main warhead charge, which can penetrate more than a metre of armour. MILAN 3 has both day and night thermal imaging capabilities, is efficient at overcoming countermeasures, such as pyrotechnic flares, and is not fooled by distractions such as the heat source of a nearby burning vehicle.

Even though anti-tank weaponry has become more and more sophisticated, there is still a place for the basic tank-stoppers: fixed barriers and mines. The tactical minefield became a defence against enemy tanks with the development of contact and pressure mines which were set off by the track pressure over the mine. The most common tank obstacles appeared before World War II at the Maginot Line in France, along the German frontier with Czechoslovakia, in the Low Countries and, later, in England. They were called "Dragon's Teeth", made of concrete, often pyramid-shaped (some rectangular) and usually about one metre high. They were laid across probable tank routes, six ranks deep and virtually guaranteed to stop any tank that dared try to cross them. Simple and effective.

TANK MAN

Government is not reason, it is not eloquence, it is force; like fire, a troublesome servant and a fearful master.
– George Washington

The tank is more than a killing machine, more than a battlefield menace. In many parts of the world since the Second World War, tanks on the streets have often been the first sign of violent political change, a military coup or the imposition of a repressive regime.

Politicians have long recognized the value of the tank in the intimidation and repression of civilian populations. Its awesome appearance can be traumatizing, especially in an ordinary urban context. Patrick Wright, author of *Tank*, a superb cultural history of the weapon, comments: "People talk about the tank as a rational instrument of warfare—you get lots of them, then you mass them together and you advance—but it's always had a symbolic dimension as well. It is a monstrous object that crawls towards you and you don't know what it can do to you, but it scares you almost to death. It would be quite wrong to ignore this. The symbolic force of this weapon makes it very well attuned to modern peacekeeping-type operations. It may take two months to get it there, but if you put a tank on a bridge things tend to settle down."

In the last half of the twentieth century, ordinary citizens of several nations faced invading tanks and, for a while at least, stood their ground in defiance of clearly overwhelming force and fear.

On 4 November 1956, Hungarian Prime Minister Imre Nagy spoke to his people in a dramatic radio broadcast as Soviet armour assaulted Budapest. "Soviet troops attacked our capital with the obvious purpose to overthrow the legitimate Hungarian government. Our troops are fighting. The government is in its place".

Shortly after the death of Premier Josef Stalin in 1953, the Soviet leadership became aware of a growing disenchantment with the oppressive communist system in the satellite nations, Hungary being a prime example. The Soviets ordered the hardline Hungarian Communist Party boss, Matyás Rakosi, to Moscow for consultation.

following spread: The tank man of Tiananmen Square in Beijing on 5 June 1989, defying a column of 18 Chinese Norinco main battle tanks at the massive protest demonstration.

He was directed to relax the pressures then being applied by his regime on Hungary's industry and collective farms, to soften his "reign of terror" approach, and to work towards a higher living standard for his people. Finally, he was required to ordain fellow communist Imre Nagy as the new Hungarian Prime Minister. Nagy was a moderate with considerable popular support. He was known for opposing the communist policies of terror and forced industrialization and collectivization. He was a reformer who wanted to liberalize communism in his country, but without any major shift towards capitalism. He began his programme in July with what he called "the new stage in building socialism".

In little more than a year after the death of Stalin, the Soviet flirtation with a more relaxed form of communism appeared to be ending as hardline policies came back into vogue. In Hungary, Rakosi saw the opportunity to regain his former stature and embarked on a programme to de-stabilize Nagy's government. In March 1955, emboldened by the Russian winds of change, he sacked Nagy and reimposed terror on Hungarians.

But with the coming of a new Soviet Communist Party chief Nikita Khrushchev, and his February 1956 denunciation of Stalin, Rakosi's little empire in Hungary began to unravel and by the summer he had been dismissed.

Unrest in Hungary, Poland and elsewhere in the Soviet satellite states was growing rapidly. On 22 October the people of Budapest learned of a change of leaders in the Polish communist party. Wladislaw Gomulka, like Nagy, a relative moderate, was the new party boss, ousting the former Stalinist regime in Warsaw. His rise to power triggered a prompt Soviet reaction. Khruschchev flew to the Polish capital as Soviet military forces mobilized to move on the rebellious satellite state. A clash was averted, however, as the clever Gomulka carefully maintained his stance within the federal system of the Warsaw Pact. On hearing of the party changes in Poland, students of the Budapest Technical University were inspired to create a 16-point list of demands. They then called for a peaceful gathering on 23 October to demonstrate their solidarity with the people of Poland and declare their demands. Walls all over the city were plastered with posters calling for freedom. The demonstrators were demanding a complete withdrawl of the troops, the abolition of censorship, establishment of a multi-party political system with free elections, economic independence and the re-establishment of traditional national symbols and holidays. They were supported by much of the citizenry. A broad spectrum of politics was represented as leftists, communist reformers, social democrats, religious leaders, conservatives and even some right-wing elements joined the movement. Ordinary citizens defied the government and got their news by listening to the banned Radio Free Europe. The Hungarian Revolution was under way.

The initial violence occurred when Hungarian secret police opened fire on activists who were attempting to occupy the headquarters of Radio Budapest on the 23rd. Elsewhere in the country revolutionary groups were quickly being formed and a general political strike was organized. Student and general demonstrations erupted in the many town squares where the protestors frequently focused their attentions on dismantling and destroying the hated symbols of repression. Down came Soviet war memorials, red stars and, in perhaps the most defiant of vandalisms, the activists set about the massive statue of Stalin in central Budapest, attacking it with hammers, toppling and decapitating it. In the wake of all this action, Imre Nagy was once again brought in as Prime Minister.

By the 25th the Hungarian situation had worsened significantly. In an ugly scene at the parliament building, unarmed demonstrators were fired on by soldiers in an effort to suppress the uprising. There, and in other parts of the country, hundreds of protestors were killed. Gradually, however, many

Hungarian soldiers began changing sides and joining the ranks of revolutionaries.

Two days after the shootings, Imre Nagy told the nation that he had formed a new government which incorporated non-communists and intended to negotiate the withdrawal of Soviet forces from Hungary. Under new management, Hungarian Radio followed the Nagy announcement with one in which it supported the protestors. But while the Soviet troops had withdrawn from Budapest, they remained poised in the countryside, ready to move forcefully against the activists. On 1 November, with the troops refusing to withdraw further, Nagy acted by withdrawing Hungary from the Warsaw Pact alliance and declaring his nation's neutrality. By doing so Nagy renounced the policies of his own party and the international communist movement. The Kremlin reacted immediately.

On 3 November, Soviet army generals were in discussions with officers of the Hungarian army about Soviet troop withdrawl. The talks were a sham and the Hungarian delegation was arrested by Soviet security forces. On 4 November, Soviet military forces moved in a savage attack on Hungary and in a few days put an end to the rebellion. Imre Nagy and his top officials, who had sought refuge at the Yugoslav embassy in Budapest, were given assurances of safe conduct out of the country. When they tried to leave, they were quickly taken into custody by the Soviets who then installed their own puppet government headed by János Kádár, who had won Soviet support by opposing the rebellion.

Now Soviet tanks and armoured vehicles clattered down the main streets and boulevards of Budapest, firing indiscriminately as they rolled. Young armed activists fought back, shooting, shouting and hurling Molotov cocktails (bottles filled with gasoline) at the tanks. Many homes and buildings were destroyed as the Soviets forceably put down the revolt. Token resistance continued until early in 1957, but the revolution had failed. A new reign of terror had begun. Some 25,000 Hungarians were arrested and

"Socialism with a human face," was what Czechoslovak communist party leader Alexander Dubcek called his 1968 effort to reform the political and social policies of his nation. The reform movement, now referred to as Prague Spring, is seen by many as the precedent for and forerunner of Soviet leader Mikhail Gorbachev's glasnost and perestroika reforms of the USSR in the 1980s.

Dubcek became party leader on 5 January 1968, replacing Antonin Novotny in that role. Novotny had been reviled by many party members for a poor economic performance during under his leadership. The reform movement under Dubcek soon expanded beyond economic reforms to demands by students, journalists and intellectuals for an end to press censorship. On 22 March, Novotny was finally ousted from his job as President of Czechoslovakia and was replaced by General Ludvik Svoboda, a respected war hero.

The reform process went forward under Dubcek and his colleague, Oldrich Cernik, with publication of the Action Program of the Communist Party, calling for a ten-year reform of the political and economic systems and referring to the "unique experiment in democratic communism".

incarcerated in the two years following the revolt; 230 were executed. Almost 200,000 refugees fled the country to freedom in Britain, the United States and elsewhere.

In 1949 Mao Zedong stood in Beijing's Tiananmen Square and proclaimed a "People's Republic" on behalf of the people of China. The square, near the Gate of Heavenly Peace leading into the Forbidden City, had been the scene of student demonstrations as early as 1919 and has, since 1949, been the venue where the Chinese leadership reviews the troops of the People's Liberation Army.

Forty years after Mao's proclamation, student and worker members of China's pro-democracy movement, gathered to take back Tiananmen Square for a seven-week period in the spring of 1989. They were joined by educators, doctors, soldiers and others and eventually numbered more than one million, many of whom had seen operating democracies while on visits to the United States and Britain.

The demonstration had started on 15 April after the death of Hu Yao Bang, the former Secretary General of the Communist Party of China, who had been demoted and disgraced when he was accused of being in sympathy with student pro-democracy demonstrators in 1987. Thousands of students went to Tiananmen Square to honour Hu Yao Bang and were soon joined by workers and intellectuals. The action of the demonstrators was quickly condemned by the government in a letter to the *People's Daily*, describing the students' behaviour as "an act of treason". Police freely used their truncheons to control the demonstrators. This caused many more thousands of students and their supporters to come to the square to denounce the violence and express their anti-government views.

The dissidents produced a daily newspaper which protested against government corruption and demanded political democracy in their country. They broadcast their message, and the speeches of

It stated that the Communist Party would now have to stand against other parties in elections. Enormous popular support for the reforms was evident in that year's May Day celebrations.

The Soviet rulers, dismayed by the turn of events in Czechoslovakia, called the Czech leaders to Moscow for a dressing down, which was followed on 29 May by a visit of Soviet military officials to Prague, ostensibly to plan upcoming military exercises. The split with Moscow was extended on 26 June when Dubcek officially abolished censorship in Czechoslovakia. The authorities in the Kremlin were not amused and ordered Soviet-led military exercises to begin in Czech territory on 4 July in a move aimed at shoring up anti-reformists there. In the next fortnight members of the communist parties of the Soviet Union, Poland, Bulgaria, East Germany and Hungary met in Warsaw to draft a harsh warning to the Czech leadership that its policy of reform was jeopardizing the vital interests of the other socialist countries. By 29 July the Soviets were in no mood to listen to Dubcek's argument that his reforms were building public support for the party. They were highly critical of his policies and beginning to threaten

223

invasion. Two days later it was announced that new military exercises were to be held near the Czech border by forces of the Soviet Union, Poland, Hungary and East Germany.

In the following week a meeting of the Warsaw Pact nations was held at which five members of the Czech Presidium delivered a note to Soviet President Leonid Brezhnev stating their fear for the socialist order and requesting Soviet military intervention. The crisis point was reached on 18 August when Brezhnev decided to invade Czechoslovakia and on the 20th and 21st, 500,000 Warsaw Pact troops entered the country. Russian tanks rumbled through Prague's Wenceslas Square and Alexander Dubcek, Cernik and the other leading Czech reformers were promptly arrested and flown to Moscow where they were required to sign a document renouncing many of the reforms they had instituted. They were also made to accept the continued quartering of Soviet troops in Czechoslovakia. By 8 p.m. on the 21st crowds of Prague citizens were being contained by Soviet troops in the Old Town and Wenceslas Squares. Tanks were firing upon the National Museum and some nearby buildings causing great damage.

The Soviet invasion of Czechoslovakia, in which more than 100 Czech

their heroes, from a radio tent in the square and they created a 30-foot statue which they named the Goddess of Democracy. It was erected to face the massive poster of Mao there. At the southwest corner of the square was a Kentucky Fried Chicken shop which the demonstrators used as their headquarters and meeting place. Their struggle for human rights had been non-violent and a remarkable expression of will and determination.

On 14 May more than 2,000 of the protestors were engaged in a hunger strike as more than 100,000 occupied the square. In the following days their numbers grew rapidly to nearly one million. They began shouting for government reforms and the resignation of the Chinese leader, Deng Xiaoping. Their calls were a supreme embarassment to the government which, at that moment, was hosting Mikhail Gorbachev, the first Soviet head of state to visit China in thirty years. In a conciliatory gesture, Deng Xiaoping called on the hunger strikers in hospital and then agreed to meet with the student protest leaders. In the meeting Deng did not accede to their demands. He warned the Chinese people of the repercussions that awaited those who became involved in the protest movement. On 20 May the hardline Premiere Li Peng branded the protest action a "riot". He declared martial law in Beijing and called in troops from the countryside. By the following day the People's Liberation Army had taken over all newspapers, television and radio stations in Beijing. On the 22nd, the government shut down the satellite feed to North America and Europe.

Key members of the government were divided over what measures they should take to quell the protest. Deng advocated suppression by the use of any force necessary, but others around him wanted no part of that. Unarmed soldiers had no effect on the demonstrators who surrounded their vehicles. By 29 May the government had declared the students and the other demonstrators "hooligans" and "bad elements"; counter-revolutionaries who were liable to be arrested and shot. On 2 June more

than 200,000 soldiers had moved into Beijing. Deng's patience was exhausted. He ordered the army to retake Tiananmen Square at all costs. By noon on the 3rd, PLA soldiers had entered the square and were hitting people with truncheons as well as tossing tear gas cannisters to disperse the crowds. In a broadcast the government then warned that it had the right to deal forcefully with the "rioters". The people of Beijing were instructed to stay indoors. At 2 a.m. on 4 June, units of the PLA 27th Field Army surrounded the square and by 4 a.m. its soldiers had opened fire on the protestors. The amry brought in tanks from all directions towards the square and hundreds of the unarmed demonstrators, including many children, were killed. The Chinese Red Cross estimated that up to 2,600 students and civilians died in the tragic action, which quickly attracted worldwide condemnation of the Chinese government.

The next day the shocked and outraged activists steadfastly refused to leave Tiananmen. Elements of the People's Liberation Army occupied the square and were endeavouring to secure their supply lines, as a column of eighteen Norinco Type 69/59 main battle tanks advanced down Chang'an Boulevard, the Avenue of Eternal Peace. The BBC's Kate Adie described what happened next: "Just after midday the tanks rolled out of the square. A lone young man stood in front of the first one. The tank faltered; came to a stop . . . . It was an extraordinarily purposeful but mundane way of doing things . . . . It seemed impromptu. There he was with his little plastic bag—such a human touch, as if he had been shopping."

Wang Weilin. It may or may not be the real name of the unknown rebel who defied the Chinese Communist regime that day in one of the most courageous acts of all time. He was a slight figure in white shirt and dark slacks. In his left hand he held a shopping bag. He moved towards the approaching tank column and positioned himself directly in front of the lead tank, which stopped and then attempted to swerve to the right around the man, who moved left to block it. It then tried to swerve to the left and he moved right. The man then climbed up onto the front of the tank to speak to the driver. The writer Pico Iyer reported the rebel's words to the driver as: "Why are you here? My city is in chaos because of you." Little is known about the young man who defied the might and power of his government that June day. *Time* magazine has cited the unknown protestor as one of the "top twenty leaders and revolutionaries of the 20th century." It is widely believed that he was a 19-year-old student. His actual identity is still a mystery, as is his fate. According to the Information Center for the Human Rights and Democracy Movement in China, the Communist Party authorities have never found Wang. They quote Jiang Zemin, the Party General Secretary in 1990, as saying: "We can't find him. We got his name from journalists. We have checked through computers but can't find him among the dead nor among those in prison." When asked about the fate of the young rebel by the American television interviewer Barbara Walters in a 1992 conversation, Jiang responded: "I think never killed."

The powerful image of The Tank Man, Wang Weilin or whatever his name may be, posed resolute in front of that Chinese tank, is a familiar one to hundreds of millions of people around the globe. It has become an icon of defiance and one of the most famous and recognized photographs of all time. Of the Tank Man, Patrick Wright has written: "The image has been subject to much interpretation in the West . . . . The military historian John Keegan declares it a merely 'poetic image', a story of 'impersonal armed might of the army lined up against the unvanquished human spirit.' He then breaks to say, drily, 'You can write the words yourself.' Some newspapers have certainly done that. Tantalised by the image of this man who is universally known and yet almost

completely obscure, newspapers have felt obliged to augment the story. One report confirmed Wang's status as a student by putting books in his bag, and there were diverse variations on the words he is said to have shouted at the tanks, from the simple 'Go away' of the *Sunday Express* to 'Go back, turn around, stop killing my people' elaborated by *Today* a week or so later." In the British Parliament, Neil Kinnock, then leader of the Labour Party, said: "The memory of one unarmed young man standing in front of a column of tanks . . . will remain . . . long after the present leadership in China and what they stand for has been forgotten." On 4 June 1998, the ninth anniversary of the Tiananmen Square tragedy, United States Senator Paul Wellstone addressed the Senate: "Like everyone who witnessed that brutal massacre, I can not forget the image of that lone, courageous figure, Wang Weilin, standing firm and holding his ground against the oncoming PLA tanks. China's leaders have tried to convince the world that freedom and democracy are Western ideals, contrary to Asian values. Their rhetoric would have us believe that maintaining repressive policies is essential to the preservation of their cultural and national identity. The image of Wang Weilin tells a different story; a story of the human spirits' incredible determination and sacrifice for liberty and freedom."

Since the events of June 1989, the Chinese government has sought to mollify the people with the prospect of greater individual material wealth to be achieved through an increase in the pace of economic development, this in lieu of greater political rights. Some personal freedoms have also come to pass, including the right to choose one's job and to relocate. Such gains have functioned as a limited diversion from the political activism of the recent past, but the memory of Tiananmen Square, of the Tank Man and the spirit of the demonstrators there, survives and continues to inspire the peoples of China and the world.

citizens died, was roundly condemned by most Western nations and by many of the communist and socialist states. By 31 August censorship had been reintroduced there and the Kremlin had reasserted its iron grip on its satellites. On 17 April 1969, Alexander Dubcek was removed from the post of party first secretary.

It is infinitely more humane to appal a rioter or a savage by showing him a tank than to shoot him down with an inoffensive-looking machinegun.
– Clough Williams-Ellis

overleaf: Innocent war games break out on an ice rink at the Songhua River in Harbin, China. For one Yuan, children can buy ten snowballs, which they can fire at each other through the cannon of their tanks.

AT THE MILLENIUM

TOO HEAVY FOR RAPID TRANSPORT BY PLANE TO WAR-TORN LANDS, TOO SLOW ON ITS TRADEMARK CATERPILLAR TRACKS, THE TANK IS BEING "MODERNISED" FOR THE AGE OF PEACE-KEEPING. – editorial, *The Times*, (London), 17 November 2000

At the millenium the United States Army completed a thorough review of its role in the world and concluded that a radical revision in its planning and procurement for armoured vehicles was essential. During the Kosovo conflict in 1999, the Army found itself in the position of having to send its massive 70-ton M1A2 Abrams main battle tanks to Albania for combined operations with its Apache helicopters. The tanks had to be brought to the battlefield one at a time by C-17 transport planes in a costly and time-consuming series of ferry flights. The contrast between what the Abrams tanks had achieved in the Persian Gulf War, destroying the Iraqi armoured force in roughly 100 hours, to the Kosovo conflict where the big MBTs simply could not be delivered in a timely fashion, was startling to American planners. They felt, too, that the Cold War-era main battle tanks, which had performed so well in the wide open spaces of the Gulf deserts, and which, for so many years, had helped to deter Soviet aggression in Western Europe, were just too big and heavy for the sort of conflicts they envisioned in the future. The Army clearly needed an alternative, and now plans an entirely new type of "medium armoured vehicle" to become its future mainstay.

Both the U.S. and British armies anticipate future conflicts being relatively small regional wars. They see their key requirements for armour as a rapid deployment capability and maximum battlefield flexibility. Failure to arrive for the opening acts in the theatre of operations could mean missing the only opportunity to bring such a conflict to an early end.

The 70-ton Challenger 2 is the current main battle tank of the British Army and will probably remain so for another quarter of a century. But, like the Americans, the British are keen to investigate the possibility of re-equipping with a much lighter and more easily deployable armoured vehicle, something they refer to as a Future Rapid Effect System (FRES). Like the Americans, they are interested in a vehicle which is adaptable to all types of battlefield, is smaller and lighter than an MBT, has substantial firepower and affords excellent armour protection for the crew. Ideally, they want it to also be capable of being assembled in sections once the "kit" has been delivered to the war zone.

According to Major-General Peter Gilchrist, Master General of the Ordnance, the British Army Board representative in charge of equipment, the Challenger 2 will be the last of the British main battle tank types and will be replaced by the year 2025 with a vehicle weighing 20 tons or less, with greater firepower and protection.

British Army sources conceive of such a FRES vehicle being made of a type of plastic and armed with an electro-thermal chemical gun. It may be either a tracked or wheeled vehicle, but will be designed to be as stealthy as possible, presenting a small radar signature to the enemy. Propulsion will probably be electric and the FRES will probably be manned by a crew of just two, possibly three. The new vehicle will undoubtedly cost much more than the current Challenger 2, probably at least twice as much, but should be easier to maintain, cheaper to operate and longer lasting.

Britain's Royal Air Force has no transport aircraft capable of ferrying a 70-ton Challenger 2 tank. It has announced plans for the short-term lease of some American C-17 Globemaster transports, but they are capable of carrying only one such tank at a time, so the British Army is keen to have a much smaller and lighter armoured vehicle which can be readily airlifted to where it is needed.

The Light Armor Vehicle (LAV), also known as the Interim Armor Vehicle, is the weapon which is enabling the American Army to convert its armoured force into a true rapid deployment force. That is not to say that the new "tank" will necessarily pack less firepower. It will begin its combat career with an updated version of the 105mm cannon that was the original gun on the M1A1 Abrams main battle tank.

After lengthy studies of all the possible design characteristics for such a weapon system, the Army came to a decision which it announced on 17 November 2000. The new vehicle is would be an eight-wheeled LAV, a collaborative effort between General Motors, the giant Detroit auto maker, and General Dynamics Land Systems which built the Abrams tank.

No more tracks. The LAV rides on run-flat tyres. With its crew, weapons and ammunition, the combat weight of the vehicle is just 38 tons, considerably below that of the Abrams. It takes only two crew members to operate the LAV and they are protected by special 14.5mm-thick armour. The vehicle runs with full-time four-wheel drive and eight-wheel drive can be selected, giving it a 62-mph road speed. It will have a range of 312 miles. The LAV has been designed to be operated independently in combat for periods of up to 72 hours.

Having made the decision, the Army has committed to an order for 2,131 LAVs at a total cost of $4 billion, enough vehicles to equip up to six Brigade Combat Teams. The order includes provision for specialized variants: fire support, reconnaissance, engineering, medical evacuation, mortar and missiles, nuclear, chemical and bioweapons detection, as well as two types of command vehicle. A Light Armoured Vehicle Company version will accommodate nine infantry personnel. Such a company will also include two LAVs armed with 60mm and 120mm mortars and another version with remote gun control for fire suppression. Finally, there is to be the Mobile Gun System Variant which mounts the type's heaviest firepower, the rifled 105mm cannon in a low-profile turret.

The switch to a wheeled as opposed to a tracked vehicle has been, and continues to be, the subject of much military, industrial and congressional controversy. The U.S. Congress has ordered that a test be conducted to find out if this particular wheeled concept is indeed superior to a tracked one.

Whatever the result of such a test, the Army insists on having the capability of inserting a combat-ready armoured brigade to a hotspot anywhere in the world in a mere 96 hours from getting the call; to put a full 15,000-man division on the scene in just 120 hours and to field five divisions in 30 days or less. The new light armoured vehicle should give it that capability.

The U.S. Marines have a specific requirement for what is now referred to as an advanced amphibious assault vehicle, or AAAV. General Dynamics has met that need with a new system that is capable of both high water-speed and exceptional cross-country mobility. The AAAV is able to launch forces from up to 25 miles from shore and bring them to the beach at 25 knots, affording the flexibility and tactical surprise, firepower and protection necessary to quickly gain battlefield dominance. With a land speed of 45 mph, a sea range of 65 nautical miles and a land range of 400 miles, the AAAV is armed with a 30mm Bushmaster MK44 primary weapon and a 7.62mm M240 machinegun. Fully-loaded, the craft weighs 37.5 tons, has a crew of three and carries 18 troops.

Speaking of things to come, the United States Army and the U.S. Defense Advanced Research Projects Agency, are developing a Future Combat System. This, it is hoped, will provide American leadership with more options when responding to

When General Eric K. Shinseki, United States Army Chief of Staff, announced in late 1999 the Army's plan for a new, medium-weight armoured brigade, it called into question the future of the Army's primary armoured weapon, the Abrams M1 main battle tank. While he asked American technology to study the possibilities for enhanced armour, electric drive and active protection systems, to determine whether advances in these areas could be brought to bear on future U.S. mounted war fighting, he indicated that the Abrams was certainly not dead, by any means. The M1 will most likely be around for many years to come.

crises and conflicts. This sophisticated concept involves a modular, armoured *wheeled* vehicle that is adaptable to various battlefield conditions. Much smaller and lighter than today's MBTs, it will come in the form of a manned command-and-control/personnel carrier, a robotic direct-fire system, a robotic non-line of sight system, and an all-weather robotic sensor. It can be delivered in useful quantities to any war zone in the world by existing transport aircraft. The aim is to provide the U.S. Army with combat superiority over all foreseeable enemies by 2025. The future is smaller and more efficient combat formations. A brigade-sized force could be deployed in under 96 hours.

It has been a long, hard road-march from the era of the Bronze Age warrior chariots to that of the Light Armor Vehicle. The Future Combat System may or may not take the form of a tank, but whatever form it takes will surely reflect lessons learned from the dramatic history of its ancestor.

left: A General Dynamics Land Systems Light Armoured Vehicle. This armoured personnel carrier is one of a family of special-purpose LAVs for the American military. Other types include a mobile gun system, a reconnaissance vehicle, a mortar carrier, a command vehicle, a fire support vehicle, an engineer support vehicle, a medical evacuation vehicle, an anti-tank guided missile vehicle and a Nuclear-Biological-Chemical (NBC) reconnaissance vehicle.

GLOSSARY

ACR Armored Cavalry Regiment.

AH-1 Huey Cobra, U.S. attack helicopter.

AH-64 Apache, U.S. attack helicopter.

AP Armour-Piercing.

APC Armour-Piercing Capped Shot with a soft steel cap over the pointed tip, to act as a shock absorber on impact with the target; improves penetration.

APC Armoured Personnel Carrier.

APDS Armour-Piercing Discarding Sabot.

APFSDS Armour-Piercing, Fin-Stabilized, Discarding Sabot round.

Appliqué armour Additional armour applied to the basic plates on a tank.

ATGM Anti-Tank Guided Missile.

AVRE British armoured vehicle of the Royal Engineers; a special-purpose tank for demolition and other duties.

Barbette Section of a tank superstructure that is raised, fixed and carries the fighting compartment.

BILL Swedish-designed anti-tank missile system. utilising a shaped-charge to attack the top surfaces of a tank.

Bins Externally-mounted boxes on a tank for storage of tools and loose equipment.

BMP Russian Infantry Fighting Vehicle.

Ceramic laminates Ceramic and composite layer armour, to make a tank more resistant to the effects of shaped-charge rounds.

Bogie A suspension wheel on a tank.

Calibre The internal dimensions of a gun barrel.

Chobham Armour A unique armour system devised by the Chobham, England, research facility of the British Army. Uses a secret compound containing steel and ceramic to improve the resistance of a tank to penetration by shaped-charge rounds.

CID Commander's Integrated Display.

CITV Commander's Independent Thermal Viewer.

CP Command Post.

Cupola A raised tank position (for one or two men) offering an improved field of vision.

Bustle An overhang at the back of a tank turret usually used for storage or radio equipment.

DU Depleted Uranium; used as a core in certain types of armour-piercing ammunition due to its exceptional hardness and density.

ECM Electronic Countermeasures.

ERA Explosive Reactive Armour; an armour system utilizing high-explosive that is sandwiched between steel plates. It is intended to disperse the force of a hit on a tank by a shaped-charge or long-rod penetrator weapon.

Fascine A roll of wooden palings carried on early tanks, to be dropped into a trench to aid the tank in crossing the gap.

FLIR Forward-looking InfraRed.

FT Flame Thrower.

Fume Extractor A system for removing the gases present after firing the gun; sucks the gases from the muzzle before the breech is reopened.

GCDP M1A2 Gunner's Control and Display Panel.

Glacis plate The sloping armour on the front of a tank which gives the driver better visibility as well as deflecting shot from the hull.

GPS Global Positioning System; a satellite-based navigation system.

Ground pressure The total weight of a tank divided by the area of track in contact with the ground, expressed in pounds per square inch.

Gyro-stabilizer A hydraulic motor used to keep the main gun of a tank levelled on a target while the tank is moving.

HE High Explosive.

HEAT High-Explosive Anti-Tank.

Hellfire U.S. Helicopter-borne Fire-and-Forget anti-tank missile.

HESH High-Explosive, Squash-Head.

HMMWV U.S. High-mobility Multi-purpose Wheeled Vehicle.

Howitzer A gun designed to fire a projectile with a high, arching trajectory.

HUD Head-Up Display.

Hull down Tactical position in which only the turret of a tank is exposed to its target, thus protecting its hull from return fire.

HVAP High-Velocity Armour-Piercing.

Idler wheel An unpowered wheel on a tank which carries the track; adjustable for track tension.

IFF Identification, Friend or Foe.

IFV Infantry Fighting Vehicle.

IVIS Inter-Vehicular Information System; a computer network for the U.S. M1A2 main battle tanks.

Laser Detection and Warning System An electronic sensor on a tank or other vehicle that is activated when hit by a laser beam from a missile or a laser illuminator/designator. It alerts the tank crew that their vehicle is being laser-targetted, giving them the direction from which the beam is being trained.

LAV Light Armoured Vehicle.

LAW Light Anti-Tank Weapon.

Longbow A type of day-and-night radar for use on the U.S. AH-64 attack helicopter.

Long-Rod Penetrator A metal dart up to two feet in length and weighing ten pounds. It is fired from the large-calibre gun of a tank to penetrate the armour

of an enemy tank.

Louvre A tank ventilation inlet that is normally protected by armour.

M2/M3 Bradley U.S. Infantry Fighting Vehicle of the 1980s.

Mantlet An area of armour protecting the space where the main gun of a tank projects from the turret.

Maverick U.S. air-to-surface laser- or infrared-guided missile which can be used in an anti-tank role.

MBT Main Battle Tank.

MILAN Conventional wire-guided missile.

MRE Meal Ready to Eat. U.S. individual rations first distributed in the 1980s and used in the Gulf War.

MMS Mast-Mounted Sight; an optical sensor device with a daylight television camera and a laser range-finder and designator, to be mounted on U.S. attack helicopters.

Monocoque A single, one-piece hull structure which bears the structural loads of a vehicle such as a tank and is employed instead of a conventional chassis.

Muzzle brake Located at the end of a tank gun barrel, reduces recoil by deflecting propellant gases to the rear.

Muzzle reference system A system for guaranteeing that the sights of both gun and tank are precisely focused on the same point on a distant object.

Muzzle velocity The velocity achieved by a projectile when it leaves the muzzle of a gun.

NATO North Atlantic Treaty Organization.

NBC Nuclear, Biological, Chemical.

NTC The U.S. National Training Center, Fort Irwin, California.

NVG Night Vision Goggles.

OPFOR Opposing Force in a training exercise.

Panzer German: armour; tank, armoured vehicle.

POW Prisoner of War.

RAM Radar Absorbent Material.

RCS Radar Cross Section.

Recuperator Absorbs gun recoil, reduces stress on the gun mounting and returns the gun to the firing position.

Republican Guard Initially the personal guard force of Iraqi leader Saddam Hussein. Later an Iraqi Army elite force of more than 100,000 men. In the 1990-91 Gulf War, the Republican Guard were thought to be the greatest threat to the Coalition forces.

RHA Rolled Homogeneous Armour; steel alloys rolled to constant thickness and uniform hardness for maximum strength and penetration resistance.

Rollers Unsprung wheels of a tank suspension.

ROE Rules of Engagement; the conditions under which U.S. military forces may fire on hostile forces.

RPG Rocket-Propelled Grenade; Russian disposable, light-weight anti-tank weapons.

RPV Remotely-Piloted Vehicles; small, unmanned drone aircraft normally used for reconnaissance.

Schnorkel A tube on some tanks to enable the crew to breathe during deep underwater fording.

SP Self-propelled.

Shaped-Charge Warhead A high-explosive charge is formed or "shaped" around the outside of a copper cone. With the explosion of the anti-tank warhead, the resultant energy is directed inwards and forwards, which creates a stream of gas and molten metal, forcing a metal slug to the front, which then melts through the tank armour.

Shot Solid projectile with no explosive charge' its effect is achieved entirely through kinetic energy.

Skirting plates Vertical armour to protect the upper portion of a tank's tracks and running gear as well as the hull.

Spall Portions, splinters or fragments of a tank's armour that break off and fly into the interior of the vehicle when the tank receives a hit by a bullet, anti-anti-tank round, artillery round, shot or missile.

Splash The same as Spall; also bullets which become semi-liquified on impact with the rim of the opening created on their impact.

SPH Self-Propelled Howitzer.

Sponson A gun mount that was attached to the sides of early tanks, affording limited traverse.

Suspension The system of linkage between the track and hull of a tank, which supports the track.

TACAN Tactical Navigation System.

TADS Target Acquisition Designation Sight.

Thermal sleeve An insulated blanket that is wrapped around barrel of the main gun on a tank to maintain a constant barrel temperature and prevent differential expansion of the barrel and a consequent loss of accuracy over longer ranges. With the muzzle reference system, the thermal sleeve assures first-round accuracy.

Tank An enclosed, heavily armoured combat vehicle that is mounted with cannon and guns and moves on caterpillar treads.

TIS Thermal Imaging Sight.

TOW Tube-launched, Optically tracked, Wire-guided missile. U.S. anti-tank weapon system.

Track link An individual element in a tank track; it is normally connected to the adjoining links by pins.

Turret A tank's rotating armoured structure that rests on ball bearings; the turret turns on a traversing ring.

overleaf: The German Leopard II is among the few modern main battle tanks that have achieved a balanced mix of firepower, armour protection and mobility. With a road speed of 45 mph and a range of 600 miles, the four-man tank is armed with a Rheinmetall 120mm smoothbore gun, a 7.62mm co-axial machinegun, a 7.62mm anti-aircraft machinegun and sixteen smoke dischargers. The Leopard II went into service with the German Army in 1980 and is also used by the Netherlands and Switzerland.

Dear Colonel Churchill,
It is with great pleasure that I am now able to report to you that the War Office have at last ordered 100 landships to the pattern which underwent most successful trials recently. Sir D. Haig sent some of his staff from the front. Lord Kitchener and Robertson also came, and members of the Admiralty Board. The machine was complete in almost every detail and fulfills all the requirements finally given me by the War Office. The official tests of trenches, etc., were nothing to it, and finally we showed them how it could cross a nine foot gap after climbing a four foot six inch high perpendicular parapet. Wire entanglements it goes straight through like a rhinoceros through a field of corn. It carries two 6-pounder guns in the sponsons (a *naval* touch), and about 300 rounds; also smaller machine-guns, and is proof against machine-gun fire. It can be conveyed by rail (the sponsons and guns take off, making it lighter) and be ready for action very quickly. The King came and saw it and was greatly struck by its performance, as was everyone else; in fact, they were all astonished. It is capable of great development, but to get a sufficient number in time, I strongly urge ordering immediately a good many to the pattern which we know all about. As you are aware, it has taken much time and trouble to get the thing perfect, and a practical machine simple to make; we

PICTURE CREDITS

Photographs by Philip Kaplan are credited: PK. Photographs from the author's collections are credited: AC. Photographs from the United States National Archives are credited: NARA. Photographs from Military Stock Photography are credited: MSP. Photographs from the Imperial War Museum are credited: IWM. Photographs from the Tank Museum Collection, Bovington, are credited: TM/BOV. Photographs from the DaimlerChrysler Corporate Historical Collection are credited: DC. Jacket front: courtesy Jeff Dacus, jacket back: NARA, jacket back flap: Margaret Kaplan. Front endsheet: NARA, Back endsheet: MSP/Sam Katz, P2: IWM, P4: MSP/Will Fowler, P6: AC, P7: IWM/W.B. Adeney, P8: TM-BOV, P9 both: TM-BOV, P10 all: TM-BOV, P14: AC, PP16-17 all: TM-BOV, P18: IWM/W.B. Adeney, P19: IWM, P21: TM-BOV, PP22-23: IWM/W.B. Adeney, P25: TM-BOV, PP26-27: IWM/Paul Nash, P30 left: NARA/August Hutaf, P30 right-both: IWM, P31: IWM/Sir William Orpen, PP32-33 all: TM-BOV, P34: AC, P35: IWM, PP36-37: TM-BOV, PP40-41: MSP/Will Fowler, P42: MSP/Will Fowler, P45: TM-BOV, PP46-47: TM-BOV, PP48-49: TM-BOV, P51: Frank Reynolds, P53: AC, P54: IWM, P55: AC, P57: MSP/Will Fowler, PP58-59: MSP/Will Fowler, P59 right: AC, P60: TM-BOV, PP60-61: TM-BOV, P62: MSP-Will Fowler, P63: AC, PP64-65:DC, P65 right: TM-BOV, P66 both: TM-BOV, P67: TM-BOV, PP68-69: DC, P70: DC, P71 left: Bill Mauldin, P71 top right: AC, P71 bottom right: PK, P72: AC, PP72-73: TM-BOV, P74: NARA, PP74-75: MSP/Will Fowler, PP76-77: TM-BOV, PP78-79: TM-BOV, PP80-81: MSP/Will Fowler, P81 right: AC, P82: MSP/J. Littlefield, P83: IWM, P85 both: TM-BOV, PP86-87: courtesy of J. Kugies, P88: TM-BOV, P89: TM-BOV, P90: TM-BOV, P91: MSP/J. Littlefield, P92: TM-BOV, P94: MSP/J. Littlefield, PP96-97: TM-BOV, PP98-99: TM-BOV/David Shepard/Royal Tank Regiment, P100: AC, P102: TM-BOV, P103: IWM, P105: TM-BOV, P106 top left: AC, P106 left: PK/courtesy TM-BOV, P106 centre: TM-BOV, P107: IWM, P108 both: AC, P109 both: TM-BOV, P111 both: TM-BOV, P111 right: courtesy Mrs Donald Chidson, P112 top: TM-BOV, P112 bottom: MSP/Will Fowler, P114 both: PK, P115: PK, P116 both: Bundesarchiv, P117: Bundesarchiv, P118 all: PK, P119 both: AC, P120 top: TM-BOV, P120 bottom: AC, P122 both: PK, P123: IWM/T.B. Hennell, PP124-125: MSP/Will Fowler,PP126-127: AC/M.C.A. Russell, P128: TM-BOV, P130 top left: courtesy Charles Shenloogian, P130 centre: TM-BOV, P131: courtesy Steve Joseph, P134 top left: AC, P134 top: TM-BOV, P134 bottom: courtesy A. Hoffmeister, P135: AC, P136 top: TM-BOV, P136 bottom: NARA, P138: courtesy Ludwig Bauer, P139: AC, P140: TM-BOV, P142-143: Flo Garetson, P145: AC, PP146: TM-BOV, P147 top and bottom: Flo Garetson, P148: AC, P149 both: TM-BOV, P150: AC, P150-151: MSP/Will Fowler, PP152-153: MSP/Will Fowler, P154: DC, P155: AC, P156: TM-BOV, P157: TM-BOV, P158 left, both: MSP/J. Littlefield, PP158-159: TM-BOV, P160 both: TM-BOV, P161: NARA, P162: NARA, P162-163: NARA/James R. Drake, PP164-165: TM-BOV, PP166-167 all: NARA, PP168-169: TM-BOV, PP170-171: NARA, P172: NARA, PP172-173: MSP/Will Fowler, P174: MSP/Sam Katz, PP176-177: Micha Bar Am/Magnum Photos, P178 top: TM-BOV, P178 bottom: Micha Bar Am/Magnum Photos, PP180-181: MSP/Sam Katz, P182-183: MSP/Sam Katz, P184: Micha Bar Am/Magnum Photos, PP186-187: MSP/Sam Katz, PP190-191: courtesy Jeff Dacus, P191: US Air Force, PP192-193: TM-BOV, PP194-195 all: courtesy Jeff Dacus, PP198-199: Robert Bailey, PP200-201: MSP/Will Fowler, P202: MSP, P203 both: MSP/A. Cors, P205: MSP, P206: MSP/J. Littlefield, P207: MSP/J. Littlefield, P208: NARA, PP208-209: NARA, PP210-211: MSP, PP214-215: PK, PP216-217: NARA, PP218-219: PK, PP222-223: Stuart Franklin/Magnum Photos, PP226-227: Reza, PP230-231: GM GDLS (General Motors-General Dynamics Land Systems), P232: AC, PP234-235: MSP/Will Fowler.

ACKNOWLEDGMENTS

The author is particularly grateful to the following people for their kind help in the development of this book: Pauline Allwright, Ernest Audino, Averdieck, Fritz-Rudolf, Jeff Babineau, Malcolm Bates, A.G. Bramble, Ludwig Bauer, Rex Cadman, Donald Chidson, Valerie Chidson, Neil Ciotola, Jeff Dacus, DaimlerChrysler Historical Collection, J. Ellison, Chris Everitt, John Ferrell, David Fletcher, Eugene Flowers, George Forty, Will Fowler, Ella Freire, Oz Freire, Flo Garetson, Gaston Gee, Hans Halberstadt, Robert T. Hartwig, Douglas Helmer, Eric Holloway, James Jinks, Steve Joseph, Hargita Kaplan, Neal Kaplan, Margaret Kaplan, Sam Katz, Johannes Kugies, Jacques Littlefield, John Longman, Tilly McMaster, James McMaster, Elise McCutcheon, Judy McCutcheon, Richard McCutcheon, Martin Middlebrook, Steve Nichols, John Nugent, George Parada, Alan Reeves, Heinz Renk, Charles L. Ross, John Schaeffer, Charles Shenloogian, David Shepard, Garry Third, George Hudson Wirth, Dennis Wrynn. Grateful acknowledgment is made to the following for the use of their previously published material:

Averdieck, Fritz-Rudolf, from his notes on World War II experiences.
Bauer, Ludwig, from his notes on World War II experiences.
Belfield, Eversleigh, and Essame, H., *The Battle for Normandy*, Pan Books, 1967.
Bramble, A.G., from his notes on World War II experiences.
Browne, Captain D.G., *The Tank in Action*, William Blackwood and Sons, 1920.
Dacus, Jeff, from his notes on Gulf War experiences.
Eshel, David, *Chariots of the Desert*, Brassey's, 1989.
Guderian, Heinz, *Achtung—Panzer*, Arms & Armour, 1992.
Guderian, Heinz, *Panzer Leader*, Penguin Books, 2000.
Hamilton, Nigel, *The Full Monty: Montgomery of Alamein 1887-1942*.
Hartwig, Robert T., from his notes on World War II experiences.
Liddell-Hart, Basil, *The Other Side of the Hill*, Papermac, 1993.
Mauldin, Bill, *Up Front*, Henry Holt and Company, Inc., 1945.
Messenger, Charles, *The Art of Blitzkrieg*, Ian Allan, (a translation from Militarwissen Schlaftiche Rundschau, December 1935.)
Perrett, Bryan, *Iron Fist*, Arms & Armour Press, Cassell & Co.,1995.
Ridgeway, Matthew B. and Martin, Harold, *Soldier*, 1956.
Rogers, Colonel H.C.B., *Tanks in Battle*, Seeley, Service & Co., 1965.
Royal Tank Regiment, *The Tank Journal*, 1920, 1921, 1922, RTR..
Sullivan, Captain S. Scott, from his speech to the final reunion of the 745th Tank Battalion, U.S. Army.

BIBLIOGRAPHY

Adams, Simon, *World War I*, Dorling Kindersley, 2001.
Ambrose, Stephen E., Band of Brothers, Simon & Schuster, 1992.
Ambrose, Stephen E., *Citizen Soldiers*, Simon & Schuster, 1997.
Arnold, James R., *The Battle of the Bulge*, Osprey Publishing Ltd., 1990.
Barker, Lieutenant Colonel A.J., *Afrika Korps*, Bison Books, 1978.
Beevor, Antony, *Stalingrad*, Viking, 1998.
Belfield, Eversleigh and Essame, H., *The Battle for Normandy*, Pan Books, 1967.
Bethell, Nicholas, *Russia Bsieged*, Time-Life Books, 1980.
Bishop, Chris and Warner, Adam, *German Campaigns of World War II*, Grange Books, 2001.
Blackburn, George G., *The Guns of Normandy*, McClelland & Stewart Inc., 1995.
Blackburn, George G., *The Guns of War*, Constable Publishers, 2000.
Blumenson, Martin, *The Patton Papers 1940-1945*, Houghton Mifflin Company, 1957.
Boscawen, Robert, *Armoured Guardsmen*, Leo Cooper, 2001.
Browne, Captain D.G., *The Tank in Action*, William Blackwood and Sons, 1920.
Bryant, Mark, *World War II in Cartoons*, Brompton Books., 1989.
Burke Publishing Company, *The Conquest of North Africa*.
Chant, Christopher, *Armoured Fighting Vehicles of the 20th Century*, Tiger Books International, 1996.
Campbell, John, *The Experience of World War II*, Oxford University Press, 1989.
Canby, Courtlandt, *A History of Weaponry*, Hawthorn Books, Inc. 1963.

Carruthers, Bob, *German Tanks At War*, Cassell & Co., 2000.
Churchill, Winston, S., *The Second World War: The Grand Alliance*, Houghton Mifflin Company, 1950.
Clancy, Tom, *Armored Cav*, Berkley Books, 1994.
Clancy, Tom, *Into The Storm: A Study in Command*, G.P. Putnam's Sons, 1997.
Clark, Alan, *Barbarossa*, Quill, 1965.
Collier, Richard, *The War In The Desert*, Time-Life Books, Inc., 1977.
Cooper, Belton Y., *Death Traps*, Presidio Press, 2000.
Cooper, Matthew and Lucas, James, *Panzer*, Purnell Book Services Limited, 1976.
Coppard, George, *With A Machine Gun To Cambrai*, Cassell, 1999.
Costello, John, *Love Sex & War Changing Values 1939-45*, Collins, 1985.
Crow, Duncan, *Modern Battle Tanks*, Profile Publications Ltd., 1978.
Davies, J.B., *Great Campaigns of World War II*, Macdonald & Co., 1980.
Delaforce, Patrick, *Taming The Panzers*, Sutton Publishing, 2000.
Delaney, John, *The Blitzkrieg Campaigns*, Caxton Editions, 2000.
Deighton, Len, *Blitzkrieg*, Jonathan Cape, 1979.
Diez, Octavio, *Tanks and Armoured Vehicles*, Lema Publications, 2000.
Doubler, Michael D., *Closing With The Enemy*, University Press of Kansas, 1994.
Edwards, Roger, *Panzer: A Revolution in Warfare, 1939-1945*, Brockhampton Press, 1989.
Eshel, David, *Chariots of the Desert*, Brassey's, 1989.
Fletcher, David, *Tanks and Trenches*, Sutton Publishing Ltd., 1994.
Fletcher, David, *The British Tanks 1915-19*, The Crowood Press, 2001.
Flower, Desmond and Reeves, James, *The Taste of Courage The War 1939-1945*, Cassell, 1960.
Folkestad, William B., *The View from the Turret*, Burd Street Press, 2000.
Forbes, Colin, *Tramp in Armour*, Collins, 1969.
Ford, Roger, *The Sherman Tank*, Brown Packaging Books Ltd., 1999.
Ford, Roger, *The World's Great Tanks*, Grange Books, 1999.
Forty, George, *Afrika Korps At War: 1. The Road To Alexandria*, Ian Allan, 1978.
Forty, George, *Afrika Korps At War: 2. The Long Road Back*, Ian Allan, 1978.
Forty, George, *A Pictorial History: Royal Tank Regiment*, Guild Publishing, 1989.
Forty, George, *Tank Aces*, Sutton Publishing, 1997.
Foss, Christopher F., *Jane's Tanks and Combat Vehicles Recognition Guide*, HarperCollins, 2000.
Gardiner, Juliet, *D-Day: Those Who Were There*, Collins & Brown Limited, 1994.
Gervasi, Tom, Arsenal of Democracy II, Evergreen, 1981.
Green, Michael, *M1 Abrams Main Battle Tank*, Motorbooks, 1992.
Green, Michael, *Patton's Tank Drive D-Day to Victory*, MBI Publishing, 1995.
Guderian, Heinz, *Achtung–Panzer*, Arms & Armour, 1992.
Guderian, Heinz, *Panzer Leader*, Penguin Books, 2000.
Halberstadt, Hans, *Military Vehicles*, Metrobooks, 1998
Halberstadt, Hans, *Inside The Great Tanks*, The Crowood Press, 1998.
Hastings, Max, *The Korean War*, Michael Joseph Ltd., 1987.
Haupt, Werner and Bingham, J.K.W., *North African Campaign 1940-1943*, Macdonald & Co., 1968.
His Majesty's Stationery Office, *The Eighth Army*, 1944.
Hogg, Ian V., *The Greenhill Armoured Fighting Vehicles Data Book*, Greenhill Books, 2000.
Hogg, Ian, *Tank Killing*, Brown Packaging Books Ltd., 1996.
Holmes, Richard, *Battlefields of the Second World War*, BBC, 2001.
Houston, Donald E., *Hell On Wheels The 2d Armored Division*, Presidio Press, 1977.
Hughes, Dr Matthew and Mann, Dr Chris, *The T-34 Tank*, Brown Packaging Books Limited, 1999.
Jensen, Marvin, *Strike Swiftly!*, Presidio Press, 1997.
Jones, Kevin, *The Desert Rats*, Caxton Editions, 2001.
Jorgensen, Christer and Mann, Chris, *Tank Warfare*, Spellmount Limited, 2001.

Keegan, John, *The First World War An Illustrated History*, Hutchinson, 2001.
Kurowski, Franz, *Panzer Aces*, J.J. Fedorowicz Publishing Inc., 1992.
Lande, D.A., *Rommel in North Africa*, MBI Publishing Co., 1999.
Lefevre, Eric, *Panzers in Normandy Then and Now*, After The Battle, 1983.
Lucas, James, *Panzer Army Africa*, Purnell Book Services, 1977.
Macksey, Kenneth, *Battle*, Grub Street, 2001.
Macksey, Kenneth, *Tank Facts & Feats*, Sterling Publishing, 1980.
Macksey, Kenneth, *Tank Tactics 1939-1945*, Almark Publishing Co. Ltd., 1976.
Macksey, Kenneth, *Tank Versus Tank*, Grub Street, 1999.
Macksey, Kenneth, *Tank Warfare: A History of Tanks in Battle*, Granada Publishing Ltd., 1971.
Man, John and Newark, Tim, *Battlefields Then & Now*, Macmillan, 1997.
Mason, David, *Verdun*, The Windrush Press, 2000.
Mauldin, Bill, *Up Front*, Henry Holt and Company, Inc., 1945.
McCombs, Don and Worth, Fred L., *World War II Super Facts*, Warner Books, 1983.
McGuirk, Dal, *Rommel's Army in Africa*, Motorbooks, 1993.
McKee, Alexander, *Caen: Anvil of Victory*, Dorset Press, 1964.
Merewood, Jack, *To War with The Bays*, 1st The Queen's Dragoon Guards, 1996.
Messenger, Charles, *The Art of Blitzkrieg*, Ian Allan, 1976.
Miller, David, *Tanks of the World*, Salamander Books, 2000.
Parker, Danny S., *Battle of the Bulge*, Greenhill Books, 1991.
Perrett, Bryan, *Desert Warfare*, Patrick Stephens Limited, 1978.
Perrett, Bryan, *Iron Fist*, Arms & Armour Press, 1995.
Rasmussen, Henry, *D-Day Plus Fifty Years*, Top Ten Publishing, 1994.
Rawls, Walton, *Wake Up, America!*, Cross River Press, 1988.
Reynolds, Michael, Steel Inferno: SS Panzer Corps in Normandy, Spellmount Ltd., 1997.
Rogers, Colonel H.C.B., *Tanks in Battle*, Seeley, Service & Co., 1965.
Roze, Anne, *Fields of Memory*, Éditions du Chêne-Hachette Livre, 1998.
Smithers, A.J., *A New Excalibur: The Development of the Tank 1909-1939*, Leo Cooper, 1986.
Sulzberger, C.L., *The American Heritage Picture History of World War II*, American Heritage, 1966.
Thompson, R.W., *D-Day: Spearhead of Invasion*, Bookthrift, 1968.
Tout, Ken, *A Fine Night For Tanks: The Road to Falaise*, Sutton Publishing, 1998.
Tout, Ken, *The Bloody Battle for Tilly*, Sutton Publishing, 2000.
Trewhitt, Philip, *Armoured Fighting Vehicles*, Dempsey Parr, 1999.
Viney, Nigel, *Images of Wartime*, David & Charles, 1991.
von Mellenthin, Major-General F.W., *Panzer Battles*, Cassell & Co., 1955.
Wernick, Robert, *Blitzkrieg*, Time-Life Books, 1976.
Whiting, Charles, *Decision at St Vith*, Ballantine Books, 1969.
Wilson, George, *If You Survive*, Ballantine Books, 1987.
Winchester, Charles, *Ostfront: Hitler's War on Russia 1941-45*, Osprey Publishing, 2000.
Winchester, Jim, *The World War II Tank Guide*, Amber Books, 2000.
Wright, Patrick, *Tank*, Faber and Faber, 2000.
Saloga, Steven J. and Loop, Lieutenant Colonel James W., *Modern American Armor*, Lionel Leventhal Ltd., 1982.
Zetterling, Niklas and Frankson, Anders, *Kursk 1943*, Frank Cass, 2000.

tried various types and did much experimental work. I am sorry it has taken so long, but pioneer work always takes time and no avoidable delay has taken place, though I begged them to order ten for training purposes two months ago. I have also had some difficulty in steering the scheme past the rocks of opposition and the more insidious shoals of apathy which are frequented by red herrings, which cross the main line of progress at frequent intervals.

The great thing now is to keep the whole matter secret and produce the machines altogether as a complete surprise. I have already put the manufacture in hand, under the aegis of the Minister of Munitions, who is very keen; the Admiralty is also allowing me to continue to carry on with the same committee, but Stern is now chairman.

I enclose photo. In appearance it looks rather like a great antediluvian monster, especially when it comes out of boggy ground, which it traverses easily. The wheels behind form a rudder for steering a curve, and also ease the shock over banks, etc., but are not absolutely necessary, as it can steer and turn in its own length with the independent tracks.
— A 14 February 1916 letter to Lieutenant-Colonel Winston S. Churchill, then in command of the 6th Royal Scots Fusiliers, B.E.F., from Sir Eustace D'Eyncourt, Director of Naval Construction and a chairman of the Admiralty Landships Committee

238